**WHO?**

It's about us!

**WHAT?**

Everything!

**WHEN?**

The last few years and a little history sprinkled in.

**WHERE?**

America and the world

**WHY?**

I started writing one page poems about news, history, race in America, and life (in general) as an autobiography to share with the future!

**HOW?**

Read it & Enjoy!

# WARRIOR CARRYING WATER

## ANTHOLOGY OF 500 POEMS & SHORT STORIES

## JASON LAWRENCE MOORE

**Lawrence Moore**

**About me**

**From:**

Indianapolis

**College:**

Hampton University

**Favorite color:**

Green

| EVERYTHING ELSE | ART & MEDIA | POLITICS & RELIGION | LIFE & LOVE | BLACK IN AMERICA |
|---|---|---|---|---|

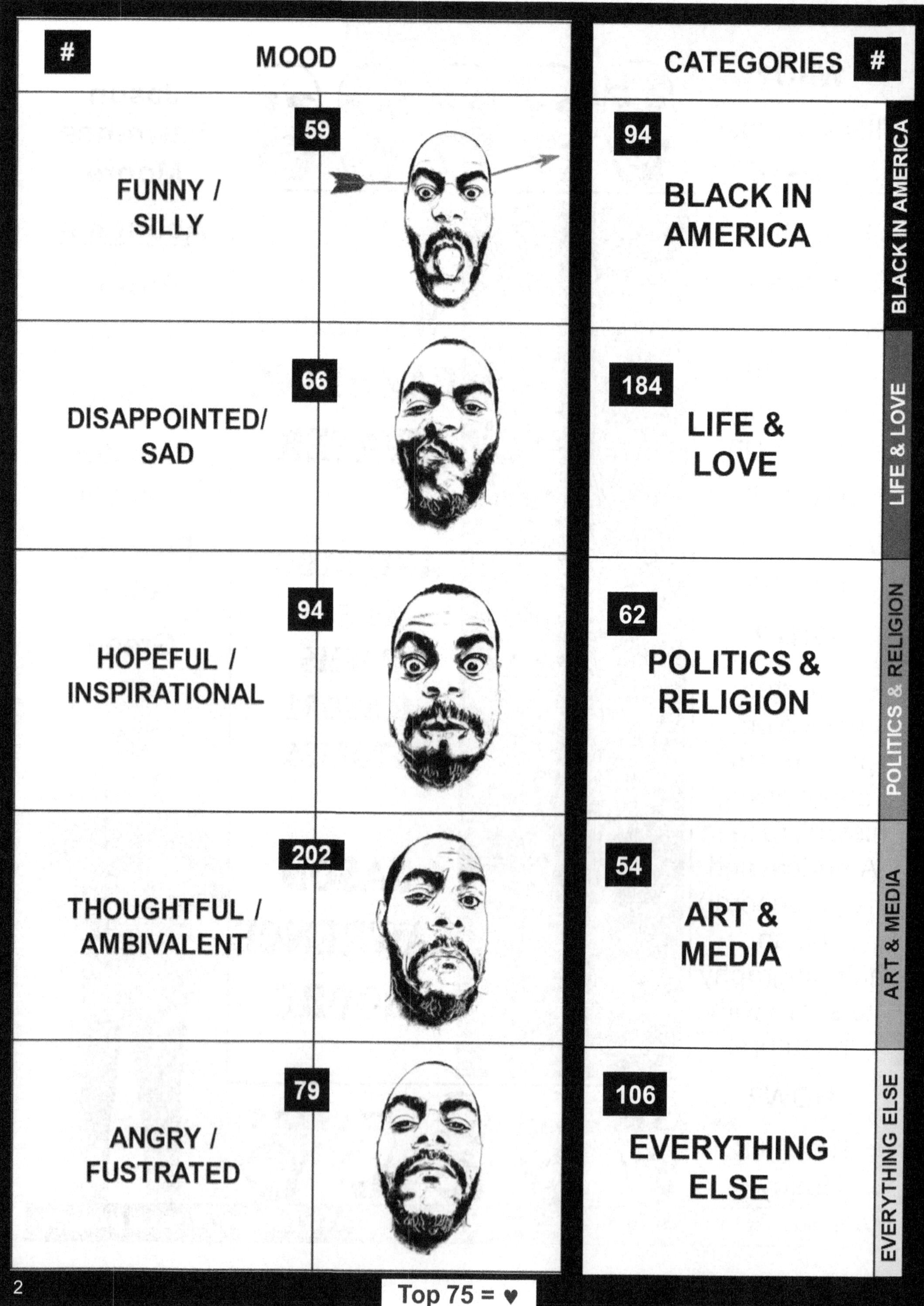

#
MOOD
CATEGORIES
#
59
FUNNY / SILLY
94
BLACK IN AMERICA
BLACK IN AMERICA
66
DISAPPOINTED/ SAD
184
LIFE & LOVE
LIFE & LOVE
94
HOPEFUL / INSPIRATIONAL
62
POLITICS & RELIGION
POLITICS & RELIGION
202
THOUGHTFUL / AMBIVALENT
54
ART & MEDIA
ART & MEDIA
79
ANGRY / FUSTRATED
106
EVERYTHING ELSE
EVERYTHING ELSE
Top 75 = ♥

# Dedication

This book is dedicated to my family

My wife (Keisha) for the encouragement
My daughter (Zoe) for the inspiration
My parents (John and Joyce) for the dedication
And my brothers (Johnny and Justin) for the motivation

Thanks for all of your support and love!

Sincerely,

Jason Lawrence Moore

To the team of illustrators who masterfully brought my stories to life,

**Thank you!**

Marcus Lorenzo Jones II

sagelorenzo.com

pgs. 198, 250, 389, 445, 515, 517, 521, 523, 525, and 529

Jonathan & Ona Riley

http://Twitter.com/nerdyboygo

pgs. 381, 484, 486, 488, 490, and 492

Keisha Marie Moore

www.getawaygardens.com

pgs. 243 and 393

Zoe Victoria Moore

pgs. 89, 129, 170, 179, 211, 264, and 375

**COVER ART**

Warrior Carrying Water
by John G. Moore Jr.
32" x 82" oil on canvas, 1990
'When a warrior is seen carrying water, it is a sign of peace.'

https://twitter.com/johngmoorejr?lang=en
https://www.instagram.com/john.g.moore.jr/?hl=en
https://www.youtube.com/user/JohnGilbertmoore/videos

# WARRIOR CARRYING WATER

When a warrior carries water, it's a sign that all is well
When a warrior carries water, know that he once faced hell
When a warrior carries water, realize that she's known grief
When a warrior carries water, it symbolizes peace.

When a warrior carries water, long after the battle is done
Lose, draw, or even if its won
With fists, rocks, spears, arrows or guns
Under attack, you either face facts or run!
Our thoughts, words, and actions will eventually become
Our measure, if you don't seek peace, then you'll never have none.

# ABOUT THE AUTHOR

## Why did I write this book?

I've been writing one-page poems over the past decade, about everything from history, life, politics, racism, daily observations, and more. From my experiences growing up in Indianapolis to traveling around the world while serving in the US Navy, and working in corporate America, I've written about my experiences and opinions about nearly everything. My journey (so far) is here for you to read. Please let me know what you think and enjoy!

warriorcarryingwater@yahoo.com

## SCAN THE QR CODES BELOW TO SEE THE VIDEOS!

Top
10

# PART I: BLACK IN AMERICA (10-103)



**Top 75 = ♥**

## #BlackLivesMatter

Black Lives Matter!
Bones dreams shatter
Crowds run scatter
Freedom justice after
Protest history disaster

Slave beats master
Charcoal on plaster
Guns cops chatter
Nothing changes laughter
Frustration lives taken
Spirits necks breaking

Acquit flip script
Distract facts quick
Soon most forget
Same old shit!
Y'all ain't hip!
Slight hand trick
Eyes disguise this
Trump bid whist!

## 13th Amendment & Prison Industrial Complex

Clauses in the law
Often cause insurrections and exceptions for y'all!
150+ years after the 13th Amendment
Involuntarily servitude, still includes, those mostly skinned with pigment!
Written in between those lines
Are loopholes, so America can leverage petty crimes
Black codes put black souls **IN** Union jails and **ON** Confederate plantations!
Free labor, under the law, and indivisible, as slave owner's reparations!

13th Amendment (Abolition of Slavery) US Constitution, section #1:
Neither slavery nor involuntary servitude, except as a punishment for crime whereof the party shall have been duly convicted, shall exist within the United States, or any place subject to their jurisdiction.

## 30 Seconds in a Cage: Whitney Plantation

On the Whitney Plantation tour with my brothers, Johnny and Justin
Only five black people in a group of 20, ain't that something?
Our tour guide was leading a group a discussion
On the ways that slaves spent their forlorn days
Then she invited us to step into a cage
Iron, rusty, hot, and confined
Less than 30 seconds in, I nearly lost my mind!
When I lost sight of my brothers, it was no longer just pretend
I saw a dozen white faces (from our group) through the cell bars, and panic set in!
I lack the words to describe exactly how it felt
150+ years ago, our cards were dealt
In spades, men, women, and children's lives reduced to economic trade
Toiling to harvest sugar, tobacco, and cotton for no wage
Even after freedom, while sharecropping, we couldn't believe them!
Same clothes, same laws, same work, same reason
My Great-Grandfather was born a slave, yet he had hope
I was born "free", but I don't.

## $4^{th}$ of July is a lie?

In this dystopian future that we're living in
Much is taken, and nothing is given
What if every truth that we ever learned was a lie?
Life, liberty, the pursuit of happiness, and the $4^{th}$ of July?
The colonies rebelled to get freedom (to protect the institution of slavery), but why can I?
I get taxed and treated whack
Make and own less, just because I'm black
Where's my apology and retribution?
Y'all more concerned about the economy and pollution
It never seems to be the 'right' time, to do 'right' by us
Rosa quit your complaining, and get on the back of the bus!
Y'all want an equal education, then get your little asses on the **back** of the bus!
There ain't no justice, there's **JUST US!**
No matter how much we fight, beg, and cuss
Nothing will ever really change much.

## 44 Million = The population of Ukraine <u>AND</u> Black America

There were 44 million people living in the Ukraine, at the start of the 2022 war
About the same as Black America's population, so what's the comparison for?
Reparations, America pays out billions of dollars each year, but we still get no love?
See for yourself and visit https://foreignassistance.gov/
Click on any country to see how much 'assistance' America has paid out since 2001
In the interest of security, the economy, religion, and wars long lost and won
America spends so much money, time, and resources to champion foreign interests
While Black Americans still get taxed, discriminated against, killed, and beaten senseless.

ForeignAssistance.gov
Data last updated on: 04/22/2022
Add Filters
$46B Disbursements
15k Activities
210 Countries/Regions
reset zoom
$3.3B - $4.9B
$1.5B - $3.3B
$501M - $1.5B
$141M - $501M
$261 - $141M
No Data
Ukraine
$534,341,428 disbursed

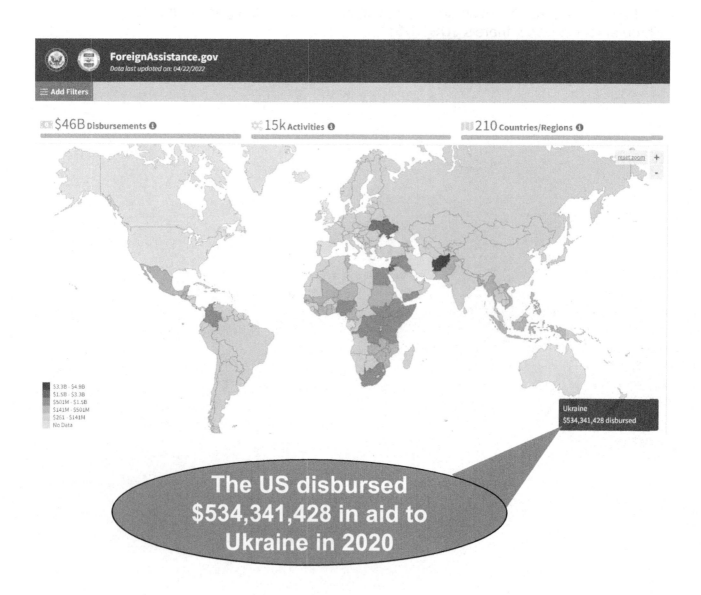

**The US disbursed $534,341,428 in aid to Ukraine in 2020**

## A pianist and a kid play at the airport

At DTW (Detroit Metropolitan Wayne) County Airport, Delta Terminal 71
There's a classically trained pianist, second to none
Playing, 'I don't get around much anymore'
I appreciated the melody, but most choose to ignore
At the Chick-fil-A, I just ordered a #1
Thinking one day, I might learn to play the piano and maybe even buy one
As he plays, travelers go about their various ways
I'm chilling, due to several flight delays
With time to burn, or is it supposed to be killed?
What a way to make a living, he's playing for tips with his skill
I would tip, but don't have any cash
'Do you take debit cards?' That would be a silly question to ask!
Amused, I see a young black kid, gleefully riding a Razor scooter past
I took a mental picture, as he nearly hit at least six people I figure
You know they were thinking, I wish security would catch this little…!
Later, I see that he's adopted, and both of his parents are white
His dad cut his hair just like his, no fade, just a stripe
Respect to him, for seeing and loving beyond color
His story will long stick with me, as I also wondered about his mother
Could I, would I, ever adopt white kid?
Maybe, I suppose that if I did
A middle aged white guy, at the airport, may also think about me and my kid...

## A slave and a queen

I had dinner with two of my ancestors, each born 1,000 years apart
A slave and a queen, I don't know who I was more in awe of
My challenges and failures seemed like utopian fiction to them
My worst day would be each's heaven
We wondered how we were able to span generations, and break the rules of time
Speaking with the past and the future in the flesh
Our words translated via subtitles in our minds
Shared facial features that ached from smiling and laughing at the impossibility of our experience
From the Queen, I learned that history edits and embellishes more often than we know
Yet when the world was smaller and younger, people were more the same
Wonderful, flawed, ambitious and evolving
From the slave, I learned how a lifetime of terror can sharpen one's mind, body, and soul
I fear they learned nothing from me
A common man in a modern world, who has flown across the globe, and has probably forgotten more things than the scholars of their time ever knew
With such an abundance of freedom that it leaves him paralyzed
While royals waste and rule, the enslaved rebel and seek freedom
In the empire of America, we don't really struggle, we just exist to consume
1,000 years from now, what will my progeny be?

## African American Emigrants?

In the nexus of my birth (Chicago)
On a business trip, so the visit was terse
I don't know which was worse
A tale of two cities one pretty (downtown) the other (Southside) hurt
I enjoyed both parts, for what its worth
But the nicest ride, of some lives, ends up in the back of a hearse!
Drugs, gangs and corruption
A lack of morals is the assumption
But its the lack of jobs and education, that caused the whole situation!
Mothers and fathers in prison, without cause or explanation
The young, gifted, and black, get processed like a raisin
In the sun, dried and blinded by all the hypocrisy
Social programs and funding cut by government and conservative philosophy
Votes and protests won't fix this mess
Revolution and looting are just symptoms of our distress
A real paradigm shift, is need to uplift
Useless, money, God, and tax deductible charitable gifts
Backpacks and free bikes won't change or save young lives
When every day, they're surrounded by struggle and strife
Historically, when the oppressed can no longer tolerate the lunacy
They leave their homelands in search of freedom and opportunity
Maybe we should do the same....

## America: lie, kill, and steal

When the last two impeached US Presidents (Clinton and Trump) were acquitted
Both vehemently admitted
Innocents, as the witnesses' lives were ruined
Counterfeit, our more perfect union
Illusions of checks and balances broken
History told the truth, but America thought it was joking!
In retrospect, we've live through countless holocausts unharmed
Millions killed, enslaved, and oppressed worldwide, but we're still not alarmed?

## America's only successful Coup d'état (November 1898, Wilmington, NC)

During a November election, nearly 125 years ago
Democrats in North Carolina, would quickly overthrow
The biracial Fusion party, made up of Republicans and Populists
Who empowered the mostly black and affluent population, of a North Carolina metropolis
Democrats deployed the Red Shirts (a para-military terrorist group) to stymie the black vote
And leveraged all of the daily newspapers, stating that quote,
'This is a white man's country, and white men must control and govern it'
The Democrats published their Handbook statewide, to make it legit
They swept every position, electing every Democrat who ran
And then, they also decided to usurp acres of black owned businesses and land
Murdering hundreds of black men, women, and children, and causing thousands more to flee
Who never returned to North Carolina, by threat of death by bullet or tree (lynching)
The leader of the resistance, Alfred Moore Waddell, declared himself the mayor
Nothing could save black folks then, the law, or even prayer!
This was 23 years before Tulsa (Oklahoma), and 25 years before Rosewood (Florida)
We can ask for reparations and fair elections, but will it really do any good?
In the last century, the parties may have changed
But our country's history of manipulation, still remains the same
We keep mastering and playing by their rules, but they just keep changing the game.

## Amistad

At Mystic Seaport, in Connecticut, looking at some old ships
I didn't expect to be reminded of slavery, chains, and whips!
Moored to the pier, in the distance, I discovered something odd
A small old ship named 'La Amistad!'
I didn't recall anything about it, on Mystic's website
It was so small (120' long by 23' wide) I kept thinking, this just can't be right?
I found a sign that confirmed, that it was the very same historic schooner
There were some people working onboard, I wished that I had noticed them sooner!
We walked over to ask a question
But busy with renovations, they didn't have time to share a history lesson
It was low tide, so the deck was a few feet below the pier
I explained to my daughter, the history of what once happened here
In 1839, 53 slaves (including four kids) taken from Sierra Leone to Cuba revolted
When the ship's cook joked that he'd be killed, salted, and cooked, Cinque* was very insulted!
The 'cargo' killed the cook and the captain, and ordered the navigator to take them back home
The navigator sneakily sailed to New York instead, impervious to 'Stockholm Syndrome'
The Amistad was seized in Long Island, and the surviving victims were charged and arrested
The merchants said that the slaves were born in Cuba, but eventually had to confess it
Cinque learned English and won his Supreme Court cases**
President Martin Van Buren appealed twice, because he was extremely racist!
Cinque and the rest of the Mende*** finally made it back to Africa, three years after they were originally taken!

* A.K.A. Sengbe Pieh
** With the help of former president John Quincy Adams (then a U.S. Representative from Massachusetts) and attorney Roger Sherman Baldwin (32nd Governor of Connecticut and US Senator) who both represented the African 'fugitives'.
*** The Mende are one of the two largest ethnic groups in Sierra Leone (West Africa)

## An analogy about racism

Racism is like the entire ocean, not just the sharks and predators lurking
A whole ecosystem that surrounds us, constantly hurting
Most of the aquatic life living, crawling, floating, and swimming discriminate
The mass majority of their lives spent stressed, the constant fear of danger imminent
Those too big to fail
The Sharks, Octopuses, Sea Turtles, Jellyfish, Sea Lions, and Killer Whales
Live their lives in privilege, ignorant, just wagging their tentacles, flippers, and tails!
The only difference in this analogy
Is that under the sea, the evolution of prey and predator is an actual reality!
But up here on dry land
The construct of race, amongst woman and man
Was simply just an incredible lie, spread by religion, sea power, and greed centuries ago
A truth that is finally being brought to light, so please let everyone else know!

## Another poem about racism

I've lost my will to make sense
Of all of the nonsense
They kill, we die, repeat, wash, rinse
Outrage, frustration, out of order and control
How can we reset, repair, and mend the broken pieces, back into a whole?
Are my questions reaching the right audience?
Are the real solutions really that obvious?
When the motto is live
Or slaughter them all like pigs!
Why do we have to get up, get over, get under, and **THEN** and forgive?
I have no answers, just stupid ideas and useless words...

## Been in the room

I've been in the room
Where I was the only one getting fired
Been in a room
When I was exhausted, but no one else was tired
Been in the room
Where my peers made more money than me
Been in a room
When racist and sexist jokes deeply offended me
Been in the room
Where HR urged me to accept a demotion
Been in a room
When **<u>MY</u>** trainee got **<u>MY</u>** promotion
Been in the room
Where management gave me an impossible task
Been in a room
When, even in a pandemic, I was the only one wearing a mask
Been in the room
When I called out a superior for being a prick
Been in a room
Where I didn't say shit
I'll stay in the room, until I can change it...

## Bill's overdue colonizers!

When hate hurts the heart
People panic, and process pain poorly
God gave us flaws, yet still reprimands cruelly
The worst win rewards, just look at the bully
They're ropes, we're cogs, and life is just a pulley
Europeans conquered the world, so half speak Spanish or English
Got Johns and Marias in South America and Asia, its so difficult to distinguish
Worried that immigrants will take back what is due
So they pass laws and build walls, against anyone with a hue
The world makes and Europe takes
When will the colonizers pay, for all of their past mistakes?
The world should reclaim half of Europe's riches, if it were any wiser
Trillions of Euros in gold, oil, diamonds, and free labor - the bill's overdue colonizers!

## Black and Bull

When black people are killed and treated unfair
The economy and stock market, goes the opposite of bear
Early July, in two thousand and sixteen
The Dow Jones hit records levels, never before ever seen!
But when terrorists threaten European kingdoms overseas
Investors get worried, and the markets begin to freeze
Economic prosperity in America, as strange as it often seems
Flourishes when black folks are down, on their backs and knees
Europe's abuse of Africa is hundreds of centuries old
Weapons, religion, and sin, three reasons why the Vatican is made out of gold!
Romans and Greeks killed and enslaved Hebrews and Africans
Then other caucasians invaded, conquered, and enslaved men
Women and children in mass
The culmination of world domination, they were very successful in their task
Are they justified in their wrong doing, because they have yet to feel God's wrath?

## Black and white friends talk about BLM

<Black>
If I protested with caution
And brought my daughter to witness
And she accidentally caught COVID (or a bullet), would you question my parental fitness?
We're in dire straits, putting it all on the line
But America is still indifferent, searching for evidence of its spine...

<White>
Jewish people are a minority, and they are doing just fine!
So why are African Americans the subject of almost every headline?
Slavery ended over 150 years ago, and what's with the BLM pound sign?

<Black>
Ethnic enclaves like Chinatown, Little Italy, Little India, Little Poland, and Koreatown still exist
Guess what happened to the African American equivalents?
Black Wall Street was burned, and the Black Star Line was thwarted
Black folks were hung, terrorized, integrated, redlined, and our history still remains distorted
Jewish people are united (in general) by a world leading religion
You and I believe in the same God, but my ancestors had no choice in the decision
For thousands of years, Jewish people have been 'chosen' worldwide
For hundreds of years Black people were stolen, raped, beaten, and then died!
All in the name of religion, economics, and a history that our nation holds so dear
America's three pillars: greed, death, and fear!
A stolen land made rich by slaves and oppression
But you still wonder if #BLM is a suggestion or a question?

<White>
I'm not responsible for slavery
And I have two friends who are black!
But I'm confused by this conversation, and honestly feel like **I'M** being attacked!
If I tweet #All Lives Matter, I could lose my job!
My wife posted #Blue Lives Matter on Facebook, and she was attacked by a virtual mob!
I just want things to go back to the good old days
When things weren't so politically correct, and people didn't get things twisted sideways

<Summary>
A familiar impasse among black and white friends
Compromise and disappointment is where it typically ends
Privilege is blinding and oppression has no remedy
Mutually beneficial solutions are fiction, the spoils belong to the victor, not the enemy

## Black and white friends talk about race

<Black friend>
At work, sometimes I go to my car to cry
Not from sadness but from anger, why?
Frustration, discrimination, comments, jokes, and utter disregard
When you are the only black person at work, you cannot 'play the race card'
When a black athlete wins a championship, **everyone** will celebrate
But when a black man kills a white cop, the media motivates America to segregate
As long as we're sweating, singing, dancing, running, boxing, and catching balls, things are fine
But when things turn sour, and black folks commit a crime
White America loses it collective mind
They buy guns and alarms, clutch purses, and lock their homes and car doors tight...

<White friend>
Defense is the best offense, I'm more concerned about my family's safety than black plight!
'Blacks,' have it better than ever, besides, I voted for Obama twice, and he was only half white!
African Americans are in movies, on stage, in plays, so they must be doing alright, right?
Whenever I travel to the airport, and stay at luxury hotels, what do I see?
Black and brown people everywhere... working... to... serve... me...
While I'm on vacation... They are working… oh wait, I see...
I'm privileged and you're not - silly me!

## Black Codes

Look up the Black Codes, to better understand American history
After you've read them, you'll be just about as pissed as me!
The US government made laws to suppress freed black folk
Today we're 'sort of' free, but still most ain't quite woke
Former slave masters forced sharecroppers to work
Or go to jail, so they toiled in the dirt
The difference between 1865 and 1866
Was subtle, and worth just a few extra cents!
Freedom still felt like bondage, for the newly emancipated
After the famous proclamation, our ancestors were still frustrated
Uneducated, broke, unable to vote, still lynched and castrated
To survive they conceded, still 'working' for their former masters
Rearing and feeding white babies while planting and harvesting crops in their pastures
Fast forward to the present day
Laws and economics are still much the same way

| Character | Binary Code | Character | Binary Code |
|---|---|---|---|
| A | 01000001 | Q | 01010001 |
| B | 01000010 | R | 01010010 |
| C | 01000011 | S | 01010011 |
| D | 01000100 | T | 01010100 |
| E | 01000101 | U | 01010101 |
| F | 01000110 | V | 01010110 |
| G | 01000111 | W | 01010111 |
| H | 01001000 | X | 01011000 |
| I | 01001001 | Y | 01011001 |
| J | 01001010 | Z | 01011010 |
| K | 01001011 | a | 01100001 |
| L | 01001100 | b | 01100010 |
| M | 01001101 | c | 01100011 |
| N | 01001110 | d | 01100100 |
| O | 01001111 | e | 01100101 |
| P | 01010000 | f | 01100110 |

**B 01000010**
**L 01001100**
**A 01000001**
**C 01000011**
**K 01001011**

**C 01000011**
**O 01001111**
**D 01000100**
**E 01000101**
**S 01010011**

## Black Confederate Solider

Black Confederate Solider
90,000 slaves, south of the Mason-Dixon border
Fighting for family and freedom
Bayonets and bullets?
Master said we don't really need them
Northern Negros is already free
So why in the hell is you fighting me?
I have freedom to gain
Or after hell, its back to whips and chains
As slaves, we had no voice
Fight for the South? Like we had a choice!
On the battlefield, I sort of free
'Bout the same as plantation misery
We cling to Old Dixie, like its Jesus Christ
As the only path to salvation - a "gift" from the whites
In the Gray Army, I got a knife
Learned to read and write
Field promotion, now I'm a medic who just saved the life
Of my master, even though he sold my wife
No supplies, eating swamp rats, with sides of moldy rice
If freedom ever had a price
I've paid it twice
With blood and sin
I shot a guy and then stabbed his twin
Stole his shoes and his ring
Then threw it all away, superstitious of what they spirits can bring
July 10th, I think I'm eighteen
This morning had a dream
A woman's touch, and sudden rush
When I woke up, A union soldier stabbed me, I'd just been stuck
Cold blue eyes
To my surprise
He felt remorse
And I of course
Just smiled
Dixie saved me after a while!
Now I'm a slave in heaven
And White Jesus is a good master....

## Black History (Back to Africa)

I insist that we, learn more black history
Our struggles and triumphs can no longer be a mystery!
America got its power off of our backs and creativity
Who farmed the land? Black folks!
Who executed the plan? Black folks!
Who fought hand to hand? Black folks!
Who gave them song and dance? Black folks!!! Whoop, whoot!!!!
Door knobs and ironing boards
Were invented by our people!
Tree trunks and hollowed gourds
Music and creativity has long been embedded in our people
I can't say for certain, but I wouldn't be surprised
If the sista' who invented peanut butter and jelly sandwiches, also came up with french fries!
You know that the first boiled egg, that was probably ever made
Was by a brotha' who was thinking, 'they gonna love this… and look at how much time I saved!'
Long before Dr. King and Malcolm X
Black folks hopes and dreams, had long been put to the test
Stolen from a foreign land, by shackled feet and hand
Identity, religion, and names all stripped
Raped, humiliated, killed, violated and whipped
Terrorized, brainwashed, like caged birds, our wings were clipped
Stressed and malnourished, yet somehow we still hip?
Discriminated against, for our hair, skin, and full lips
Black is beautiful, my people, let's take a trip!
Back to Africa, Marcus Garvey was our forerunner
We can live in America in the spring and summer
Then fly or sail to Africa in the winter and fall
America would crumble, and say, 'We can't lose all of y'all!'
That Black Star cruise liner would be so lit!
Entertainment and barbecues for weeks, across the Atlantic!

This dream can be a reality
If we just brush up on some new languages, and put away some of our salary
And invest in a black bank, like One United
I'm just writing down my dreams and getting all excited!
Wakanda forever!
Fiction to reality, fam we so clever!
Our destiny is only limited, if we say and think the word 'never'
Give us free? Who are we?
Kings and Queens!
Whenever we dare to endeavor!
Stars aligned, when our kind, built pyramids with just our minds and a lever!
When we shoot for the stars
We'll heal most of our scars
The path to the future, is back in our past
Black History my people – we are free at last!!!

## Black is mouse, white is elephant

I guess how **WE** feel is just irrelevant (hun?)
Black is mouse, white is elephant
Some may say that they're both gray
But that's when I jump into the fray!
Imma stay hell-bent for justice
When the powers that be, 'bum rush' us!
Did you see Ieshia Evans, standing strong and serene?
As the heavily armed police, rushed toward her at full steam!
While the cowards and photojournalists waited behind the scene
To capture and sell, our patented design
You'd think we'd revolt, but it happens almost every time!
It's like they have a monopoly
On our souls and intellectual property
Still, we infinitely overcome adversity, making dollars out of dimes
Fuck pulling up boot straps!
I wear wingtips, and I want **MY GOT DAMN** country back!
America's superpower came from our ancestor's strain
Slaves harvesting cotton, tobacco, and sugar cane
Crispus Attucks lived and died for America's Revolution
Unappreciated patriots stay agitated, because our liberty should never be prorated or debated, but our freedom and opportunity always ends up getting confiscated, when we get money and power, it always gets raided, RIP Black Wall Street and Black Panther Party Incorporated, decimated like cancer, grief paralyzes our ambitions, chasing education burdened with hella debt and tuition, not confident as the token black, subtle now when they attack, just joking, but then you realize that you've been the butt all along, stay strong, credit to your race, don't let a 'nigga' moment be your disgrace, our boss, money, and God all bear a white face, Europeans possess 9/10$^{th}$ of the world's wealth and law, they even seized make-believe, got my seed writing a white Santa Claus! Damn they hold all cards, gamble/deal/steal/spar its a fixed game, nothing will change... unless...yes... Revolution!

## Black Nationalism 2.0

In May two thousand and fifty three
The president signed an executive decree
Awarding 'reparations' via government land
In Nevada (80% Federally owned) 40 acre plots were nothing but useless rock and sand
Most folks sold their rights back to the state
Earning just enough money to keep food on their plate
A wise few claimed their ‘reservation’
And profited greatly from their exploration
A year into the President’s unexpected fourth term
A powerful group of black folks, represented by a famous law firm
Held a press conference announcing their succession
From the United States and the world, leaving a strong impression
A new nation, far beyond Marcus Garvey’s wildest dreams
A place for people to escape from one of the world’s most racist regimes.

## Black people are magic

There is a unique power, that black people use
To make a lot money for others, who then abuse
Our magic, talent, and ability to make things cool
Like Mr. T, 'I pity the fool!'
Without 'Black Twitter' for instance
There might not be any new hashtags and trends in our absence
But we never really 'own our own,' we just beg for 'their' permission
Our oppression is a cancer, in and out of remission
We been schoolin' America, but still pay the highest tuition!
And accumulate various debt and fees
While these thieves hold our promissory notes, deeds, and keys!
Our chronic disease conditions us to service and please
Those who left Europe
Who tap our sap, then bottle and sell our syrup!
Bodies, souls, music, culture, and P.O.V.
They don't see us as human, because we're such an invaluable commodity...

## Census

When a census taker tried to quantify me last
I pushed her old ass out into the grass!
And slammed the front door
Screaming, 'Don't come 'round here no mo!'
Trying to raise my taxes and gentrify our district
Actin' all surprised when they get cussed out quick!
Once they see too many 'negros'
Suddenly there goes the quality of our roads!
They never plow or fix shit!
Sidewalks look like a gravel and sand pit!
Why all the hood streets gotta bend rims and break suspensions?
Cuz' our tax dollars get moved from infrastructure to build them new prisons…
Then they stop and frisk
Us 'niggers' and 'spicks'
Oh don't get pissed!
They call them 'perps' at Police Academy, but it's all the same shit!
When white folks brag, I get pissed quick
How they speed without fines and talk their way out of tickets and shit!
I tried it once, the officer was like 'Nigger please'
There's a website on the back of this ticket, now go and pay me some fees!

UTION, MILITARY INSTALLATION, ETC.
Name
Type
Line Nos. ________ to ________, inclusive

CONFIDENTIAL This inquiry is authorized by Act of Congress (46 Stat. 21; 13 U. S. C. 201-218) which requires that a report be made. The information furnished is accorded confidential treatment. The Census report cannot be used for purposes of taxation, investigation, or regulation.

FORM **P1**

U. S. DEPARTMENT OF COMMERCE
BUREAU OF THE CENSUS
**1950 CENSUS OF POPULATION AND HOUSING**

| FOR ALL PERSONS | | | | | | | | | FOR PERSONS 14 | | | | | |
|---|---|---|---|---|---|---|---|---|---|---|---|---|---|---|
| RELATIONSHIP<br>Enter relationship of person to head of the household, as Head, Wife, Daughter, Grandson, Mother-in-law, Lodger, Lodger's wife, Maid, Hired hand, Patient, etc. | LEAVE BLANK | RACE<br>White (W)<br>Negro (Neg)<br>American Indian (Ind)<br>Japanese (Jap)<br>Chinese (Chi)<br>Filipino (Fil)<br>Other race—spell out | SEX<br>Male (M)<br>Female (F) | How old was he on his last birthday?<br>(If under one year of age, enter month of birth as April, May, Dec., etc.) | Is he now married, widowed, divorced, separated, or never married?<br>(Mar, Wd, D, Sep, Nev) | What State (or foreign country) was he born in?<br>If born outside Continental United States, enter name of Territory, possession, or foreign country<br>Distinguish Canada-French from Canada-other | LEAVE BLANK | If foreign born—<br>Is he naturalized?<br>(Yes, No, or AP for born abroad of American parents) | What was this person doing most of last week—working, keeping house, or something else?<br>(Wk, H, Ot, or U for unable to work) | If H or Ot in item 15—<br>Did this person do any work at all last week, not counting work around the house?<br>(Include work for pay, in own business, profession, on farm, or unpaid family work)<br>(Yes or No) | If No in item 16—<br>Was this person looking for work?<br>(See Special Cases below)<br>(Yes or No) | If No in item 17—<br>Even though he didn't work last week, does he have a job or business?<br>(Yes or No) | If Wk in item 15 or Yes in item 16—<br>How many hours did he work last week?<br>(Include unpaid work on family farm or business)<br>(Number of hours) | 1. If employed (Wk<br>2. If looking for work<br>3. For all other<br>What kind of doing?<br>For example:<br>Nails heels on shoes.<br>Chemistry professor.<br>Farmer........<br>Farm helper........<br>Armed forces........<br>Never worked........<br>(Occup |
| 8 | A | 9 | 10 | 11 | 12 | 13 | B | 14 | 15 | 16 | 17 | 18 | 19 | 20 |

## Droitwich (the get-past-you-shuffle)

Droitwich is the term for the 'get-past-you-shuffle'
In the street dance/pedestrian hustle
I scared two strangers
Walking around a corner, in each other's path – 'Danger!'
Blue and green eyes both opened wide
A white man and woman's true feelings, in this split, second could not hide
Co-workers that I'd known for a few years
Panic and control, lost in inches of personal space, and surfaced latent fears
Never once in my 40+ years
When I cross paths with a 'non-ethnic' or non-black
They never say my bad, or get out of **MY** path
Once they realize who/what I am
Awkward silence
No threat of violence
The expectation is that I should acquiesce
So I first say excuse me and then walk around
And they just walk away without a sound.

## Emancipation

150+ years ago, we were freed
Fresh off the plantation, there was an overwhelming need
Searching for a sense of identity
We had a hard row to hoe
Writers like Harriet Beecher Stowe
Defined the modern 'Negro'
Sharecroppers toiled long hours to raise dough
Imagine picking cotton, tobacco, and wheat
Many earned just enough to eat
Fast forward 100 years, when 'colored' people got rights
Still, civil struggles caused much strife
Segregation moved to integration
Dreams of slaves and MLK, became a manifestation
Obama's ascension, was a result of the culmination
Of generations of men and women, standing on the shoulders of thousands of unnamed leaders
Standing tall with pride, like Redwoods and Cedars
Our roots are strong and nourished us well
The future is here and now, can't you tell?

## Emotions, restrictions unfair

No justice, no peace, no freedom, emotions, restrictions unfair
My skin, features, and hair
Check, check, check, identified threat, yet why do I try?
I have some opportunity and access, but my limit is still just up in the sky
Banging on a glass ceiling, as I continue to fly
Success is still high above me
Plain as day, I can still see
Invisible barriers, how frustrating they can be
Why is this system still in place?
Forcing me to labor, in an infinite race
With rigged rules, no clues, or hope for a victory
Going in circles aimlessly, repeating history

**Everybody got reparations except...**

Slavery, sharecropping, payday loans, and jail
Bondage, perpetual debt, cheap labor, and personal hell
Drugs, gangs, and cops who often stop and frisk
White folks, too privileged to even wonder why we're still pissed
Broken families, social calamities, and overburden grannies
Baby daddies making infrequent visits in vintage Caddys
The faults in our stars, materialistic and misogynistic
Looking future rich, but past broke, a walking contradiction
A charlatan president, in this dystopian fiction
Up is down, smiles are frowns, and celebrities are as high as college tuition
Pharmaceutical snake oil, disbursed with amoral prescriptions
Opioids fill voids, like Netflix subscriptions
Have nots binge watch, while the rich take their crumbs
Mortgages, bills, phones, and media, are all just making us numb!
Fewer people know Jesus
Charities pocket profits, then become more egregious!
They'd rather just 'save the planet' and drive a Tesla or Prius!
And kill us, as the cops, crips, and bloods keep pulling those triggers
Everybody got reparations except for them...

## Fight Wokes

So many of you everywhere
Driving in big vehicles, with small dogs, without a care
At the airport, in Starbucks, and at Whole Foods
Yet I rarely see y'all being embarrassed, on the evening news
Getting got or getting shot
Safe, tucked far away, in your place behind a key and lock
Suburban, or moving downtown to be more ‘urban’
Gentrified, with four times the earning
And net worth your of your ethnic' neighbors
They take the bus to work, while you read about their despair in the funny papers!
Some are liberal, while others are conservative
But most get nervous when
We walk by, they clutch purses and lock their doors
Your ancestors took mine, so what, now I'm some how gonna take yours?
Black Americans give to a fault
But we keep get charged for things that we haven't even bought!

## Fleur-de-lis
(Saints' Logo/Mark of Slaves)

Walking around the French Quarter in a daze
Crowds in bars watched the Saints game being played
While rich Negros were bought and sold via online fantasy trades
An echo of slave days, when massa used **Fleur-de-lis** to mark the hides of his and her slaves
Few know this logo's significance and story
The 'Redskins' weren't the only franchise that was derogatory…
For hundreds of years, Black Americans slaved and sharecropped sugar cane
Yet even after freedom, we gang bang and slang cane
Worked for the white and made the white, that caused our plight like diabetes and addiction
Mental, spiritual, emotional and physical diseases plague us, but America still thinks it's just fiction!
These long term effects, still curse us like a voodoo hex
Plantations were replaced by the industrial prison complex
Our future should be a destiny manifest
Being survivors, from a long line of survivors, was the ultimate test
Against all odds, given nothing, we built America... Yes…
But they keep us uneducated and depressed
Frustrated and in debt
Doped up and locked down, because they're afraid of what's next.

## fuck europe!

How come nobody ever says it?
I'm surprised (that) no one's has ever really done it!
I'm about to change public opinion and keep it one hundred!
europe was a deadly virus, that made the whole world sick
Am I the only one whose fed up with all of this bullshit?
The world has 37 billion acres of inhabitable land, ain't that a bitch?
So why does 'queen' elizabeth own 18% (6.6 billion acres) of it?
We should all gather up a bunch of pitch forks and torches, and then steal back **ALL** of that shit!
If a 400 year slave trade from Africa, 200 years of british rule in India, and **TWO** Opium Wars in China doesn't make you mad
europeans also murdered millions of people in 'America' just to take all that they had!
So here we all dwell
With these europeans, who still make life on earth a living hell!
They are living in paradise
While the rest of the world **STILL** pays the price!
Consuming all of the world's natural resources, gold, cobalt, lithium, cotton, rubber and rice
Because they aren't abundant on the 'continent'
Of their origin, where they've spent
Centuries hoarding and stealing art, culture, religion, science, and wealth
The world lives and dies twice, while most europeans are the 'picture' of health!
Karma and retribution simply just don't exist
If they did, the count of european graves would be a very long list
But it ain't, so they just keep on stealing, killing, and living well
A life on earth for most europeans is a paradise, but for the rest of us, its just a living hell!

(I just didn't feel like capitalizing or making 'europe' a 'proper' noun above, since my ancestors and I were forced to speak and write in 'english' when we were kidnapped and forced into slavery...)

♥

## Gaslight Slavery

Gaslight slavery
Fear, the absence of bravery
So pissed, that they can't admit…
Their privilege, so they resent…
Our history and mystery
Love my culture, but, they're constantly pissed at me!
A system of lies, from education to laws
Believe our future is grim – **PAUSE…**
Power and money is 100% fiction
Make believe, written to deceive, so that people will listen
Columbus and Washington killed people and owned slaves…
Both are still celebrated as national holidays
Psychological warfare, like Patrick Hamilton's play
Dim the gaslight, then flip the victim's plight
Like… 'damn, maybe Kanye was right?'
Slavery sounds like a choice...
Not!  That negro's been crazy, gotta mute that voice!
Don't fall for the 'okie doke'
When the media's blowing smoke
Shell games, while they re-arrange the names
Three Card Monte, keep your eye on the **Spades**!
**Diamonds** cut, **Clubs** hit, as your **Heart** bleeds with rage
Four suits proves, that the fix has been in!
The game's rigged, those who dealt the cards, just pretend....

## Give them the Samuel L. Jackson face!

Being the only black person (at work) sitting in a cubical in the back, allows one to hear
What Caucasians, Asians, and other racial persuasions say, whenever we ain't near
Gone is the guard, long disappears the fear
Most times, I'm just quietly working in PowerPoint and Excel
Then they whisper or blurt out some racist shit, and I'm like, what the hell?
Occasionally I have to intervene, when they the start to cause a scene
Using our slang, saying, 'Guurrl', 'Ratchet', 'Bae', 'Bye Felica' or 'Yassss Queen'
Other times I cringe, when they tend to offend
When one's true colors emerge, it's too hard to pretend
During President Obama's election and re-election
They'd hem and haw, in their biased reflection
Now with Trump, they vomit all the fake news that they hear on TV as gospel
Trevon was high on weed, Sandra Bland they still don't understand, and Black unemployment is at its lowest level in decades, so how/why is that so awful?
Their reasoning and justification is completely logical (not!)
Because they've never been turned down for a job, or a loan, or been harassed by a cop
But it's not my place to educate my boss and others who control my corporate fate
So I just give them the Samuel L. Jackson face, whenever they discriminate
Snakes on a Plane, Do the Right Thing, and Patriot Games, with a Nick Fury take
Dead stare, foul cowl, says, 'get the Fuck outta here,' like Django Unchained
Make them ashamed, with a John Shaft wrath, like, 'White bread, is you insane?'

**Global Majority**

I'm a Global Majority
Refuse to be a color or minority
Acting locally and thinking globally, grants me authority
Race is an iceberg, far beneath there's much more to me
And you - boxes, adjectives, and labels are lunacy!
Those who use them, simply have no class, truancy
Suggest progress, and watch them scratch their heads cluelessly
This ain't the way that it is supposed to be
Degree, presence, or absence of melanin, ain't really a reason to boast to me
Nor is one's wealth, place of birth, or current vicinity
What is God's hue, is it a he or she, singular or a trinity?
We ask the wrong questions, and then accept truth horribly
We need to unlearn and return
Question the 'facts' with which we're most concerned
Because it's pointless, none of us are anointed
Or special, as the powerful become self appointed
Some nerve, as their personal disasters curse the masses
Forever frozen by fear, trapped and passive
Like Lions and Elephants, choked by a tiny rope
At all of the zoos and circuses, they've lost all hope!
If they could only remember, the feeling of freedom
Then they could break free from their cages, but who would feed them?

## Granted

Granted...the planet's slanted
Subliminal thoughts implanted
Gas ain't cheap, we need electric!
Bet this?
Politicians neglected
To share power with the people
Separate and unequal
Privilege is a HUGE a blind spot
Backing up in luxury SUVs, not using the mirrors and cameras, 'Honey, did you hear a knock?'
'He just jumped out of nowhere, do you think this is some sort of a scam?'
Is that blood **AND** a scratch on my bumper? Damn!
Shouting obscenities at the injured pedestrian, because you have dinner reservations at 8!
Driving away without saying sorry, because you don't want to be late
This hit and run scenario is an analogy for racism's cause and cure
The next time y'all 'driving in privilege,' check your cameras and mirrors, just to make sure!

## How the 'underclass' will overcome

Without salvation or divine intervention
We overcame fears of whips and lynching
Jim Crow now, still barely gets mentioned
Billy clubs, fire hoses, and riot fights
Civil rights stymied by elections, insurrections, and police lights
Decades of integration and crack pipes, decimated black life
Causing high cholesterol and hypertension, symptoms of our strife
Technology is obviously a double edged knife
Producing the illusion of inclusion
Sans WIFI and a payday away from losing (everything)
Life is a game, but the cost of admission is never free
If the odds can somehow outweigh our inequity
Trust in God, then bet on me!
Your tired, hungry, and poor
Huddles masses, still deeply indebted, to a society that's cashless
The sons and daughters of slaves, who built the world's greatest civilization
Have the power and ability to destroy its very foundation...

## If Kavanaugh were black and Anita Hill were white

If Brett Kavanaugh were black and Anita Hill were white
Things would have turned out exactly the same way, right?
Man, Clarence and Brett wouldn't be sitting on that bench!
Double standards, wash, repeat, and rinse
The more things change, the more they just don't make any sense!
We hope that people will do good, but they probably won't
We're at the pinnacle of cynical
Don't need parables that are biblical
A lot of guys use public restrooms, but hardly ever use soap!
To wash their hands, but we demand, and hang on to slivers of hope
I often wash and dry mine
Then I have to use the same door, that they left covered in germs and slime!
What's the use, when we care, but they simply don't?
Ignorance is bliss, and the system is broke!
The greater good, being misunderstood, it's a cruel joke!
We all have reverence for the POTUS and the Pope
While both have robbed, killed, and abused people for generations
All the gold in the Vatican and Fort Knox, won't cover the cost of reparations!
While candidates debate, to control the fed and the state
Most Americans think that everything is just great!
And that the concept of 'race' is an archaic construct
The 'haves' said the 'have nots' are simply just out of luck

## I'm my ancestors' wildest dream

I'm my ancestors' wildest dream
Slaves who survived by any means
Necessary, freedom was a sweet blessing
Angels cheering for me, down from heaven

We can't imagine living each other's life
I can't fathom their daily pain, struggle, and strife
So every class, test, event and game
I work hard and smart so that I can claim
Success for them, me and my family
Their survival and sacrifice is what made us free

So I make a daily vow
To make them proud
Me, a rookie on my family's team
I'm my forefathers' wildest dream
I'm my ancestors' wildest dream

Middle class, but my great grands think I'm a king!
Slaves made this country great every beyond measure
Died broke but gave all us invaluable treasure
I share their hopes, blood, dreams, and genes
What didn't kill them all, made them sing
Spirituals of low sweet chariots
They slept on the floor, now we stay at the Marriotts!
I thank them daily for their sacrifice
They all paid the ultimate price

I time travelled back into the distant past
150 or so years ago if you do the math
To see my great grandfather* who was born a slave
An asset, his second Master's $1,500 mortgage paid

He died free, so they put a different name on his grave
Than the one that his cruel captors and masters gave
Branded, bought and sold with a bank approved mortgage
Then discarded like lost goods, for years left in storage
The 'land of the free' was a Ponzi scheme
But it's okay and why I say that I'm their wildest dream.

## I'm my ancestors' wildest dream

# My Great Grandfather was a slave for 12 years

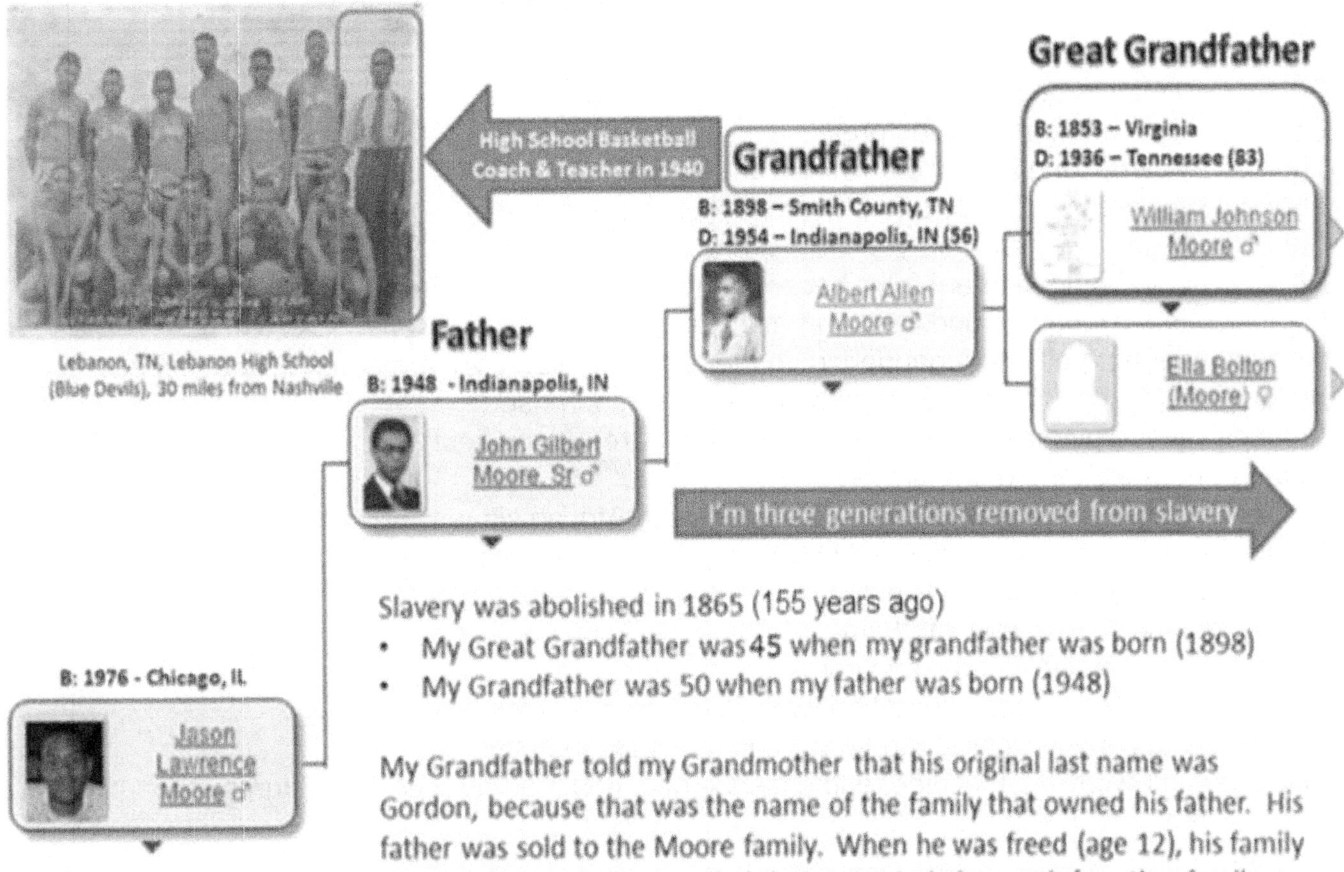


Slavery was abolished in 1865 (155 years ago)

- My Great Grandfather was 45 when my grandfather was born (1898)
- My Grandfather was 50 when my father was born (1948)

My Grandfather told my Grandmother that his original last name was Gordon, because that was the name of the family that owned his father. His father was sold to the Moore family. When he was freed (age 12), his family decided to keep Moore as their last name to help search for other family members who were sold to other families.

THIRTEENTH CENSUS OF THE UNITED STATES: 1910 POPULATION

**In the rearview, slew two, armed and racist cops**

We went from 'Distinguished Gentleman' and 'Head of State'
Comic movie plots became reality in 2008
Obama's hope and change was great!
Then 2016 came, and I felt like a college graduate
Thought my votes for Sanders and Clinton would be adequate
But 'Great Again' was familiar, yet strange and cold
Rich, privileged, and ignorant folks became empowered and bold
Gentrification, alienation, and random traffic stops
Gerrymandering, politicians pandering, in the rearview, slew two, armed and racist cops...
Building walls, shock and awe, so only a few remain surprised
America's just a pyramid scheme, built on hatred, greed, and lies!
Home of the free, land of the brave?
Rather decimated Indigenous people and exploited African slaves!
Yards below Central Park, once held hundreds of unmarked graves
Gotham's first gentrification problem
Simply displace, rape, and 'off them'
Americans denied life, liberty, and joy
Jim Crow, civil rights, and integration was all just another ploy
To divide and conquer, black and brown communities and cultures
Still today our words, art, bodies, and essence gets poached by soulless vultures.

## Life beyond black and white

Written prose for my foes
Discriminate, while washing my clothes
Whites and darks remain separate
The former, gets heat and bleach
The latter is us, understand my speech?
Universal rules are pointless, no need for religion to preach
Now we're begging for forgiveness, no need to beseech
The wing span between my hands, is still far beyond my reach

Ideas in mustard seeds, yield actions in trees
Yet, they bend in the wind, then surrender their leaves!
Nature sheds its coat in the winter, while we put on our sleeves
Another paradox, we rob mother nature, like we hate her, pitiful thieves!
Opposable thumbs, separates us from pond scum
Intellect allows us to recollect, what's already been done
Gifts from millions of generations, since we were crustaceans
We did not create everything, so we ponder our foundations
If we had all of the answers to life's mystery
We would be disappointed, and then change our history.

## Linconia and Monrovia

In 1862, Abraham Lincoln wanted Black Americans to emigrate to Panama
Told the 'would be' Central American colony (Linconia), 'y'all can have them all!'
Lincoln invited Fredrick Douglass and others to the White House to discuss his plan
In total disgust, they replied to Lincoln, 'We ain't getting on no more boats white man!"
Costa Rica, Nicaragua, and Honduras felt the plan would end with America attacking
500 black families were willing to go, but the plan never ended up happening...

...Monrovia (the current capital of Liberia) is named after James Monroe, America's 5th President
In the 1820's, the American Colonization Society (ACS) sent thousands of free black Americans to become African residents
The American government preferred their emigration, in lieu of emancipation
As more 'negroes' gained freedom, America gravely feared widespread interracial integration
Monroe and the ACS treated black folks as goods and Africa as their lender
We got all that we need, now please return to sender!

JAMES MONROE
5th PRESIDENT
TERM: 1817-1825
ABRAHAM LINCOLN
16th PRESIDENT
TERM: 1861-1865

## Living with history's worst

Imagine that Nazi Germany never ended its reign of terror
Picture King Leopold II's Belgium still exploiting and killing 10-15 million men, women, and children in the Congo (all for Ivory and Rubber - Google it!)
How much more land and riches would the Queen Elizabeth II have (she currently owns 6.6 Billion acres of land - again Google it!) if the British Empire never relinquished its hold on (large) parts Africa, India, Hong Kong and Australia?
How much more gold could Italy have possible taken from Africa to decorate the Pope's Palace?
What if the Spanish, French and English still owned and shipped in replacement slaves to run their sugar cane plantations in Haiti?
What could be worse than Italian grave robber Giuseppe Ferlini destroying 40 Nubian Pyramids in the 1830's?
What if I told you that America became a world superpower because it murdered, enslaved, segregated, integrated, incarcerated, drugged, tried, lynched, beat, raped, mutilated, subjugated, terrorized, burned, castrated, cheated, lied, redlined, and stole from black people for centuries, but was never was once forced to stop, apologize, or atone for its past actions? Kind of fucked up ain't it?

## Matchstick!

Being black in America is like having a fuse
Racism is a match that some white people use
They incite, we ignite
We beg, they refuse
31 traffic stops? He was only 32!
Newt Gingrich is right, white folks have no clue
We move on, grin and bear it, and ultimately lose
I lick my thumb and finger
To put out the spark, but the anger will still linger
But my wick's getting shorter
I hope I don't explode.

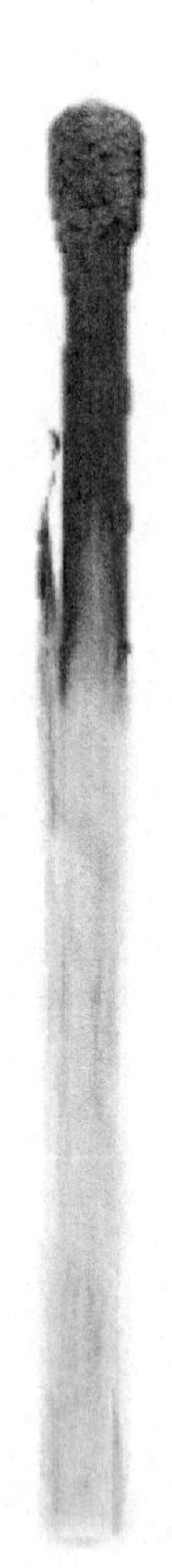

♥

## Middle Passage Martyr

Trapped, hot, and nauseous, eight weeks at sea
Naked, chained, unbearable shame, no longer free
Blood, shit, tears, vomit, and pee
Everywhere around me
Arms, legs, hands, and heads, writhing in pain
Curses, prayers, nonsense, going insane!
Will they beat me?
Will they eat me?
Deathly smell
This… Is… hell…
Why have we all been cursed?
Life or death, uncertain which is worse
Bruised, branded, and whipped, I can't stand it!
The skin on my back, got cracked by the devil's whip
After the third hit
I caught the tip, with a desperate grip!
We outnumber them - let's takeover the ship!
Put them below in chains, to lie in our shit!
Most ignored my plea and call to revolt
Too petrified to push, too broken to hope
Heads bowed and eyes darted down to the deck
As the sole mutineer, my fate was set
Still chained to bodies to my left and right
I pushed them behind me, with all of my might
As fire and smoke spewed from a cannon, I wasn't too surprised
A flurry of rocks and metal was my untimely demise.

♥

## Misnomer = Black Privilege

Being Black in America (no privilege) some just can't stand it
Change won't happen, until we force and demand it
Those with money and power, are oft too heavy handed
When black folks get fed up, they just don't understand it
The ghetto's good enough, and who gives a damn about the planet?
Greed is good, I wish a 'Nigger' would
Demand another red cent, because it won't do any good
They'll just buy drugs and Jordan's, and hang out in the hood
With this 'us' versus 'them' mentality
Inequality and discrimination will long remain our reality
Why is the top public school in NYC (Stuyvesant High School) only 4% Black?
Why, to be successful, do our kids have to play basketball or football or rap?
Chris Rock said it best
Talking about his neighbor in jest
Same homes, but one is a movie star, the other is just a dentist!
Better health, less stress, and generational wealth
Some 'fight wokes' got what I got, and barely made it past the 12th
Grade, in this day and age, the America Dream
Is a nightmare for most, as we cry, die and scream!
African Americans, the soul, builders, and pariahs of these great United States
Are in an abusive relationship with a country that constantly hates (us)...

## Mortimer and Randolph

I accept your opinion and understand your truth
It's not my job, or desire to provide you with proof!
To retort what you accept as reality and fact
If you really believe that Trump isn't full of crap
Then there is not much that I can say
You'd probably disagree with me anyway
Then you said NFL players must stand
And pay their respects, or else we must demand
Their resignations and rescind all of their endorsements
Call the owners, the POTUS, and other reinforcements
And later muse that Trump deserved the Nobel Prize for Peace?
For the historic meeting with North Korea at the least
Talking points from Fox News and the Daily Beast
I was quiet when you further bragged about jobs and the economy
I chewed my food, more than I normally do honestly
But then when you quipped, 'I don't understand why Kaepernick is so pissed?'
Over that little incident?
I took the bait, 'Oh you mean Ferguson?'
Well, you reasoned, that kid shouldn't have reached for the cop's weapon then
Besides, the officer was found not guilty…
I look around for the waiter and beg him to bill me!
The table looks to me, for some type of reply
I sarcastically say well at least the cop didn't die!
Conversations about bad areas of town
Privilege, the lack thereof, and how the disenfranchised act and sound
Boot straps, gun racks, and the media's quest to keep the rich/white man down
It's just like Mortimer and Randolph are back in town!
Trading places, anti-racist, their game changed with a dollar bet
After they tasted defeat, they got right back up on their feet, and bought a brand new jet!

## Murder Porn

Graphic images constantly being played
News and social media posts, like bullets being sprayed
White crime and death is well protected
And hardly ever displayed, replayed, or disrespected
But when Black lives die
It's highly publicized
America has long been desensitized
Mass media hangs strange fruit as a sadistic prize
We've seen George Floyd die at least a dozen times!
And that sets a dangerous precedent
We're being brainwashed, with all that time spent
Is it for justice, or just laws and rules being bent?
Innocents lost, as the police commit
More crimes for which they'll never repent
More preacher prologues from busy pulpits
Different times, same shit.

## My shit hard and my dick soft!

I'm stressed out and I'm pissed off
My shit hard and my dick soft!
Pulled over by an angry cop
Passengers' wife and daughter's respect lost
When he called me boy, I could have mouthed off
Instead I said, 'Yes Sir,' like I was taught
Stayed alive and paid the ticket cost
Now when I try at home to command
My wife and seed plead, 'Why you ain't pop off like that to the man?'
So eyes and necks roll, double standard
Had I talked back they'd be stranded
Widow/single mom/daddy issues/headstrong
So I lost the battle, still fighting to win the war...

♥

## Myocardial infarctions

Knowledge is pain, ignorance is bliss
I was 'today' years old, when I realized this
The more I learn, the more I get pissed!
Re-read American history, for the irony and plot twists
Abraham Lincoln paid reparations of $300 per slave, to all DC slaveholders
We keep asking for reparations, but politicians tell us to wake up and smell the 'Folders!'
Black Americans die early, often, and heartbroken
From myocardial infarctions, patiently waiting for pardons, apologies, and tokens
**The revolution was televised, but we can't afford Wi-Fi or cable!**
Why settle for crumbs or a seat, when we can just build our own table?

## New Africa

In the not too distant future, an earthquake instantly creates a new land
Less Atlantic Ocean, more African sand
An entire new island, about the size of Japan!
Full of oil, gold, and trillions in other natural resources
Dozens of European, Asian, and American army, navy, marine, and air forces
Try (in vain) to claim the world's newest continent
But New Africa belongs to old Africa, justice for centuries of time spent!
Mistreated, enslaved, robbed, killed, and haunted like a ghost
The world's most valuable place (and people) finally gets what it deserves most
When a new world appears off of Africa's west coast!

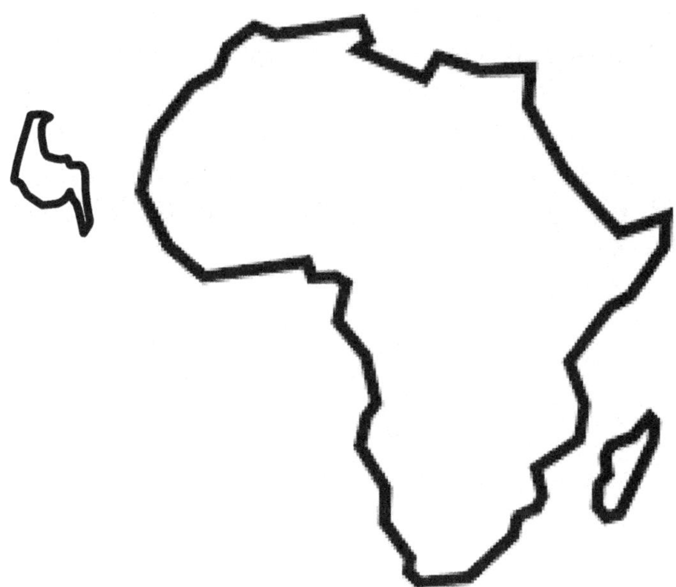

## Nigger in the woodpile

'Nigger in the woodpile'*
A phrase that we haven't heard in awhile
The origin of the phrase comes from slaves running away from their master
Now it is a 'British' term for a snafu, problem, or disaster
In July of 2017, Anne Marie Morris** an member of the UK's Parliament
Used the phrase, 'Nigger in the woodpile' in her argument
Those bloody blokes started to squirm
Tasteless expressions like 'African Booty Scratcher' and 'Indian Rug burn'
What's that? Would you like to know how it ended?
She apologized and was temporarily suspended
Don Imus posted 'color' commentary about 'Nappy headed hoes'
Apologized and then went back on the air with two new radio shows...

*The phrase 'Nigger in the woodpile' means "some fact of considerable importance that is not disclosed—something suspicious or wrong". The phrase can be traced to the United States, when the phrase was used in song lyrics to reference slaves who hid in piles of wood while fleeing north to freedom.

**Anne Marie Morris is (as of August 2022) currently a Member of Parliament (MP) for Newton Abbot (since 2010) and a member of the Conservative party. Discussing the impact of BREXIT on the UK's financial services industry, she said, "Now I'm sure there will be many people who'll challenge that, but my response and my request is look at the detail, it isn't all doom and gloom. **Now we get to the real nigger in the woodpile**, which is, in two years what happens if there is no deal?"

## No more MLK quotes

When will we get a definitive win?
Where justice prevails and intolerance ends
If race and class are just two made up constructs
Who has the power and ability to say game over, time's up?
The abolition of slavery and voting rights
Are ancient and hollow victories to young protesters demonstrating under broken streetlights
Prisoners making street signs and license plates for pennies in prison
Share similar fates as their ancestors were living
The current system is broke, and unchanged by our votes
We need real solutions today, no more MLK quotes.

## No problem

You don't want no problem with me
I might only be a buck and half plus three
But I really wish you'd test me
All this rage that I suppress, just like Banner, Bruce
As I transform into a beast, who proceeds to cuts loose
Watch my reality become your worst nightmare
I see the fear in your eyes, as I proceed to tear
Your life, piece by piece
Nothing but pain, blood stains, and a future of family grief
I was mild mannered, but you just had to poke and provoke
Damn, this rage calms my nerves, like some cigarette smoke!
As your moans and groans crescendo, so goes your hope
Pulse goes, life ends, as you take your last gulp
Of air, no, I don't care, cuz you didn't heed or believe
When I said at the start, that you don't want no problem with me...

## No reparations

Five hundred and seventy eight pounds and twelve shillings
Was the sum that the families of Salem witches got in reparations…
The morals and irony of our proud Christian nation
Native Americans and black folks only got reservations and complications
If it sounds like I'm complaining, then you're damn right!
Protesting is pointless, it would be foolish for us to put up a fight
History is filled with injustice and lies
I have no hope that the future won't be otherwise
I'm still steaming from those missionaries, who converted us 'heathens'
Who enslaved, conquered, and waged war for dubious reasons
For centuries, decades, and scores, they bred, worked, hung and raped us
Changed our names, berated, castrated, and hushed us
Mistreated us, beat us, stole our art and our souls, regulated us, discussed us, bussed us,
Fear us, lust us, cuss us, distrust us, mock us, judge us, lock us, con us, curse us, and kill us.

## Ode to the Black Panthers

Them against the world
Proud, loud, men, women, boys, and girls
Social programs, pamphlets, and guns
Feeding and educating our daughters and sons
Afros and dashikis, uniquely displayed Black pride
They even made Dr. Martin Luther King move to Chicago's Southside!
Fighting for education, healthcare, and piece of mind
Great ideas and intentions, just in the wrong place and time
For our civil rights, some paid the ultimate price
To get the freedoms and opportunities that we all now have in this life!
So proud of them and so ashamed of us
Today we complain, refrain from change, and barely vote
We have not overcome, still victims of the gun, and the system is still broke.

## OJ's Parole Show

OJ's Parole Board hearing was just sad to see
Why won't the media just let him be?
Whatever you think about Orenthal James
Consider the fortune that the mass media has made on his name
I've had a lot of dreams, where I've felt trapped
Like OJ, explaining myself and taking a bunch of crap
Wondering why do these motherfuckers keep messing with me?
If he were white, they'd probably just let him be
He reminded me of Morgan Freeman in that movie, Shawshank Redemption
The white dude escaped, while he's all old, holding onto his hat, still begging for permission....

## On the EL Train – Chicago, June 2018

I was on the EL train
Riding to a Cub's game
There was this young brother, talking some crazy yang
He spit for emphasis, after every other point
Then he pulled out a lighter, and then sparked up a joint!
He continued to talk about the government and God
When the contact buzz hit me, I felt a bit odd
Then some of the points that he made, didn't sound so crazy
He spit on my shoe, but I was just too tired or lazy
To interrupt his entertaining monologue of conspiracy theories
If he were more ambitious and charismatic, he could have a show or web series
His friends shared his chronic, and nodded in agreement with his every proclamation
The future is doomed, stay in school kids, and get a trade or an education!

## Onus / Owned Us

The onus, ain't on us
As we die, cry, fight and cuss
The government can't legislate morals to make you just!
And the ‘gods’ ain't at odds with your mistrust
We're so tired of the way that you treat us
But all we can do is fuss
The onus is yours, because you once **owned** us!

## Piece vs. Police

I wish a joker would
Try to step to me and mine
When these busters step out of line
It gives me reason to break their spine!
I try abide by the law, and walk the moral line
But I'm so tired of the police harassing me all the time!
All my stored up hate's ready to explode
They call me boy again, I'm gonna be bold!
I've had it up to here, so I'm finna go dumb!
Might just go crazy, so dem jokers better run!
They got a gun, so I got a gun
Allergic to malevolence, it makes my trigger finger itch
This fool in blue, will be lying in a ditch!
When I scratch and squeeze
The trigger on my Dessert eee's
Witness the bullets spray, like a sneeze!
Snotty slugs striking they mugs
Shells fell like phlegm, spat from street corner thugs!
My clip's congested
Filled with hate and biologically infected
Its weapons of mass destruction, whenever I'm disrespected!
Safety's never selected
My pistol's always loaded
Cellphone videos are useless, damn I should've voted!
Cuz they shoot first, and then ask questions later
Now Mama's in church, praying to our Lord and Savior!
And I'm just another nigga on the 11 o'clock news
My first, middle and last name under my mugshot, in red and blue
Black on Black, Blue on Black, White on Black crime
We don't fear death, just hope for reduced jail time

## Plantation Perdition

Our ancestors must never be forgotten
Their story was purgatory, picking sugar cane, tobacco, and cotton
As masters surveyed and inventoried their chattel
Enslaved human beings were treated worse than cattle
Whips sting, sweat streamed, agony under burlap
When scabs on backs cracked, bloody cloths had to be rewrapped
'Water Boss?' cautiously requested, seconds away from heat stroke
A overseer drank from a canteen, then simply replied 'Nope.'

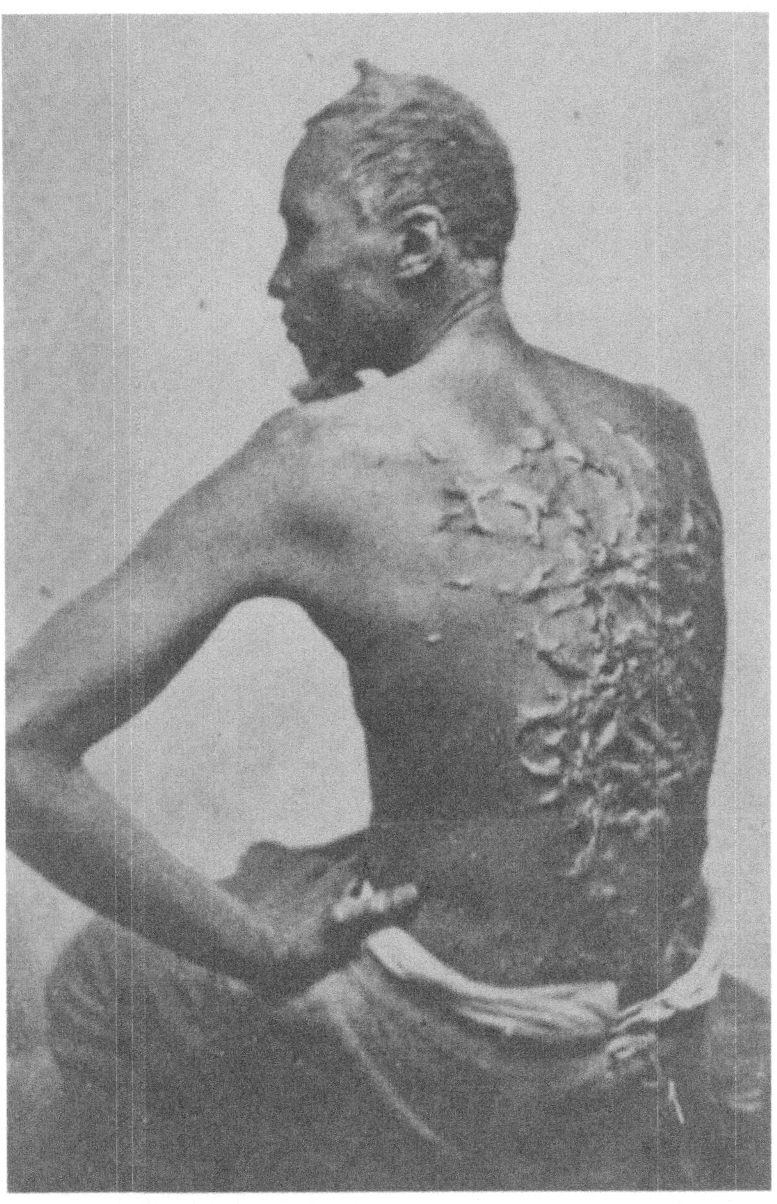

*An escaped enslaved man named Peter showing his scarred back at a medical examination in Baton Rouge, Louisiana, 1863.*
*Library of Congress*

## Privileged folks

Ever listen to the conversations of privileged folks?
It's like they enjoy egg white omelets, without ever breaking the shells or the yolks!
All of the rigmarole that most people endure
Is their biggest drama in life, nothing like the poor
Disenfranchised and marginalized masses
Who do more with less, as the world beats their asses
Imagine if spending money and time was the bane of your existence
Given everything, without hard work and persistence
Those they hate and can't understand, kept at a distance

## PTSD (Post Traumatic Slave Disorder)

Post Traumatic Slave Disorder (PTSD) is real
That haunting sensation we feel
When police lights glow, in the rearview mirror
Heart rate increases, hairpin trigger?
Starting gun's cocked, ready, aim, fire
Run nigger run, no alibi, you're a guilty liar!
Hurdles stacked in our path, so we must jump higher…
Fight or flee, either way we get caught
The system's been rigged, since we were sold and bought.

## Racial Resentment

We keep taking, but you still thrive
You're never invited, yet you still arrive
We keep killing you, but you're still alive!
**YOU** people are like weeds, no matter how hard we try
Like dandelions, you pop up unexpected, grow, and refuse to die!
We wiped out the indigenous people and bent Indian and Asian cultures to our will
But **YOU** people refused to break, regardless of how many Africans we'd steal and kill
For centuries we kidnapped kids as slaves
10 to 15% of our human cargo, now all share an ocean grave
But **YOU** people transform despair into music and art!
**YOU** people built this country, but here's the crazy part!
When I see you in my office or living in my neighborhood
Instead of waving hello, I think that you somehow cheated, and can't be up to no good!
How is it possible, that you and I can be in the same time and space?
My ancestors **OWNED** yours, so how can you even afford this place?
We copy and steal your magic
Yet here **YOU** are, your life should still be tragic!
The way that the media paints your narrative, describes a living hell
You should be poor, dead, in debt, from a broken family, illiterate, in a gang, on drugs, AND in jail!
So I'm puzzled whenever I see you
You must the exception, **YOU** cannot be the rule?
We forced you to speak our languages and believe in our gods
But **YOU** 'magic' people put your own spin on things, and still defy the odds!
Maybe we're just too insecure, uncomfortable, or unwilling and unable to face this inevitable fact
Why haven't **YOU** retaliated? Why don't **YOU** get revenge? When will **YOU** finally attack?

**Rent's due motherfucker!**

If I represent myself, there's no chance they'll acquit!
Most of my peers, are already dead or doing years
Unfair trials yield more smiles than tears
The prosecutor winced, at my clever defense
So your best and brightest is Trump and Pence?
Flesh gets ripped, on this barbed wire fence
Taking all of your scratch, like payday loans and rent!
I'm out of order?
Its useless, trying to secure the boarder
Karma from when y'all ordered the code red
Centuries of millions enslaved, and even billions more dead!
With the audacity to fear your final demise
Now y'all nervous of a revolt and timely up rise?
A stolen land and people is the foundation of your legacy
All in the name of 'God' and a manifest destiny!
Sitting up high with a gavel, and the nerve to be testing me?
Rent's due motherfucker, your time is over see?

## Repeated history?

What if North Korea secretly kidnapped thousands of American kids, all under the age of five
Then shipped them across the Pacific, assuming that 85%-90% of them arrived alive
840,000 American kids go missing each year, one every 40 seconds, according to the FBI
Only a fraction ever make the news or Amber Alerts, have you ever wondered why?
Milk cartons no longer have pictures of missing kids anymore?
Now let's get back to that, cold North Korean shore
Millions of former Americans, now slaves conditioned to serve, labor, and fight
An 'underclass' building a new foundation, to challenge America's might!
Stolen humans, long neglected and forgotten, just as soon as they sailed across the sea
This is fiction, but with all that we know about history, who's to say that it could not be?

## Revenge of the Peckerwoods

Years ago, my Grandfather told me
That one day, left unchecked, all of the 'Peckerwoods' would finally break free
And when they started yelling 'Yeee-Haaw!' you better get!
'Cuz they're either on the warpath, full 'liquid courage,' or about to start some real shit!'
'Once,' Grandpa whispered, 'When I was confronted by a pack of Peckerwoods in the wild, here's what saved me!'
Grandpa continued, 'I didn't run, I don't know Karate, but I do know **CRAZY**!'
'I looked up at the biggest Peckerwood, and stared him dead in his eyes…'
Said 'I'll whup yo' country ass, long before you get any help from those other guys!'
'The head Peckerwood flinched, because he didn't want to catch these hands!'
'He knew the tune that I was playing, but he really didn't want to dance!'
'I didn't even need to pull out my piece, I just told them all to go on about their merry way.'
'If you ever run into a pack of Peckerwoods in the wild, now you'll know what to do and say!'

## Robeson vs. Robinson

Robeson versus Robinson, both icons have my upmost respect
A young Richard Nixon got Robinson to do something, that he'd long live to regret (twice)
In 1949, before the House Un-American Activities committee
Robinson was pitted against Robeson, it was such a pity
Robeson said that Black Americans should not fight against the Russians
And was called before Congress, for a around of humiliating discussions
Robinson disagreed with most of Robeson's views
And argued that he didn't represent, nor walk in all black people's shoes
As America's hero reluctantly testified
Brothers and sisters across America, each died a little inside
Some called him an Uncle Tom
As an Anti-communist, Mr. Robinson was wrong
But the black community knew all along
That there would be no winners
To be the first and black, there are no free dinners
In 1960, Robinson choose Nixon over Kennedy for POTUS
In his final years, Jackie Robinson was bitter and refused to stand for the flag, but nobody noticed.

♥

### Ronald Reagan (born February 6, 1911) and Harriet Tubman (died March 10, 1913) were alive at the same time...

Slavery was not that long ago, so stop playing with my mind!
Ronald Reagan and Harriett Tubman were alive at the same time!
America want us to think that slavery and Jim Crow is ancient history
Then when I say that 'Black Lives Matter,' America wants to get pissed at me!
Part of me wants to continue the fight
Get into some 'Good trouble' and help make to America right
The other part of me is like, let's move to Africa, Canada, or Mexico
If I had the ability to emigrate half of Black America, how many people would go?
If America ever 'gave' black folks 'Reparations'
It might look a lot like indigenous reservations
With the construct of race
They never gave us a chance or a place
Unlike Italians, Polish, Jewish, German, Irish, and Asian immigrants, who were able to integrate
And establish generational wealth and carve out their own towns
Have you ever seen a little Africa around?
But there is still a Little Italy, Greektown, and Chinatown in nearly every major American city
Our communities were burned down, redlined, flooded, <u>AND</u> divided by highways, what a pity...

## Seeking the 'Golden Ghetto'

I told my realtor that when he searches for me
That I don't want to 'Be' diversity
Rather, I want to 'See' diversity
I've been the only 'brotha' in the HOA
Where neighbors smirk whenever they wave
Giving our daughter the best, we believed
Wise, through her eyes, whenever she sees
Disparity, isolation, and clarity
Worried that she wouldn't do well in the hood
Some folks incorrectly believe that schools with brown teachers simply aren't rated as good
Rather well, most "affluent" schools are rated 'swell'
With the students' and teachers' complexions mostly pale
At home we can supplement
But there would be arguments, if we get
Anything but a quality education
See the conundrum that we're facing?
It's not right
Our problem is black and white
The right choice is a must
Like flying in a plane or riding in a bus
Both will get her to where she needs to be
The latter will have more people that look like her and me
But it will be much less comfortable, convenient, and on time
And those passengers on the plane might treat her unkind
We won't complain
Maybe we can find a train?
A middle ground, with people of all hues, white, black, yellow, and brown
Not the greatest, but the best to be found...

## Separate and unequal

My great-grandfather was a pastor
Grandpa was a deacon
Mom took us to church
Maybe that's what got me seeking
Answers to the best and worst
History's narrative, for what it's worth
Lies multiplied to hide crimes
Genocide, apartheid, social and economic lines
Gaslights, civil rights, overtaxed, and fined
Separate and unequal
No justice for our people
Protests, distress, we've already seen the sequel
Their language and religion
Was our ancestors' punishment and prison
When I express myself and pray
Is it my bloodline that I betray?
Assimilated, displaced, cultural nomads
Protesting old flags
Entertain the masses
Filling half full glasses
Because there's a hole in the cup
Too much, yet never enough…

## Slavery was so fucked up...

Slavery was so fucked up...
**How fucked up was it?**

When the Emancipation Proclamation was signed in 1863, Texas slave owners didn't tell their slaves until June, 19, 1865!

Slave owners would split up families at slave auctions, selling them to plantations in different states just to maximize their profits!

When George Washington lived in Philadelphia (America's first capital city in the 1790's), he'd send his professionally trained enslaved chef (named Hercules) back down to Virginia every five months to ensure that he would not become free (Pennsylvania state law allowed any slave to declare freedom after living in the state for at least 6 months)! Martha Washington (the 'first' First Lady) was world famous for her 'recipes' that were really created by Hercules!

The life expectancy of the average American slave from birth was 21 to 22 years old, while that of a white person in the south was 40 to 43 (double)!

One third of slaves died within the first three years of their arrival to the United States.

Infant and child mortality rates for slaves were twice as high as southern white children!

In 1830, 36% of American households had slaves. By comparison, in 2017 40% of US households paid for lawn care services.

U.S. Supreme Court Chief Justice Roger B. Toney referring to the 1857 Dred Scott case, said "A Black man has no rights a white man is bound to respect." This became the law of the land.

The U.S. Constitution designated black people as three-fifths of a person for the purposes of determining congressional representation!

The term 'lynching' and possibly the town of Lynchburg, Virginia are named after one (of two) military officers with the last name of 'Lynch' (no relation). Captain William Lynch and Colonel Charles Lynch's methods torturing of British soldiers and slaves alike, that not only coined a new term, but also created a level of domestic terrorism so enduring, that it outlasted slavery, several world, domestic, and international wars, Jim Crow, and every other major event in American history since!

## Storms of injustice

Vicarious trauma
From years of discrimination
As we die, defend and dread in the US nation
More visceral than driving again, after a horrible car crash
Pinned by a knee, that's empowered with a badge
That ominous cloud, that reappears every other year
Storms of injustice, rain drenched with fear

## The 2nd Amendment

The second amendment
Was designed to kill 'Indians' and control slaves
The document that we all hold so dear betrays
The very ideas that it promotes!
So miss me with all the false aspirations, and promises of hope
It calls for a 'well regulated militia' and the right to keep and bear arms
If the police ever stop me, with a gun in my car, it will justify **them** causing **me** harm!
In 60 seconds, an AR-15 can fire 600 bullets!
One 'gun person' can kill everyone that they've ever known, whenever they pull it!
The trigger, as the bullets and guns got bigger
Now cops just shoot first, instead of calling us nigger...

## The 'Caucasity'...

She had the 'Caucasity'
To tell 'ole boy to 'act white,' whilst in 'their' white neighborhood (at his front door!?)
The unmitigated gall
To not put any black people on the wall - Sal's, Do the Right Thing
The nerve to cast white actors as Egyptians in the year of our Lord 2016!
In the movie The Gods of Egypt, it makes me want to scream!
The cognitive dissonance to accept an apology, hug, and get their hair fixed as a former police officer who murdered an innocent man in his own apartment!
The testicular fortitude to utter the phrase
'All lives matter,' it never ceases to amaze!
I stood beside myself and laughed
When old boy tested 'Hard Iced Tea' man's wrath
'What, you gonna smack me that?'
Wish granted, 'liquid courage man,' I told you not to call me that!

## The Cautionary Tale of Brother Shazu

The story of brother Shazu, is a cautionary tale
Of what not to do, and how to fail
An internship in corporate America
As an African American, it's a test of character
I only spoke to him a few times, a good guy, he went to Howard U
I went to Hampton, clearly the better school (LOL!)
His actions and termination, are the stuff of corporate lore
Before I tell you what happened, allow me to illustrate what happened before
I was assigned to mentor another intern, who was Asian and had a pleasant disposition
She told me a few days prior, that brother Shazu was offered a full time position!
He boasted about his achievement to all his peers, and one must have been crossed
Someone knew about brother Shazu's secret, and promptly notified his boss!
He'd walk past my cubicle daily, in the early afternoon
He must eat lunch late, I reasonably assumed
The next day, everyone was talking, with a hint of glee and shock
Shazu's new boss found him sleeping under desk, and fired him on the spot!
If you are ever tired at work, drink some coffee and remember the story of our fallen intern star
Take a half sick day, or go take a nap in your car!
Years later white folks at work, still can't believe his unmitigated nerve
It's a running joke, if someone looks sleepy they're about to, 'do a Shazu,' dude became a verb!

## The melanin and culturally deficient 'global minority'

Before the fabrication of racism, religion, and debt
The world would change, and long live to regret
Dozens of deadly sins
Crisis caused by vices, war, sex, drugs, and gin
As eggs break
We learn and make mistakes
Knowledge peddled by cunning snakes
Afterlife reservations
Disguised as spiritual manifestations
The melanin and culturally deficient 'global minority' used manipulation
To spread lies, greed, and weapons like a plague
'Whiteness,' land ownership, and money is ALL man made…
Courtrooms, credit scores, and zip codes limit hope
Life, liberty, and the pursuit of happiness for us brown folk
Assimilated aliens, with no specific place of origin, rather a vast continent
Neither African or American, blood mixed with our captors, eye and skin hues of various tint

## The progeny of product

Imagine being bought, sold, and traded
Killed, raped, and confiscated
More valuable than gold, yet treated like an animal
African slaves made the 'American Dream' tangible
For everyone save themselves
Laws forbade reading, voting, and marriage, made life a living hell!
America wanted independence from Britain, **to protect the institution of slavery**
Crispus Attucks only got death for his bravery!
The engine of the industrial revolution
Was powered by slaves picking rice, cotton, tobacco, coffee, and sugar in perpetual destitution.

## The sleep of reason produces monsters

The sleep of reason produces monsters often
When masters become captives, they'll soon fear the coffin
Demanding mercy, how soon they forgot
Necks cracked by gravity, and a vicious noose knot
The rage of the enslaved
Begins with revenge, and ends with a blade
Thousands of lies painted in pictures of 'God'
The construct of race, their foundation's a fraud.

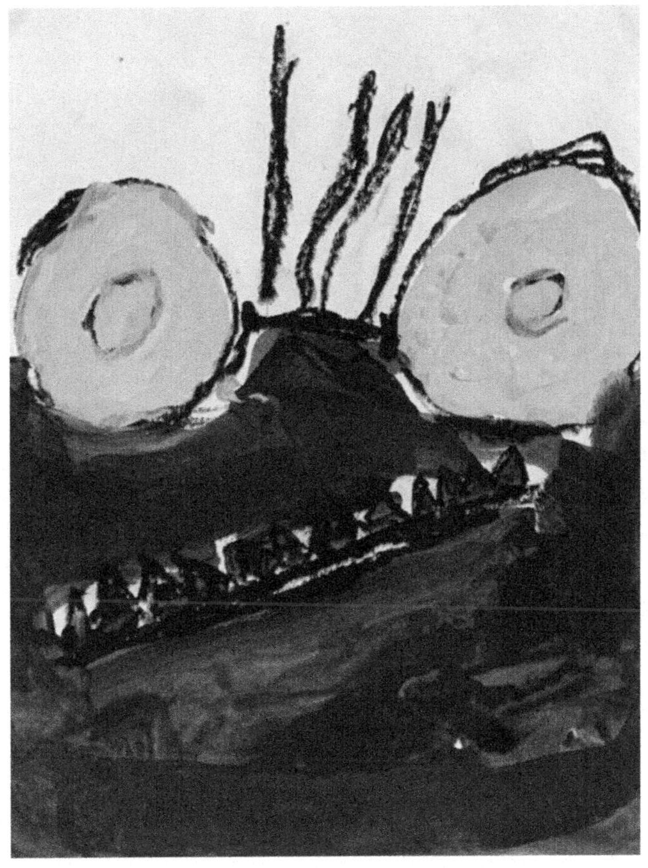

Illustrated by
Zoe Victoria Moore

## The War of General Malaise

An epic battle against General Malaise
Began as an ember and ended with a blaze
The nation was swept with a newfound craze
Where lies replaced facts, and left the masses in a daze
Both sides fought aimlessly, for causes in which they did not truly believe
While the instigators played from a safe distance, pulling tricks from their sleeves
The poor and less educated, risked limb and life
As all of America paid the ultimate price

THIS PAGE LEFT INTENTIONALLY BLACK

**Tiananmen/Ferguson**

25 years span their past
Facing a tank and a bottle of tear gas
Extraordinary citizens, both carried bags
Groceries and potato chips
It only takes one person to say, fuck this!
I read people's comments online, and most are crude
Their statements pale in comparison, to these icon's testicular fortitude!

## Uncle Sam, Uncle Tom

Uncle Sam, Uncle Tom*
Uncle white, Uncle wrong
Oh brother, sister, mother, mister, your auntie & cousin wasn't jokin'
When they said that the system was broken!
They must be trippin' or buzzin' off somethin' potent
The last GOP Convention was peppered with a dozen tokens
Just how much does a sell-out make?
And how many souls sold and owned will it take?
I know the answer is no, but please give me a break!
I can see the tide turning, "let them eat cake!"
Complain then change everything on a whim
Pitting us against them
There's more of us, plus were rich so we'll win
Trust, there's no penalty for this type of sin
White lies, hands tied, welcome to the beginning of the end!

*Uncle Tom is a misnomer – in the book Uncle Tom's cabin, Tom refused to become an 'overseer' and was killed by Legree's hand.

## Up until last week

Up until last week
Things were tough, but I had hope
That the future would be better, and that I could cope
I still have trouble getting loans
Even though I've owned five homes
I used to think that when I got stopped by the police
They might just beat my ass, and maybe knock out some teeth
Up until last week
I never thought that they could kill me, while my daughter was in the back seat.

## Watermelon & Ribs

This past weekend, my wife cooked a delicious rack of ribs
From the most tender, juicy, and tasty of pigs
When there were "leftovers", left over, I called dibs
And brought them into work the next day
Lunchtime came, to my dismay
I'm the only black person on my team, despite decades of Civil Rights
I can't heat, eat, and enjoy my rib tips, without confirming certain stereotypes
Imagine me in the cafeteria, or at my desk
With the judging looks from my co-workers thinking, "Just as I suspect!"
So I grabbed my lunch bag, and began to search
For an empty conference room, so I could get to work
Out of the way, sneaking and hiding like a felon
Then I discovered another brotha in conference room 1A, eating some watermelon!
I said, "Deion, why are the lights off? And how did you find my secret lunch spot?"
He replied, "I caught you in here last week eating bean pies, so I figured why not!"
We laughed and talked about life and the rest of the food that we brought
And prayed that we wouldn't get caught!

## We get shot

We get shot
We get got
We confess under duress
We get jail time
We are guilty until proven innocent of crime
We protest
We turn the other cheek
We get the other cheek beat
We talk revolution
We demand restitution
We point fingers
We blame as the pain lingers
We kill each other
We blame guns, gangs, drugs, slavery, government, and the single mother
We "talk" about problems in terms of black and white
We need to "make" solutions in gray with oversight
We hope for change and vote
We know that the system is beyond broke
We settle for something
We do everything and nothing
We continue plan and plot
We still end up getting shot.

There have been over 28,000 fatal encounters with police in America since 2000.

## What if Batman was racist?

What if Batman was racist
And the Joker was black?
With both in your scope, which one would you attack?
The lesser of two evils, villain or hero
The answer is always undefined, whenever you divided by zero
Seems like the hero always wins
And the villain lives, only to commit more 'sins'
This cycle repeats, each depending on the other for purpose
Both are the same, if you look just beneath the surface

## When black folks sell their homes

Black folks selling their homes, have to remember one thing
The only things some white people love black, are coffee and Dr. Martin Luther King!
When you stage your house, you must be keen
Take down all of your pictures, and please hide that afro sheen!
No wave brushes and cocoa butter
Or pictures of your sister, brother, father, or mother
Remove all African American people, places, and things, double check, and then think
See, you almost forgot that can of magic shave underneath the sink!
Hide your books and music too
Pack away the autobiography of Malcolm X and D'Angelo's Voodoo
Remove everything in your home, that's a reflection of you
Why do I have to lie to you, and then lie to me?
Just to sell my home in this "post racial society?"

## When tanks drove down my street (Indianapolis - 1995)

Some people mock the inner city, and chastise other poor parts
Calling them 'seedy,' 'sketchy,' and 'ghetto,' like we don't have souls and hearts
I grew up in the same places, that they constantly dread
Cracked sidewalks, liquor and dollar stores, crime maps labelled in red
In the summer of 1995, Danny Sales was beaten by the police
A riot ensued and they drove tanks down my street...
The tread damaged more than the asphalt and concrete
It shattered any illusion
That they saw us as human
Tax paying citizens, fought 'Billy Clubs', K9 dogs, and tear gas by hand
Those 'dangerous' people in 'Chi-raq' and 'Napghanistan'
Who keep 'killing themselves'
Don't lack morals and wealth
Rather economic injustice, school closings, gentrification, prison, and drugs in combination
The culmination, caused generations of disruption and the manifestation
Of the same disregard/apathy for us, that the whole US nation
Has for all of the victims and survivors of countless school shootings
They shrug and blame music and video games, instead of implementing solutions
And nothing ever really changes, and history repeats, because we're all complicit
The media, elected officials, social organizations, and corporate America if I'm getting specific...
'Us' against 'them,' the 'haves' versus the 'have nots'
Once thriving communities (Tulsa, Ocoee, etc.) were killed, and they took everything we got...
Just like land and names from America's Indigenous people
Reservations were first, then the 'project,' were sequels...

## When will it end?

Don't make a scene
Or Imma scream
Vanilla chocolate
As the world ends, you make a profit?
Mortgaging dreams for optics
Fits and starts
Equity is sparse
Hollow platitudes are a farce
I've seen this movie before
We don't want no more
Nightmares, injustice, hate, screams, tears, frustration, discrimination, and funerals...

## White Privilege Day (January 6$^{th}$)

January 6th, I say
Shall henceforth and forever be known as 'White Privilege Day'
As thousands of 'Patriots' marched in ranks
I was confused, wondering where in the hell are all of the water hoses, dogs and tanks?
As thousands of middle aged men and women stormed into the Capital chambers
They were not the least bit concerned or in danger
They chased that poor black Cop, up three flights of stairs!
There was no audio, but we all know the words used for their dares
You can't touch me, you might be a cop and your stature is bigger
But I'm a proud white man, and you're just a....

## Whitey found water on the moon

Whitey found water on the moon
Millions of people worldwide are dying of COVID-19
(But whitey found water on the moon)
The president said he's completely immune
(While whitey found water on the moon)
The polar ice caps have melted
But NASA's going back up there real soon!
They still haven't prosecuted the cop who killed her!
(But whitey discovered $H_2O$ on the moon)
Millions of children are starving!
(But whitey's bragging about water, thousands of miles away, on the moon)
They are locking up kids in cages on the border!
(But luckily for us, whitey's got water on the moon!)
Millions have been unemployed for months!
(But whitey's hiring engineers, to extract drops of frozen water, on the moon)
Your cousin's been in jail for years for selling weed!
(While Whitey's selling weed legally, and reading about NASA finding water on the moon)
Step and Fetch-it worked hard to get Black people to vote against their best interests!
(So that Whitey could find some water on the moon...)

## Zombie apocalypse or alien invasion

Zombie apocalypse or alien invasion
Might be the only cure for violence and racism
Are death and annihilation?
The only things that'll stop us from hatin'?
Judging, abusing, robbing
Killing, lying, raping?
Why do we repeat this vicious cycle time and again, instigating?
Mental, chemical, and environmental issues and influence
Some maintain and use these conditions as excuses
Others are guilty of information and power misuses
To spin, upend, abuse and confuse us
Like you, I want to set the best example for my kid
But I seldom take full responsibility, for all the wrong that I did
Beyond conversations and accusations, action is what we need
What's the point of turning over a new leaf, if we don't first plant a seed?

# PART II: LIFE & LOVE (105-288)

Top 75 = ♥

## #Socialdistancinghaikus

We wear the mask so
Others may live and prosper
Real heroes wear scrubs

I get déjà vu
I know I was here before
But what happens next?

Eat, sleep, watch TV
Non-essential employee
Nobody is free

I spent time today
Watching clouds float in the sky
Change is beautiful

**7/26/2057**

35 or so years from now
I'm an octogenarian, sitting in a park, wearing a smile!
Enjoying time with family and friends, just eating some barbecue
Everyone's clothes are so odd, we looked like some animals at the zoo!
Stripes, spots, fur and feathers, all over my shirt and shoes
The little ones are all so proud, that Grandpa's got on the same gear too!
Keisha is a few yards away, talking with our daughter
Zoe's hidden from my view, as I tried to focus, my eyes began to water
When she finally appeared to me, from behind a tree
I saw the little girl that I once knew, and now the woman standing before me
A spitting image of her mother, she said, 'Daddy, what's wrong?'
Suddenly, I felt as if, I haven't seen her in so long
As I experienced this vivid, futuristic déjà vu
I wondered, was it time travel or just a dream, I still have no clue?

## 10 things that Medicare doesn't cover
## (a Public Service Announcement - PSA)

There are ten things that Medicare doesn't cover
Important services, that your dear father and mother
May one day desperately need
But thanks to government and corporate greed
You, he, she, and the rest of your folks
Will have to pay for the following services, with cash or credit, and then go broke!

1) Glasses (and eye exams),
2) Hearing aids,
3) And most dental work, Medicare Advantage plans will only pay for one row of dentures, now my feelings are hurt!
4) No overseas care,
5) Or **any** medical care for your feet! Because hammertoe, bunions, and heel spurs are just like a trip to the beach!
6) No cosmetic surgery,
7) Acupuncture,
8) Prescription drugs,
9) Co-pays,
10) Or Nursing Home Care

If you don't like America's healthcare, just move to Canada, I hear that everything is 'free' up there!

## 12 Questions from my daughter

1. Why do I have to make up my bed?
2. Why is there crust on our bread?
3. Why are there braids in my head?
4. Why can't I watch YouTube?
5. Why is the sky gray today, but sometimes it appears blue?
6. Would you like to play a game of Clue?
7. Why is Barbie so skinny?
8. Why didn't Mickey marry Minnie?
9. Why are some people starving, but we have plenty?
10. Why do you work so much?
11. Why can't I bring my lunch?
12. Is it Colonel Mustard, with a knife in the hall, because I have a hunch?

## 2020 Quarantine

150+ days in quarantine
But who's really counting?
My poor kid is for sure!
With no end in site, can she endure even more?
Oh, the places we can't go
How many more bubbles can we blow?
Walks around the neighborhood, games, books, puzzles, crafts, math, and TV
Mommy's an essential worker, so at home, it's just her and me!
Five months on a 'virtual' house arrest
Is like 18 months full of Saturday's and Sunday's, no jest!

## 20th Wedding Anniversary

Made it past security
Waiting for our flight
I once dreamt about maturity
Now it's my everyday life!
Holding the world, in the palm of my hand
Time flies, seconds pulled by gravity, like sand
In an hour glass… her figure
Keeps me mesmerized
But my lust for her wit, makes me bigger!
She caught my shine, in her moon bright eyes
Heading to Havana, Cuba on vacation
20 year wedding anniversary celebrating!

## 2B who you were destined 2B

Believed in my dreams like scripture
So vivid, they painted a picture
While others debated, my goals were illustrated
Leaving foes so frustrated
That they were surprised that we made it!
See, me and success is related!
Hard work and I often dated
Opportunity and I eventually mated
Luck, I intentionally impregnated
Dedication and I, wed in holy matrimony
So failure doesn't really know me!
I keep fear and hate so lonely,
That self doubt's about to owe me!
An apology, and frustration's about to see
The other side of misery!
Because Joy is our baby!
Never no, only yes and maybe
A confident and positive attitude is key
To be who you were destined to be!

# 3$^{rd}$ Quarter

Six decades into this 'adventure' called life
One fourth spent with my daughter, one half with my wife
It's nearly halftime, as these wrinkles and gray hairs multiply
Spending less time on the 'hows' and more energy on the 'whys'
I'd never imagined how viruses, racism, and the geopolitical climate would evolve
All of the challenges we face, each of the problems that we must solve
But I'm content with who and where I am, in the present day
The third quarter has just begun, and I'm ready to play!

## 5 Boro Bike Tour

I rode my bike 40 miles around NYC
Five boroughs, bridges, and a ferry with 30,000+ bikers – it was a site to see!
As a novice, I was nervous that I couldn't go the distance
Training months prior, clouds could not rain on my persistence
I could barely do a mile at first
Before I'd cramp up, get winded, and parched for thirst
Finding time to ride my bike was the pits
In those rare spare hours, I really just wanted to watch Netflix
But I committed to participate and decided that I was going to do this!
With a $99 bike from Walmart and my Adidas kicks
In time, I could ride further and faster
Fate, is seems, can still be controlled by its master!
A lesson I needed a reminder of, in my middle age
We are all the authors of our own story - what's written on your next page?

## 50th Wedding Anniversary

50 years married
Anniversary gold status
Some say it's an institution, mixed with bliss, compromise, and madness!
Other say it's a friendship, hardly ever a 50/50 split
For better or worse, kids, work, mistakes, and **<u>ALL</u>** of the rest of it!
Love, happiness, commitment, communication, and laughter
Footsteps on a journey, where soon thereafter
You realize how your relationship has grown throughout time
Every memory a page, each experience a line
A dual biography, half a century in the making
Happy 50th Anniversary Mom and Dad, your story is breathtaking!

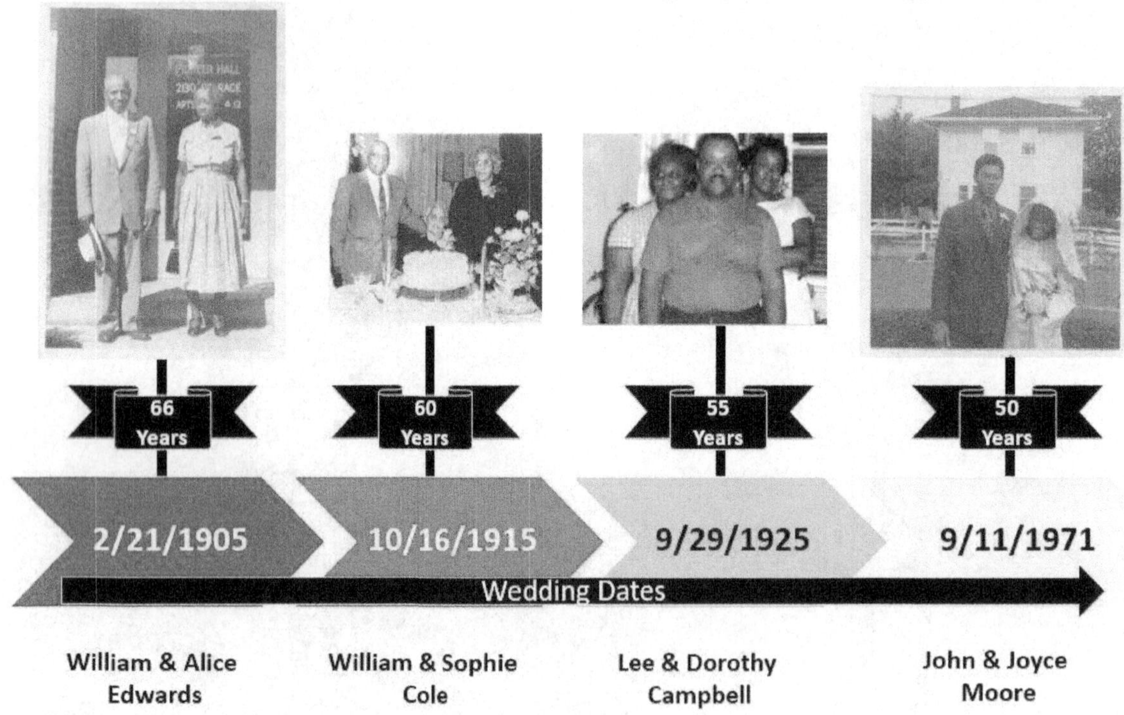

## 8 on a scale from 1 to 10

On a scale from 1 to 10, I'm an 8
Good at most things, but never quite 'great'
Flawed, but I'm not appalled
Perfection is fiction, even if it exists at all!
Above average in height, but not tall
Intelligence is several points below genius
Mild mannered, but have moments when I'm the meanest!
In the 'tennis game of life,' I'm like Venus
I appreciate the greatness of my kin
Congratulate, but never player hate, whenever they win
The point that I'm trying to make
Is that I'm okay with being good, but I really appreciate those who are great!

## 86,400 seconds

There are 86,400 seconds in each day
Make each one count, please don't let them waste away!
Time goes by quickly, so remember, whenever you pray
To be thankful, for each second used and remaining
Life isn't fair, so why keep complaining?
**<u>Nothing is simple, no one is in charge, and none of this is real</u>**
Sickness is rarely cured with just a pill
When your days are numbered, and you're reminiscing and crying
How much of it can you say wasn't wasted, without lying?

## A trip down the stairs

I slipped and tripped
Wearing dress socks while walking down the stairs, the moment I flipped
I was shocked and caught unawares, I think I broke my back and my hip!
The moment my head hit
My iPad left my hand, so now I'm pissed!
I'm never going to be able to recover that playlist!
Thinking this is it…
As my life just flashed before my eyes
This the type of gift, given a choice, I'd never take the prize
Family and friends were all there, a foreshadow of my demise?
This will take months to repair
It was crazy, hazy, as I collected myself, at the bottom of the stairs
Blessed like church folks, with bumper stickers, that arrogantly capture
That this car will be empty, in the event of the rapture!
Sweet Love, Anita Baker, I feel no pain!
That dull sinus pressure, that I've come know and expect
On account of seasonal allergies, was absent, and difficult to neglect
The out-of-body experience you read about, is impossible to explain
I heard my wife and daughter behind me, scream out my name
I turned to see that my lifeless body was the spectacle of their fright
As my spirit became a manifestation of pure light
I instinctively thought to jump back, into my former shell
Not thinking that I earned heaven, or was trying to avoid hell
My body rejected my soul, with a shock of pure pain
Tormented by (what seemed like a lifetime) my family wailing my name
I prayed that they could see me, but soon realized that it was all in vain...

### A woman walking...

Early this morning, I saw a young woman walking down the road
She didn't have a coat on, but it wasn't too cold
I noticed that she wasn't wearing a mask, when I drove by
In my rearview, I saw a face that favored my daughter's in a decade (maybe), but why?
Was she crying, I wondered what made her sad?
I doubled back, due to the pandemic and an appointment, all I could spare was some cash
Which I rarely carry, but I had a $20 bill hidden in my glove box stash
I pulled over and handed her a $20, no questions asked
I said 'God bless you,' through my cloth face mask
As a drove away, I still felt bad
Maybe she'd call a friend, Uber, or a cab?
I wondered what lead her to be alone, on the road, so early that day
I hoped and prayed that she'd be okay.

## Access and exposure

While taking my daughter to school, we parked, because we had some extra time
I told her that her Uncle Justin was in the future, visiting Africa, and it blew her mind!
How could it be 8am here and 4pm there?
Whenever her wheels start turning, she twirls a braid of her hair
Where in Africa is he, what is he doing there?
He's buying an investment property and visiting some friends
For centuries the world has viewed Africa through a deceptive and depressing lens
As my second grader mused about her uncle's latest adventure 'through time'
Her access, exposure, and questions, allowed her to reach heights I'd never climb!
Knowing what is possible, where, when, and how
Is the secret to success, God bless - Caio!

## Adverb kick that knowledge!

Adverb kick that knowledge
Rewind then spit shine, with black kiwi polish
Boot leather express, unknown answers, so you just have to guess!
Question history, then solve each mystery, unless
They cheating, time is fleeting
Cover your test, they competing!
The final score is graded on a curve
Road blocks lie ahead, so you must quickly swerve
Dot every I, cross every T, and conjugate every verb
Juggle all of your classes, swallow lunch fastest, then quickly flush that turd!
Absorb ounces of knowledge
Earn scholarships, then attend a college
Life as an adult, ain't quite like it's promised
Used to strive to be the best, now I work to be the calmest
Used to be a fan, like I dig a mosh pit drama
Blended genre, inspire like Obama
Work to live, believe in Jesus, but I also practice Karma
9 to 5 is more like 8 to 7
401k pays, but I still tithe my way into heaven
Vote, volunteer, and try to vacation often
Before you know, we will all go from lying in bed, to rotting in a coffin.

**Ali running in Zaire**

I feel like Ali, running thru Zaire
Realizing my purpose in life, without a care!
Before the biggest fight of my life
Worried, I sense doubt in my wife
But the people believe in me
And I want the world to see
Their hopes and dreams, manifest in me!
Beating George Foreman to smithereens!
Running with thousands, I heard them say
'Ali! Bumaye! Ali! Bumaye! Ali! Bumaye!'
I'm older and faster
He's younger and stronger
Invented the Rope-A-Dope style, so that I'd last longer
All this talent and charisma's a curse
All of this money and fame, all of these skirts
'Only in America,' Don King is a jerk
Rumble in the Jungle, watch me work!

## Almost anything is possible

The past was ordinary
The future's extraordinary
The present isn't predictable
But your dreams aren't fictional
What you wrote, spoke, or willed into existence
Can still come to fruition, with focus and persistence
If you believe that you can do it, and your attitude is good
Then almost anything is possible, is that understood?

♥

## Alone

I woke up from a long coma
In my bed, and smelled a strange aroma
Years had past, and everyone was gone
Extremely thirsty, my hair was gray, matted and long
I search for some water, but the faucet was dry
My limbs were weak, then I started to cry
When I read a letter from my daughter saying goodbye
Where did she and my wife go, and when?
As I pondered their whereabouts, I picked up her pen
Snapped out of my sorrow, I recalled a bag, that I prepared for the end
In the basement, I once joked that we'd be ready for the Apocalypse
No electricity or communication, but I never considered this twist!
Packs of food and water secured
I gathered my thoughts, and faced what I most feared
A glimpse in the mirror, revealed a full white beard
What was the last thing, that I could recall?
Orange Leaves blowing in the wind, it was early in the fall
Junk mail was dated, 10 years beyond what I could recall!
The front door was ajar, why?  I didn't know
A familiar voice nervously cried, 'Hello?'

## Arguments

Arguments, no one wins
Feelings bruised
Words thrown like rocks
Pelt her, tears fall
Walk away and pray
In the dog house again
Past problems unearthed
But we keep digging
She's so stubborn, I'm always at fault
Its never the major things
Just the smallest of straws that tip the scale
We could make bricks, with all of our mud
To rebuild our foundation
But we can't get past our pride
To work together
So we point out each other's flaws, and wonder what if...
We could start over
If we had more money
But we just keep quiet, and do nothing instead
Guilty of being honest, at the wrong time
Love is pain, routine, fantastic, boring, healing, and toxic in one word
A war of words where someone has to win and the other must lose
I don't want to win and lose you.

## Autobiography

I write, because I have more questions than answers
I could live another 60 years or in six months succumb to COVID or cancer
I've walked this earth for nearly half a century
Been trying to write something significant, so that history may one day mention me
Or that my stories and thoughts may be appreciated as art
Or even one day, provide a spark
To the future of humanity
I hope that they'll learn something, from my autobiography

## Avant-garde

Avant-garde, mold breaker
Level obstacles like road pavers
Tried to be garden variety
Too high on life for creative sobriety
Judge the unorthodox, from their locks
Down to the design of their socks
We can't be defined, or placed in a box!
Vision is a blessing and a curse
Drink life until you DWI, in a hearse

## Back to school – 1984

New clothes, fresh fade, fly shoes
Shopping bags and sales tags
Old friends in a new class
He grew and she blossomed
Summertime flew by fast, but man was it awesome!
My book bag is filled with paper, pencils and books
He-Man lunchbox, because I hate what the school cooks
Go through habitual rituals, like a baseball player
Typing 9x9 = on my calculator
81, to bless and test my lucky charm
Organized with a Trapper Keeper, tucked under my arm
The first week is always sweet
Everyone starts with an A, so we're all geeks!

## Bath Night

Every other day, I have Bath Night
Taking turns with my wife
Precious time with our toddler daughter, brushing teeth
Drying feet
Reading books
Singing songs, exchanging silly looks
Wash your elbows and the rear
And don't forget to get behind both ears!
Sharing hopes, dreams and fears
And the sum total of our day
The fun and challenges
The silly things that people do and say
No more time for play
It's getting late, energy wanes
Double blinks
And yawns above the sink
Choose a sleeping toy, and turn off the light
Say your prayers and tuck the covers in tight
We love you Sweet Pea - Good night!

## Beach Dreams

A late August afternoon, laying in the sand
On a beach towel, holding a few seashells in my hand
Lullabied by the sounds of the wind and the waves
Seizing the last of our fun summer days
Even with my eyes closed, the sun burns so bright
Aware of its movement, a few hours before twilight
Rubbing grains of sand between my fingers and toes
As the sweet salty air, seduces my nose
My family's building a sand castle, just a few feet away
I can hear their voices, but can't quite make out what they say
Giggles and questions mean that both are content
Relaxing and enjoying our time well spent
That day at the beach, now seems like a dream
No masks, no pandemic, man I miss 2019!

Illustrated by
Zoe Victoria Moore

## Beast of the sea

When they dragged me from the sea
I lost all of my power and glory
Whenever I try to get ahead, I get knocked on my behind
But I get back up, and stay on my grind
Refuse to give into my doubts and yours
I'd rather be free at sea, not stuck somewhere ashore
I won't drown you in a bunch of nautical analogies
But when the enemy docks, their nightmares become our reality
Poseidon ain't got shit on me!
Gods rule the land, but I'm the beast of the sea!

## Being Broke

I don't make money
I drive old cars
Nobody knows me
It's like I'm from plant Mars!
But late at night
See that's when I write
Versus on Twitter, and my tablet's like a mic
The twitterverse are my fans
I do this for the art
Ain't got no money making plans
But for real, being broke in America is hell
Can't recite it good, but I learned to write it well!
Some say my pen's sick
Guess one can accomplish the impossible with just a Bic!
Mightier than yo' dagger
Nobody likes a bragger
Drugs, cars and women, figga, if another nigga mention swagger
I'm gonna lose my damn mind
So I stay on my grind, and try to stay on the page
Imagine how a brotha feels, driving a car half his age
Engine light glowing, while wack raps on the radio cause me rage
Can't afford a habit, and nobody even knows my name
How can I ever be a player, when can't even pay admission to see the game?
Forget the fortune and fame, I wrote this to set the mood
Poor folks who can't afford to eat organic healthy food
Working 80 hour weeks, to almost pay my bills
Should be living large, but a nigga still eating Ramen noodle meals!
Ole girl's so broke, she busted the piggy bank open to barely make change
Have to choose between gas or preschool tuition, damn its ashamed!
Forget the fortune and fame, my checking account causes major pain
I feel like my exemption status on the taxes I claim
Zero, but still covet material thangs
Cable, internet, clothes and diamond rings
Add it all that stuff up, man its really insane!
To maintain, I borrowed from my 401K
Credit cards maxed to the limit, my savings is like an ashtray
Payday's no longer a cause for celebration
Always a day too late, 2am and I'm pacing
Trying to figure out which bill to pay first
So I'm starving and dying of thirst
I would get a fifth of liquor, but $20 I dearth!

## Bending into boxes

The enemy is kin to me
We discriminate, then pretend to be
Different, but we look the same to aliens see?
When the invasion begins
The enemy, of my enemy, will be my friend
And the human race will run without regard to pigment
Until then, this 'dream' is just a figment
Of my imagination
Our participation
In discrimination
Is most unfortunate
Lies and bias, are like a contortionist
Bending unnaturally into boxes
CNN's and Foxes
Elephants and asses
Rich, poor, religions and classes
All that divides us, is simply made up
Like a card game, we decide what's Trump...

♥

## Beneficence

The need to be successful
Is my heirloom and creed
To inspire my seed
To dream and believe
In her self-determination and talent to succeed
Not for fortune or fame, accolades, material things, or greed
But simply because she can and has a desire to feed
An insatiable drive within, to be the best that she can be
And years from now, when I'm long gone, hopefully when she thinks of me
She'll have the love, health, and wealth to be totally free!

## Black Barbershop

Sitting in a new barbershop, on a Saturday
I don't have an appointment, but it won't matter anyway
You don't want to get a fade, from the Barber with the empty chair
There's a good reason why, nobody else is sitting there!
A kid is getting complex graphics, cut into the side of his head
Its going to be awhile, so I'm listening to what homeboy just said
Talking about the real NBA G.O.A.T. - Jordan or LeBron?
This conversation will never end and obviously he's dead wrong
...LeBron is clearly, the better player of the two
If King James had Phil Jackson **AND** Pippen **AND** Rodman, imagine what he could do!
A mother arrives with appointments for three kids, and they all want to get something cool
But they all getting the #1 guard and a line up, because she's nobody's fool!
Old school wants a Jeri curl and a fade?!?!
And Old school's brought his daddy along, he's getting a straight razor shave
The youngest barber is talking loud, about his Friday at the club
Hustle Man is selling bootlegs from the trunk of his truck, out front, sitting on dubs!
The 'good' barber has a half-eaten fried chicken leg, in one hand
And his clippers in the other, do you understand?
There are only four barbers for 30 customers man!
And one is on a break, playing a game on the Xbox!
I wave over Hustle Man to buy a mixtape and some tube socks
I get a nod from the barber in chair #1, with a confident look in his eye
That means I'm next, so I put down their Jet magazine from 1995!

## Bleak future

New year, but no resolution
Tragic oceans filled with plastic pollution
Smog, $CO_2$, oil, fracking, people, what are we doing?
The future looks bleak
Lies, no surprise, whenever politicians speak
Fame, money, debt, gadgets, and sleep
What we gonna watch and eat?
Seems to be the primary focus
From the eyes of the youth, it's all just hocus pocus!
When the sun becomes blocked with bats and locusts
Then the illusion becomes real
Food gets recalled, while we find salvation in a pill!
We no longer read, think, or debate
Rather sit in a vegetative state
Watching Netflix
To get a fix, too bewitched, we begin to tolerate
Injustice, in lust with gossip
As entertainment masters profit
We're no longer soul searching, because we all lost it.

## Blind eyes shut with crust

Another winter's here
Colds and flus, fluid inner ear
Congestion, sore throat, with a bad cough
Energy sapped, moving like a sloth
Aches and pains, from dawn to dusk
I woke up blind, eyes shut with crust

## Blowing bubbles in the park

Blowing bubbles in the park, inspired the following verse
My young one, runs in circles, to make each one pop
The wind does most of the work!
She's disappointed, when I suddenly stop
I managed to get some soap in my eyes!
After 20 minutes of dips and blows
The bottle was still mostly full, to my surprise
Amused as she balanced a bubble on her nose!

## Boo Radley

On a plane at night thinking
Watching the lights, on the wing blinking
30,000 feet, from my window seat
Typing words into notes, each
Line has to rhyme
Not a quite a game, but it's my favorite pastime
Silly and pensive
Vague and specific
Freestyles with a twist, its
A journal of my journey
Where I can plead my case, like an attorney
Master this like Atticus' doubts
When Jem, and his sister Scout
Asked me to step out of the house
I obliged, timid but gladly
Out of my shell, like I'm Boo Radley
My past casts shadows without light
The longer and stronger I fight
Haters and instigators want to relinquish my rights
Full of doubt, but I still live my life
So I'm supposed to write about what I know, and don't know now… right?

## Boulder Back Down

Yesterday is gone, and today is nearly over
Tomorrow is nigh, so we're all a little older
Tempers get hot, whenever hearts grow colder
Victory is sweet, defeat's an unpleasant odor
News remains bleak, stacking chips upon your shoulder
Sisyphus on a hill, perpetually pushing a boulder

## Break Away

I spit, piss, sweat, and bleed on the page
Feel my skill, love, pain, frustration and rage!
Another innocent beast, locked down in a cage
Suppressed, but I never confess under duress
Nor give up the location of our hidden address
And the code to the vault, so they can press
And launch another long range attack
They stole our country, freedom, and most recently rap
Still thought that they had the upper hand
But here's what they failed to understand
The illusion, and their conclusion, was that I was at their mercy
They got hip, and realized real quick, that <u>**THEY**</u> were locked in there with <u>**ME**</u>!
Attacked with words, on the verge of body and mind control
Hypnotized ears and eyes - I made them let me go...

## Break of dawn

Dawn breaks like eggshells and corn flakes
Reflect on harsh words and past mistakes
Lessons really, so I eat them like cakes
But I always get lost in the frosting
When you whip those hips
I love to see you leave, but can't wait to taste your lips
So I give chase, post haste
If you leave angry, then I can't replace
That beautiful smile, so stay for awhile
Words divided our love, like fractions
No more talk, let's heal and love, with erotic actions
The sum of our parts, ignite sparks
Remember the embers from the very start?
Passion sets ablaze, our blood into flames, hot enough to melt a frozen heart
When your gasoline and my dynamite mix
We erupt in a cataclysmic twist…
Until the day ends and begins again
We're not perfect, so let's just pretend
Fake it until we make it
Kiss and make up, I can't wait to feel you naked!
In this game of life, my wife
I don't want to win no more
So I'm no longer keeping score
The same arguments, kids, money, and work
The feeling is mutual, you think I'm a jerk
You push my buttons, and your feelings get hurt
My neck's still sore, from sleeping on the couch
I vow to restrict dick, but can never hold out
I try to be cold, and act all pissed
Then you start acting all sweet, and rubbing on my shit
I'm just a mortal, so I can't turn off that switch!
So I'm dick deep in your love again, ain't this a bitch?

♥

**Change is hard!**

Change is hard
Starting over, cancelled card
New location, same issues
Friends forget, but ‘yo momma miss you…
New boss, mail box, ID badge, and dress socks
Values, loose change, and time lost
Embrace rain like peat moss
When storms form and it gets warm
And the clouds get ugly, floating high above me
Abuse love, God, and need.

**Chariots of firecrackers**

As a kid, I was so free
That I'd find a stick, and just beat the bark off of a tree!
Repeatedly until my hands were numb
Or the stick would break, making rhythm without a drum
To let my brothers and friends know, that it was time to battle and bike
Each armed with bottle rockets and a metal 'U' shaped pipe
Seven deep in the street
Six BMXes, but I still had the one with the banana seat!
Off to battle older kids, who all had 10 speeds
With a trash can lid shield strapped to my back, and mouth full of sunflower seeds
Then my chain popped
Steering control was lost
And a pedal crashed into my shin!
So I limped to the side of the road, yet I still managed a grin
And a thumbs up to my homies
I quickly put the chain back on, and then I quickly caught up with the Tonys
A split second before a loud whistle, I felt a Bottle Rocket
Buzz by, just inches from my eye socket!
I relit the incense, and clipped it to my handlebar
Then aimed two rockets toward our enemies and then yelled, charge!!!

# Choices (Nope/Yup) after E-40

Nope!
Yep!
Nope!
Yep!

Do you ever act bad?
**Nope!**
Listen to Mom and Dad?
**Yep!**
Never wipe your feet?
**Nope!**
Wash your hands & brush your teeth?
**Yep!**
Pick your nose for gold?
**Nope!**
Help with laundry, fold clothes?
**Yep!**
Forgot to take out the trash
**Nope!**
Clean the sink and the bath?
**Yep!**
Steal money out mom's purse?
**Nope!**
Volunteer and go to church?
**Yep!**
Lie about your report card?
**Nope!**
Rake the leaves in the yard?
**Yep!**
Forgot to do the dishes?
**Nope!**
Say Sir, ma'am and misses?
**Yep!**
Always playing in the street?
**Nope!**
Floss and brush your teeth?
**Yep!**
Play outside in good clothes?
**Nope!**
Ignore internet trolls?
**Yep!**
Bully?
**Nope!**
Silly?
**Yep!**
Hater?
**Nope!**
Got flavor?
**Yep!**
You a thug?
**Nope!**
Say no to drugs?
**Yep!**

Every kid's got choices
Do the right thing and make Mom and Dad glad
Every kid's got choices
It's better to be good than to be bad

no no no
yeah, yeah, yeah
no no no
yeah, yeah, yeah

Still suck your thumb?
**Nope!**
Like to work out and run?
**Yep!**
Get in fights?
**Nope!**
Like to ride bikes?
**Yep!**
You make fun of the less unfortunate?
**Nope!**
Save more money than you spent?
**Yep!**
Run away and join the circus B?
**Nope!**
Attend a university?
**Yep!**
Do and say things mean?
**Nope!**
Got hopes and dreams?
**Yep!**
Play video games all day?
**Nope!**
Go outside and play?
**Yep!**
Eat a lot of junk food?
**Nope!**
Smile when you get booed?
**Yep!**
Take candy from strangers?
**Nope!**
Yell Stranger Danger!
**Yep!**
T-Ped the neighbors tree?
**Nope!**
Be the best you can be?
**Yep!**
Lie cheat and steal?
**Nope!**
Keep it real?
**Yep!**

4 hours of Candy Crush?
**Nope!**
Read books much?
**Yep!**
Cemetery?
**Nope!**
Library?
**Yep!**
Keep to yourself when you're blue?
**Nope!**
Ask family and friends what to do?
**Yep!**
Talk back and don't listen?
**Nope!**
Earn respect/ask for permission?
**Yep!**

Every kids got choices
Do the right thing and make Mom and Dad glad
Every kids got choices
It's better to be good than to be bad

no no no
yeah, yeah, yeah
no no no
yeah, yeah, yeah
no no no
yeah, yeah, yeah

**Nope!**
**Yep!**
**Nope!**
**Yep!**

## Civil Rhymes

I'm a mutant, my power's with words!
It's a gift and responsibility, so it's my pleasure to serve
No Kryptonite, when shit ain't right, my rage finds a page
Turn green with envy, then in battle engage!
No capes, masks, or technology, just wit, will and might
I only need a pen in a gun fight
With spectacular ebonic vernacular!
I recite lines by chapter, like an actor
Until the plot thickens
And your heart rate quickens
As my lyrics explode
Blood flows out yo' nose
Your crimson covered hands shake
As you realize your mistake
You just got served a cold plate!
My lyrics turn those who hear it
Into stone spirits
Dem verses curses foes, like Medusa's dreadlock hisses
Injecting venom from hollow fangs, like Vampire kisses!
No antidote, against my lethal rhyme quotes
Splitting dome pieces, like ripe cantaloupes!
So Imma share my CIVIL RHYMES
To express my thoughts and opinions, on these most heinous of crimes
To educate, inform, and scorn wicked behinds
I need to do something, my patience is growing thin
In the past, I ignored my conscience, but today I listen to him.

## Clean Car

I vacuumed out our car, after a long road trip
My daughter dropped a whole bag of cherry fun dip!
My wife lost a few sunflower seed shells, every other spit
I dropped my phone in the space, down by the seat buckles
When I pulled my hand back, I had a bunch of bloody knuckles!
Wiped away a lot of dust and greasy fingerprints from the touch screen
Got my rag and armor-all, to get the dash real clean
A toothbrush for the crevices, vinegar for the glass
No quarters for the machine, all I have is cash
I put a vanilla air freshener around my rear view mirror
Poured in some rain-x in the reservoir, to make the windows clearer
Wiped down all the trim, gaskets, and door sills
Shined up the emblem and polished the grill
Then I detailed the rest of my ride, and cleaned each tire and wheel

## Clouds and chips

Why am I so down?
Blessed, yet I still frown
Stressing all the small stuff
I realize that my life really ain't that tough
But with the mood that I'm in today
I just can't seem to keep all the clouds at bay
No matter where I go, there they stay
Above me hovering, dark and grey
Eventually they'll go away
But as their frequency and duration increase
I find it difficult to find inner peace
So I've learned to love my nebulous neighbor
Cherish its absence, and enjoy the fruits of my labor
When doubt transports me back to these dark places
I realize that I'm just cargo, and my clouds are like cases
Inside this chrysalis, its dark, but protective
Metamorphosis can be seen as life or death, from a larva's perspective
Bliss and sorrow, are two sides of a coin that we all must flip
Your shoulder can be free, or it can have a chip.

## Con Science

There is a time, when you can no longer just read
You must act, you must think, you must write, you must lead!
We expect God, government, and others to meet our needs
Then get upset, when things don't change, and history repeats
You have no say, in your direction or destination, if you aren't in the driver's seat
I'm just as guilty as most, full of complacency and greed
It takes energy, it's uncomfortable, and it's not easy to succeed
So many distractions, wrong and right actions, who should you trust, what should you believe?
The old platitude, that it is you, is not always true
But that small voice, called your conscience, is far from a fool!
Listen to him/her, to understand exactly what to do.

## Consume history

I chew innovation
Choke on lies
Drink knowledge
Gulp statistics
Lick music
Breathe art
Nibble politics
Savor truth
Sip peace
Smoke war
Snack news
Spit inequality
And swallow injustice.

## COVID-19 ain't got shit on me – King Leopold II

Salut! I'm King Leopold II of Belgium.
I murdered 10-15 million men, women and children in the Congo from 1885 to 1908.
And nobody has yet to label me the 'most evil person' in history.
Belgium made hundreds of billions of dollars off of ivory and rubber in the Congo.
The Congo did not become independent of Belgium until 1960.
Belgium never paid reparations to the Congo for its decades of massacre and exploitation.
But in 2020, my direct descendant, King Philippe wrote a letter of apology to President Félix Tshisekedi on the 60th anniversary of Democratic Republic of Congo's independence.
Expressing his 'deepest regrets' to the Democratic Republic of Congo for his country's colonial abuses. The total exchange of resources from Belgium to DR Congo = $0.
I'm King Leopold II of Belgium, and COVID-19 ain't got shit on me!

Background: At the Conference of Berlin in 1885, European powers all met to carve up the continent of Africa. Belgium got the Congo, France got most of West Africa, Britain got Egypt and most of South Africa, and the Italians, Germans, Portuguese got the rest!

## COVID-19 Self-Test

I washed my hands, very well
The instructions were in Spanish, what the hell?
I jammed the stick, far up my nose
Spun it around a few dozen times, I suppose…
Grabbed the vial, and extracted my normal flora and D.N.A.
Plopped three drops of my sample down, onto the tray
Then set a timer for 10 minutes, and what did it say?
'COVID-19 Not Detected,' hip hip hooray!



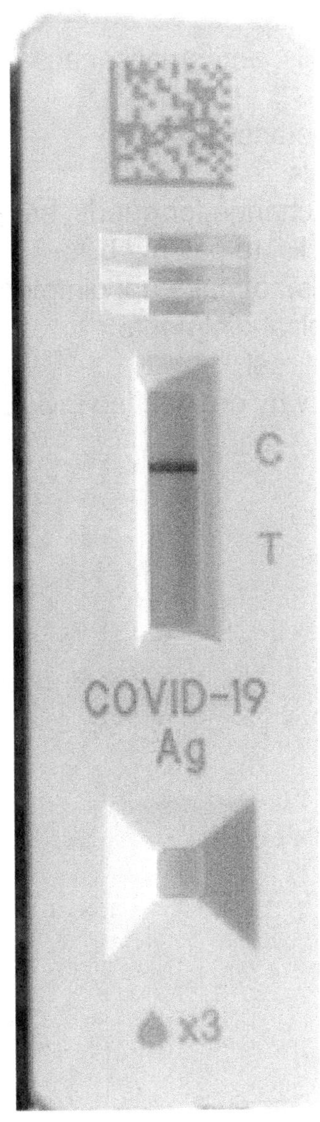

## Cray day

This long day was Z to A, 'Bass Ackwards,' ludicrous, absurd
Rare for me to be at a loss for words
But when the day broke
I was in it, up to my throat!
As I choked, I felt as if I were stuck in quick sand
I tried get free with my left hand
Then I grabbed for a life line, with my right
I pulled on that vine tight, with all of my might!
Exhausted, I tossed it, with a tinge of spite
The second I was free, I still felt anxious, like I had to pee
It's never life or death
Blessed with the best
Still quotas, spreadsheets, video calls, and emails, cause hella stress!
It's not like I'm curing cancer
But I still pursue clues, until I find the answer
Making and taking calls to work deals
To save up, to pay down debt, in exchange for goods, services, and meals
Every 1st and 15th, I leverage my skills, to pay my bills
And taxes, sending faxes and emails, to make appointments
To fill prescriptions, potions, and topical ointments
Popping pills to dull pain, and to feel real
Time's divisible, ads are subliminal, why do I feel so invisible...

## Crossing the Tappan Zee

Crossing the Tappan Zee
I had an epiphany
Here's exactly what happened see
First, a horn I heard
Then a semi swerved!
Then, I yelled some explicit words
Then I hit the breaks
My car shuddered and shaked
I was about to fall into that river or lake
But instead of my life, ending or flashing before me
A mysterious voice, suddenly implored me!
To turn the wheel and then hit it fast!
So I swerved and then stepped on the gas
I nearly hit a truck, as I slid pass
Smoke and shocked drivers, laid behind in my wake
As I yelled for joy, with a smile on my face
I realized that I could only be saved
Not by fate, others, or luck, but by the path that God made
That voice in my head, that told me what to do, was right on time!
It was divine, sublime, and definitely not mine!

## Cyclops

Got my eye on you like a Cyclops
Undivided attention, but might need some eye drops
Can't blink 'cuz you think like a sly fox
Met my match, giving you mad props
Got me tripping, like some wet mops
Hugging soles like a pair of high tops
I got no depth perception, like a Cyclops
I'm a monster, always misunderstood
Down for the cause, but some say that I'm up to no good
We're different, but we're also the same, whenever y'all wink
One's outlook, ain't always as bad you think
Labels mislead and feed discrimination
Even if we were the same, there's always gonna be some playa hatin'
Religion and prison, two man-made institutions
Cause more hate and problems, than love and solutions
Freedom and enlightenment, can't be given and taken
It's all a matter of perspective, blessed or forsaken
Pairs of limbs, eyes, and ears, but only one heart
Was it for a purpose or just symmetry and art?
Balance is an equation, logic undefined
Right and wrong ain't a circle, rather just ends of a line
Us against them, pick a side, and hope to win
It started with a bright bang, but it will all end soon, and quite dim.

## Daughter

My precious little baby
Mommy and daddy's wildest dream
Although you were born in October
You arrived, in our lives, like the sweetest spring!
A new promise of wonder and growth
On the day of your birth, I whispered this oath
I promise to teach, protect, and love you
Place only God and your mom above you
Vow do right by you and your moms
Reward all of your rights, and discipline most of your wrongs
Let you be you, and listen to your concerns with patience
Support your hopes and dreams, yet ensure that your time ain't wasted
You make my day, with just the smallest smile
I love you daughter, my only child.

**Daymare**

I woke up in the future, a relic of the past
Ordered a coffee, but they refused to accept my cash
Everywhere I went, people worshiped tiny little screens
Taking pictures, blowing kisses, news and gossip feigns
Up was down, and left was right
As facts were questioned, as the masses blindly believed the hype!
Millions were made and lives were destroyed, by a single finger swipe

## Dear Zoe

16 months have passed
Seems like you just had your first bath
Time is moving too fast
I hope you've had a blast!
But you probably won't remember
So I record these silly videos, that I suppose
I'll show you in about six Decembers
Whenever you smile at me, my eyes leak and my heart melts
Like that bag of Hershey Kisses, at Christmas
By the flood lights, that I left on the top shelf
Seeing the future through your eyes
Is the greatest gift to me
Earthly immortality
You'll bring pieces of me and your mother, into the next century!
Blessed with limitless gifts, brains, beauty, and boldness
I'm working on a plan, to make you the oldest
Of two siblings, had no idea of the gifts that you'd bring
Can't wait until the world hears you sing
Like a Yo-Yo, you'll have me and them on the end of a string.

## Death's payment is due

Headaches are chronic
Energy's fleeting
Fat displaces muscle
Hairline's receding
Old man musk
Acid reflux
Fate
Mistakes
Self hate
Opportunity, fortune, and bets, became debt, frustration, and rage!
All losses, deducted from a lifetime wage
Death's payment is due…

## Déjà vu and technology too

I get a lot of déjà vu
Random daydreams, where me and you
Did exactly what we just did before
Actions scripted, from the moment that you opened that door!
I know the words that you and I say, to the 'I' and 'T'
Maybe its a script, zeros and ones, subconsciously programed into our reality?
And some artificial intelligence can control our 'game of life' like a Nintendo
Wii, PlayStation, and Xbox applications, quickly descend into a crescendo
Using software stored in a cloud, browsed via virtual windows
As Apples and Androids, subtly avoid, our suspicion, and then clandestinely listen
Spyware declares victory, as we cower and hopelessly beg for permission
We all thought that the next threat would be alien or mankind
Yet our conqueror and master's domain remains online.

## depression

I used to take these long walks
And feel real sorry for myself
Never opened up my feelings, kept them all away on a shelf
Now I know it's depression, and a part of my health
This chronic condition exists, despite love and wealth
When I smile or laugh, it lurks behind my face
A thought or reaction away, causes clouds to crowd, post haste
Desires for food, sleep, and success quickly disappear
Like dark magic, I succumb to this doubt and fear
Present and past mistakes become more pronounced
No longer a lion, I'm as timid as a mouse
There, in this darkest pit of despair
Search along the edges, until you find a tear
If you pull at it, with all of your might
It will open the door to freedom, and control over your life.

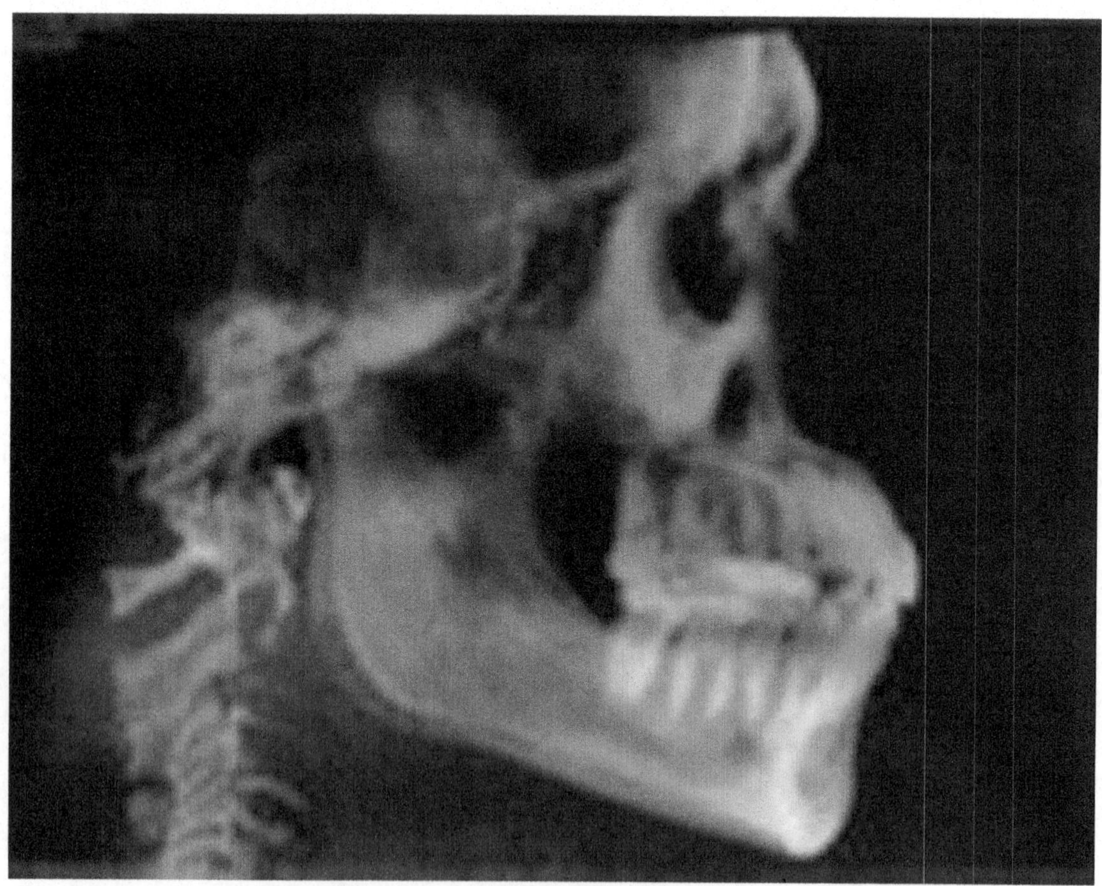

## Detroit

In the D, the only bank we know is "ruptcy"
Its been hell here for years
But the media's just now recognizing it publicly!
White flight took the jobs and tax revenue away
They visit the hood, just to judge and complain
Abandoned buildings, make Iraq aftermath look tame
Kilpatrick's indiscretion and Bing's inaction ain't all to blame
They got a Whole Foods a block away from Wayne State
Black folks work there, but can't afford its organic taste
These roads eat tires like bad habits
Several snowy winters and rock salt just ravaged
Replaced four new tires and bent my chrome rims
Political ass-fault and broken promises, I can't believe y'all voted for them!
Now I'm part of the problem, as I reside outside of the city
But home is where your news is, its such a pity!
TV broadcasts crime, poverty and corruption
They gotta use their platforms, to show people the positive side of something!
Daytime commercials urge us to '800-sue' them, get a payday loan, or don't even bother
Those talk shows, just suppose, that that nigga ain't the father!
Our stress and cholesterol levels be getting too high
Consuming media and getting fat off the devil's pie
Pursuing pleasure while barely avoiding pain
We suffer losses, not being cautious, wasting more money on PowerBall again!
Overloaded with pointless information, got us all going insane!
I'm trying to teach my daughter about life and other 'thangs'
She 5, I'm 40, and we're both going through growing pains!
We're all getting older each day, old folks say
So we fight, love, and pray toward the righteous way
As our problems keep getting more difficult, like college math
Solving for X, while making more than one gaff
Tested by God and scolded by the devil's wrath
We're not well trained
Committing sin is similar, to cleaning carpet stains
Like you accidently spilled Kool aid or red wine
On tan carpets, in the rooms, in which you rarely dine
Vinegar works, but may leave traces of your errors behind
Stepping on our mistakes
It soaks through to your socks, wait
Is that a fragment of your soul? What is this strange place?
Is it a dream, death, or some other worse fate?
Reality can change by years, via a court date
The judge and jury holds all of the cards, in spades
Dealing Kings, Queens and Jacks, multitudes of time
Travel in your mind, to the past, back on your grind
Work smart not hard, whip your own behind!

## Difficult times end, you're living proof!

Covid-19 has changed life as we know it
Wash your hands, wear masks, please don't blow it!
The past, present, and future all share a common truth
Difficult times end, you're living proof!
Faith, science, and the will to survive
Three reasons why we're all still alive
Famine, slavery, discrimination, poverty, and injustice
Is all temporary my people, have faith and trust us!
Read the word, learn the world, and free your mind
The world is yours, now's our time!

### Dime commits a 'crime'

Practicing their jump shots, outside one day
Dime and his friend Dre, heard tires screeching from around the way
But they didn't pay it no mind, as Dime grabbed a rebound
On the edge of the court, he saw a gun laying on the ground
Then he heard a familiar sound and Dre's Head was wearing a laser red dot
Sirens blurted, with no time left Dime thought
'We're about to get arrested...' as Dime sighed (in frustration)
Dre countered, 'Not again, man we gotta hide!'
'Lay on ground with your hands on your head,' Dime barked
'What?' Dre said confused, 'Are you some kind of Narc?'
'Trust me,' Dime whispered, as he rolled his ball behind the gun
'Lay down and whatever you do,' instructed Dime, 'Don't Run!'
Immediately a spotlight from a helicopter appeared
Along with dozens of police officers with assault rifles, in SWAT tactical gear
Dime yelled, 'There's a gun over by the ball, and it is not ours'
'Show me your weapons,' a Cop spit, 'Where's the rest of your gang and the cars?'
'They don't exist,' explained Dime, 'we were just playing a game'
'It's **SIR** to you **BOY**,' growled another Cop, 'Why are you both on the ground, lame?'
'**SIR**', Dime replied, 'It's the best way to not get shot in this town'
The boss Cop reckoned, 'Let's frisk them both, while they're still down on the ground.'
'Boy don't you dare put up a fight'
'If you value your worthless life'
'You'll tell us what really happened, before the end of the night!'
Dime motioned to Dre, not to speak another word
Dime and Dre would demand a Miranda, until justice was served
In the back of separate musty patrol cars
Dre and Dime the Hooper, our neighborhood star
Got booked quick, for nothing specific
No benefit of the doubt, just another statistic
Handcuffed quick, with an itch that he couldn't scratch, on his forehead
But at least Dime and Dre were still alive, had they run, they both might be dead...

LIFE & LOVE

**Dime da Hooper**

In my neighborhood, once upon a time, there was a kid whose nickname was Dime. His 'government name' was Virgil, some thought it sounded like a girl so…

The hood named him for the shots that he made. He dropped dimes so many times whenever he played, that the hoop's net chains sounded like cash registers making change! He wasn't particularly tall or very quick, but his crossover and jump shot was crazy sick!

When I first guarded him, he made me jump, with a stutter-step and double pump, Swish - Nothing but net! The game was over, and Dime was like, 'NEXT!'

We were like Lemmings, in line every time, thinking that we could best Dime at least one time! But we were wrong, because Dime's Jumper was always on fire. I only saw him miss twice, though some still call me a liar. Once, a huge gust of wind, caused Dime's arc to bend. But he got his own rebound, and then dunked it in!

I'll never forget when he missed a second time, we were playing H.O.R.S.E., in my yard around dinnertime. Dime would never admit what we saw, he threw it up, and a bolt of lightning struck the ball! The shock knocked us down, and the thunder rung our ears. We looked around everywhere, but the ball disappeared!

Dime was in shock, to his knees I saw him fall. He said, 'that was my last shot with my favorite ball.' I passed him my ball and made him a bet. He called glass, and banked it in - nothing but net!

Dime played basketball all of the time. He practiced until he was one of a kind. Old and young alike, loved to watch him play. Dime never missed a shot again, since that day. Dime has no special powers you see. But he's a great example of what we all can be. Neighborhood famous, he's a household name. You'd be a fan too, if you ever saw him play a game.

Beyond the court, Dime is a class act. He does his chores and homework and never talks back. Respects his elders and volunteers in the community. Dime the Hooper strives to bring the hood unity. Dime doesn't drink or smoke and says no to drugs. Never late for curfew, Dime stays away from gangs and thugs. When Dime grows up, he wants to own a business and work with kids, and play basketball, just like his mommy and daddy did.

## Dime the Paperboy

Dime would spend his last two nickels
On a bag of sunflower seeds and slices of dill pickles
The only kid with a discount, not from the corner store
But at Mrs. Lawrence's house, counting change at her door
And she was the only customer on his route
That received the daily newspaper, at a 50% discount!
Everyone else had a full price to pay
Whenever Dime stopped by on Saturday
He accepted money that jingled, but preferred the kind that folded
For news in the hood2, Dime had either heard or told it!
If someone's old lady was having a baby
Dime made sure that nobody was acting shady
If cars were driving down the street too fast
Dime threw newspapers at them, whenever they'd pass
He was rich, with change in his pockets
From his paper route collections, he never minded the optics
He used Duct Tape, to line his pockets
His only fear, was if he ever dropped or lost it
Carrying more than your rent weekly, Dime couldn't be safer
Nobody ever tried to stick him for his paper!
Out of respect and admiration
Never with fear or retaliation
Dime was cool with Cops and gang bangers
Maybe it was his charisma, that kept him safe from danger
Dime never met a stranger
Winter, Spring, Summer, and Fall
Delivering papers on a bike that held his Basketball
Between the bars
People admired pro athletes and TV stars
But everyone in the hood knew that Dime the Hooper/Paperboy was in charge.

## Dirty

Not depressed
I just don't want to get dressed
I kind of enjoy my grime and funk
No shave, nappy hair, I'm in a hygiene slump
How many days can I wear the same stuff?
Picking weeds in my yard, people reacting like 'he looks rough'
In a suit and tie, the hood ain't impressed with me
But with beard and a hoodie, the cops just might want to arrest me
Back when we were kids, we used to play so hard
The sweat mixed in with the dirt, and made our arms and legs look like tattoos and scars!
The aim was to have fun and play in the dirt
Now it's all about getting dressed and going to work.

## Does death renew time's lease?

At a loss for words
More or less
Blessed be
We, the envy of
Souls below and above
Burdened with nothing
But time, watching us waste something
That don't cost a dime!
Life is a crime
Committed by mortals
Aging fast, passing through portals
Until fate makes time cease
Or does death, just renew time's lease?

## Don't Believe the Hype (C'Mon!)

All those wants that we fiend
The most desirable of people, places, and things
Once we feel, reach, and use them, it seems
Less grand and important, than we originally deemed
Hype is the biggest crack pipe
It lifts us up, pushes our luck, and makes us do things that just ain't right!
So selfish, despite worldwide poverty and blight
As we wait in lines (for days) for tickets, gadgets, and Nikes!
But seldom pray, volunteer, vote, and work for what's right
Do we not care? Are we too lazy? Or do we just believe the hype?

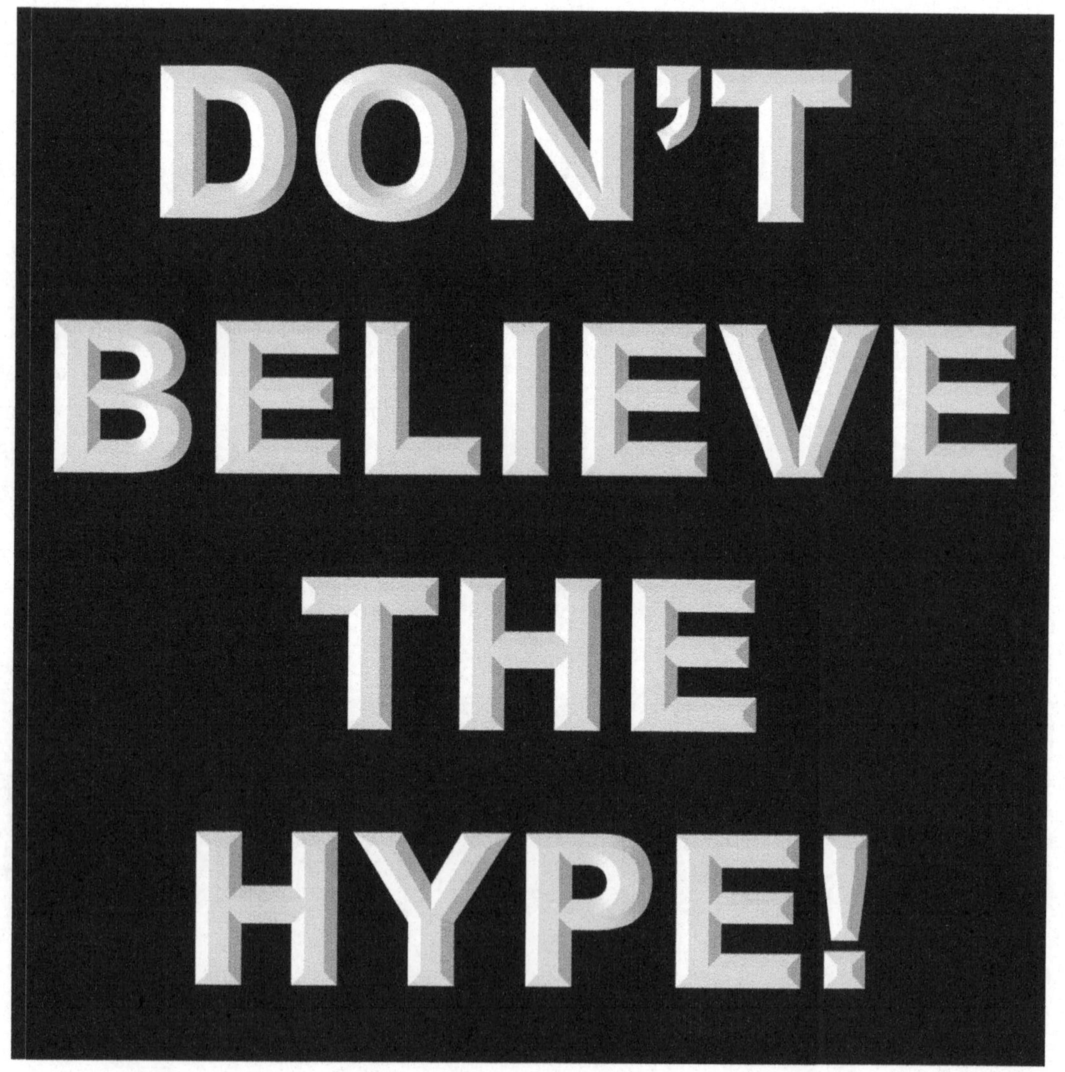

## Dope fiends die with antennas in their mouths (after E-40)

Sometimes these rhymes cut like scissors
Across paper and wrists, cold blooded like lizards
And hex like a curse
Foes think I'm a jerk
While they get screwed by management
Career disappears quickly like summer, then they wonder where the money went
A mix of drugs, booze and private schools, while they are still paying rent
Crazy how history repeats
Doo-wop crews, left with nothing but the blues and receipts
Hugs and drugs came with fortune and fame
Now no longer hot, everyone forgot, their talent and name
Like Eddie Kane, sometime they wish that rain drops would fall, hall, hall, hall, hall....♩♩♪
Instead that narcotic made them beg, borrow, steal and crawl
Addicted to drugs, fortune, and fame
They died with antennas in their mouths and dope in their veins.

## Ego Boxing

Deciding to go left or right
11 rounds of a subconscious fight
In limbo and at a crossroads
Contemplating 'maybes' and 'alsos'
On the ropes, as my ego landed a series of combos
My body's weak, drawing labored breath
Counting and trying to focus, on the eyes of the ref
Why continue? The pain, fame and money don't matter
Sharp chest pains, absent a dagger
Cold water and ice quench thirst and reduce swelling
Words hurt, but fists are much more compelling
The bell dings to start the final round
Vision blurry, eardrum busted, droning sound
No fear, as my opponent draws near
Adrenaline sobers and motivates me, as my mission becomes clear

Illustrated by
Zoe Victoria Moore

## Emotional forecast

I start the end of my day, thinking about all of my mistakes
Sometimes I never go to sleep, it takes
Patience to calm my emotional storm
As clouds casts doubt and form
I don't complain about the inevitable rain
Nor abhor the meteorological metaphor, that constantly replays in my brain
I watch everything, over again and again, until it's all done
Then my mood brightens, enlightened by my internal sun
As I witness (from a different perspective) today's blessings, one by one...
Love, life, God, and things yet to be done.

## Emotions

Pleasure is fleeting and simple to measure
We wear our anger, like coats made of leather
Love is volatile, like tropical weather
To the rich greed is good, to the vain envy is better
Pride can evoke tears and warm the soul like a sweater
Stress robs us of our best, and oppresses like a fetter
Compassion inspires one, to forgive both trespasser and debtor
Guilt makes us wilt, like a flower who wishes to be wetter
Hope inspires all kinds to join as one, together…

## Entrepreneur

When the Carney brothers started Pizza Hut (1958, Kansas)
They borrowed $600 bucks
From their parents, to start their dream
That's about $5,000 in today's green
Do you think that you could do the same thing now?
There's over 15,000 Pizza Huts around (the world)
It's not impossible, but $5K and a dream is quite a tall task
Unless you create a new app, or invent a device that rivals an iPad
Suppose you start small, and have some skill
Own a Barber Shop, or rent some mom & pop spot, for a good deal
You'll need employees, customers, and a website
Your dream's success, will certainly keep you up at night!
So you work hard and put up a smart fight
Target Direct Mail, pushing retail
With digital and social marketing, you can't fail!
But some days are slow, so as you read your mail
You notice bogus demands, bills and taxes
To bide your time, you feed them lines, like Hollywood actresses
Stalling, until you get ahead of your overhead
Your dream, it seems, fails to make substantial bread
You were meager, yet eager to succeed
You can't sell your phone, communication is a vital need
So you abandon your social life
Plans with family and friends, time with your kids and your wife
Investing all of your time, body, and soul
With a singular goal
To make your small business successful and profitable

## Every storm runs out of rain

Every storm runs out of rain
Maya Angelou once claimed
But without an umbrella, cold and miserable
Life seems so unfair and abysmal
It's difficult to see yourself dry
So you wipe your brow, fix your posture, and lie
And tell yourself that this ain't so bad
Then a bus splashes you, standing on the sidewalk, all drenched and mad!
Ice cold water, drips down your back
Down into your underwear, via the crack
But you continue walking, inexplicably pigeon-toed
Bent but not broken, frustrated and cold
Your mind punishes you with negative energy
'Why are you such a loser?' and 'it sucks to be me'
Then a small voice jokes, to lift your spirit
'Snow might be worse', you chuckle when you hear it
Perspective and time can turn challenging situations into lessons
The tomorrows of your worse days, are nothing but blessings

**EZ Passes, freedom, and power**

So this is the enlightened American age?
Time flies but still burns slow, with disenfranchised rage
Unable to change history or habits
While ignorance reigns and multiplies like rabbits
Pests best the least who show fear by squirming
Men and women afraid of mice and other vermin
Setting traps and buying semi-automatic straps for no reason
Laws legislate morals and promote hunting season
Not for beasts, but for burdens of society, economically on wrong side of the tracks
Those Latinos, indigenous people, and of course 'the' blacks
In prison making street signs and license plates, for ten cents per hour
So the fortunate 'quiet' majority can have EZ passes, freedom, and power

## Floating Cigarette Butt

Dreams extinguished, like 'Lucys' once lit
Floating in toilets, full of piss and shit
Broken, I'm floatin' in a nightmare that won't quit!
Commodes hold us back, like crabs clawing for preservation
Random dicks keep aiming, trying to piss me off, then flush, to undermine my determination
But I keep treading this foul water, 'cuz I don't belong in no fucking sewer!
With the dead fish, phlegm, urine, and manure
So pick me up motherfucker, and flick me in the trash where I belong!

♥

## Fly Away

Butterfly, butterfly
Flutter by, flutter by
Your metamorphosis, is like that of a tortoises'
So slow, that nobody ever notices
Got us all confused, like dolphins and porpoises
But it's not what you think
See, they tried to conquer us, but we're far from extinct!
Fly in the sky, but refuse to be shooed
Flap your wings, and just do what you do!

## Free throws

I went to a local basketball court
And shot 100 free throws, here's my statistical report:
I missed 74 of them!
Quite a few 'almost' went in
But none of those would count
My confidence was soon replaced with doubt
But didn't blame the wind
For the reason, as to why, my shots didn't go in
Maybe my ball had too much air?
Perhaps the rim wasn't level up there?
When I missed a dozen shots in a row
I was about ready to go!
As I ran down each of my own rebounds
Here's what I found
Whether I'd hit or miss a shot
I'd retrieve the ball and go right back to the same spot
Making only 26% from the line is whack!
I'm only half as good as Shaq!
I may never improve, but I'll try again and again
The odds aren't in my favor, but at least a quarter of the time, I'll win!

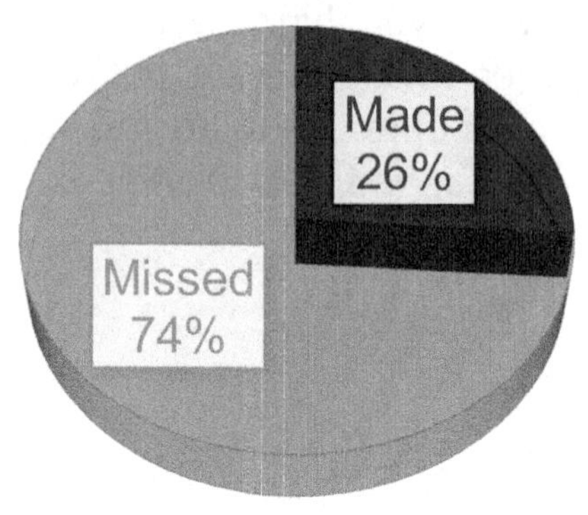

**Frog & Dog**



Frog and Dog became fast friends
They did everything together, even dressed up like twins!
Even though one is a mammal, and the other is an amphibian
They treated each other and everyone else the same
And believed that others who didn't, should be ashamed!
When their kin, asked why they tend, to befriend another kind
They would reply, that friendship comes from the heart, not from the mind!
Fear and hate are caused by ignorance, and a lack of understanding
Besides, constantly being angry and afraid, is way too demanding!
Frog and Dog rather just be
Best friends, living life happily!

Whenever Frog and Dog play
They often cause shock and dismay!
How can a Dog and a Frog be best friends?
And why would enemies, dress up like twins?
Frog and Dog never question other animal's hows and whys
They just play, do, be kind and try
There is no rule, that says that Dogs and Frogs can't be cool!
If there is, it hasn't been taught at their school!
Boys, girls, and species of every size and hue
Can learn and play together, without a big too do
So why can't a Dog and Frog be best friends?
And why should it bother you. if they dress up like twins?

Frog and Dog's example has changed others hearts and minds
Now you see Pigs hanging out with Porcupines!
Birds flying with Butterflies
And Cats running with Mice
Scratch that - one was just chasing the other one
Nothing is new under the sun
But Dog is cool with some Cats
And Frog will hang out with a few Owls and Bats
If predators and prey, can be friendly and play
Then why can't some people get along to this day?

Illustrated by
Zoe Victoria Moore

## Frustration taken out with belts

A fire blazes before me
Timbers ember, into ash once a tree
From lush to dust, time's impossible to flee
Youth is wasted wanting more
The lack of responsibility and the occasional chore
Would be a welcome burden for most adults
Fear of the mortgage past due, causes frustration taken out with belts…
Bad behavior and poor report cards
Undisciplined mouths end up with scars
Retaliation at school, she plucks at other's strings like guitars
Bored with discord, she channels her anger
And hangs up her feelings, like coats on a hanger
In closets full of junk and bones
Then gets cyber-bullied via social media on her phone

## Gentle Finger Friction

Palms itch,
hands shake,
The anticipation is sublime…
You're blowing my mind!
Without speaking a word
I listen,
Referencing erotic descriptions,
From nasty past pornographic fiction
Translated your script, with gentle finger friction…
You're the author of my dreams,
Boundaries surpassed,
As inhibitions give way to absolute permission...

## Glossophobia (fear of public speaking)

The feeling, on the cusp of failure or greatness
Is the same
Not sorrow or acclaim
But butterflies, discomfort, and pain
Moments before eureka
Like the deafening silence from a speaker
On a stage with a microphone, forgotten words
The crowd senses the tension, man this is for the birds!
Fear is a phantom, but youza Ghostbuster!
He finds his nerve, her spirit she musters
In a calm and even tone, the speech begins
Good evening enemies and friends...

## Good grief

I've only been to a handful of funerals
So I don't have much experience with grief
Dreading sorrow, from life lost to time's thief
A friend described a sad scene, that hit me like a rock
At a cemetery, on Mother's Day, four spaces from his mother's plot
He arrived with flowers, to pay his respects
And saw a toddler with a tea set, dressed in her Sunday best
She cried, 'I miss you mommy, so I made you some tea'
I felt heartbroken for her, and embarrassed by my trivial 'woe is me'
A few yards away stood her father, with a tearful and watchful eye
As his daughter asked to be alone by the grave, all he could do was cry
My friend left, so that the father and daughter could grieve
I said a prayer for the unknown family, as a chill ran up my sleeve
What if we were the bereaved?
Could my daughter process my loss with such grace?
If my daughter lost her mom, could I give her time and space?

## Grateful & Glad

Time flies by so fast...
It's like driving on ice, then you suddenly crash!
60 to zero, as the airbags explode from the dash
Witness your whole life, fast forward in a flash!
In a just split second, relive your entire past
Peaks and valleys made the picture so pretty, alas!
You took it for granted, but how long did it last?
All the conversations, frustrations, inconveniences, and tasks?
You'd embrace it all for another chance, but now you're just mad
The two biggest changes that you'll ever have
Life and death, for the time in between, just be grateful and glad.

## Grateful for another year

46 years
My birthday nears
With age comes more fears
Regrets, loss, and tears
All the potential and could have beens
Are just history and dust in the wind
Alas, don't worry about the past
And other things that you can't control, instead just ask
What can be done?
Reflect on all of the battles won
Be grateful for all that you have
You can try counting all of your blessings, but you ain't that good at math!
Every accident avoided, every day spent above ground
Those billions of seconds gifted, it's really quite profound
I'm grateful for another year

## Greener grasses

Ever think about this?
The burden of bliss
Royal blood lines, trapped in an abyss
Hemophilia by incest, centuries in the making
Heavy weighs the crown, as lives are forsaken
So blinded by the power, glory, and fame
That their royal subjects, never noticed their struggle and pain
King Tut died at 19, and walked with a cane!
Those we idolize, would gladly trade in their money and fame
Gods, Kings and Queens trapped in hell, because we worship their name…
Greener grasses, with no clue of the true hue
Each wishes to walk a mile in the other's shoe

## Haze Gray

A Navy warship's color is called Haze Gray
Overcast on a dreadful, rainy summer day
The sky, water and ship's hues all look the same way
The humidity and heat make the paint sticky
Camouflaged in a 'paint boat,' so you might miss me
While my shipmates go out on liberty, to find a date
I'm busting rust, with a wire brush, to prep the surface for some more paint!
A deck Seaman's fate on duty, dirty, hot and pissed
Alone in port, painting the side of my warship

## Herbicide

They grow relentless, in bitter spite
In my garden, all day and night!
Around the corn and tomatoes
And under the strawberries and potatoes
Some with thorns, poke through my gloves
Deeply rooted, tiny insolent shrubs!
Outnumbering my crops 10 to 1
Usurping invaluable nutrients, water and sun
Row by row, large and small, I routinely pluck
Tomorrow even more will appear, and it sucks!
The opportunistic and tenacious bastards of unwanted seeds
Perpetual herbicide against formidable foes called weeds

## History's authors

From blank pages to thoughts, ideas, and situations
A writer's best weapons are solitude and patience
Tried a pen and pad, but could barely read what I wrote
Frustrated, I contemplated, before losing all hope
Illustrated my narrative, in every spare minute
Typing notes on my iPhone, pushing every limit
Short rhymes of these times, the who, what, when, where, why, and how
My words make some cry, and others might even smile
Making something from nothing, is such a rush
Ain't even gonna lie, most of it sucks!
Then, every now and again
I write a real gem!
Treasure by any measure, from one's mind is win!
I didn't need a class or a book, to tell me where to begin
I found it buried deep, from somewhere within
A spell in me, compelling me, to rhyme on a whim!
Of these times that we're currently living in
History's writers, lit my fire, so we can blaze once again!
It's imperative, that we control the narrative
Otherwise history lies, and skews our heritage...
Holocausts vanish and wrongs are ignored
When the righteous are resented, the radical will be adored

## Hospital Stay

Lying in a hospital bed sick, as nurses bantered with candor
Dazed, as I gazed at the light above in amber
'Sir, I need you to void your bowels', barked loud
No good morning, hello, kindness, or smile
That must be beyond the cost, of my insurance price
Feeling woozy as I stood, my knees shook like dice
Crap, the toilet seat was as cold as ice!
How did I get here, taking my health for granted?
Sides in pain, as I strained, eyes watered and slanted
Looking damn ridiculous, in this hospital gown
Pride humbled, as I stumbled back, my IV stand fell down!
The nurse was terse, as she assisted, and held back a curse
I was ashamed and felt worse
When I told her, that I could not poop or pee…

## How Scantron tests ruined America

When Michael Sokolski invented the Scantron, back in 1972
He had good intentions, but never realized what he helped to do
Or ruin, American mediocrity began with millions of #2
Pencils, on forms circling bubbles
And began our nation's troubles
A machine reduced the youth, to zeros and ones
Data extracted, classifications and transactions, mere currency, our poor daughters and sons!
Dreamers to consumers, thinkers to workers, successfully transformed
By a machine and a form, designed to make us... conform....

## How to Swim

Here's how you can learn how to swim
First you must jump in!
Swallow water, stinging eyes
Tread by moving your arms, feet, and thighs
Close your eyes, and then hold your breath
Practice the four strokes: crawl, butterfly, back, and breast
Cup your hands and push the water back
Stab the surface with your hands, in lieu of a smack
Do the same when you dive
Don't welcome the pool with two high fives!
Rather cut the surface, palm over palm, like your arms are knives
When all else fails, and you lose control
Roll over onto your back, push your chin and butt up, and move your arms and legs around, slow.

**Humanity is so new…**

Five billion years from now
The sun may envelope our planet
How on earth will people manage?
Travel through time and space?
To find a new place
To call home, but we're not alone
Ungrateful tenants, renting an unmerited home
If earth's whole history was just 12 months
Dinosaurs didn't arrive until December then became oil and dust!
Humans appeared late on New Year's Eve
If I told you that humanity was only '24 minutes old,' would you believe?



**DECEMBER**

| S | M | T | W | T | F | S |
|---|---|---|---|---|---|---|
| | | | 1 | 2 | 3 | 4 |
| 5 | 6 | 7 | 8 | 9 | 10 | 11 |
| 12 | 13 | 14 | 15 | 16 | 17 | 18 |
| 19 | 20 | 21 | 22 | 23 | 24 | 25 |
| 26 | 27 | 28 | 29 | 30 | 31 | |

WE
ARE
HERE

♥

## I didn’t fully understand

I didn't fully understand
love
frustration
patience
humility
pain
anger
sorrow
pride
joy
success
and failure…

Until I became a parent.

**I don't get enough pussy for this!**

Got me actin' all domestic in shit
I'm not saying that you owe me a hit
But you never in want fo' some dick!
Gotta beg, borrow, and steal it like a trick
When I try to say no, you start grabbin all on my nuts
Two seconds later I'm dick deep in yo' snatch, rubbing on your butt
Like weekends, it goes by too fast, then I bust a nut
It's insane, and you never complain, cuz I puts it down!
Then you good for days, but I'm still feening for some round brown
So I walk around with blue balls while you ask for favors and cash
That's bullshit, cuz I can't get a lock on that ass!
Shit, I don't get enough pussy for this!

## I failed as a father today

I failed as a father today
Because my kid did her homework the wrong way
I tried to keep my cool
And calmly explained, three times, what she should do
She failed to listen and rudely snapped back
'We're not supposed to do it like that!'
A bubble away from boiling, I growled 'It's still not right...'
Frustrated, she cried and put up an emotional fight
With a hand on my belt, I directed her to her room
Opted for a time out, to cool off, instead of spanking her too soon
I don't want to associate discipline with homework
But I won't allow my kid to mouth off, and act like a jerk!
After as many minutes as her age passed, I asked her to return
I erased the wrong answers, and explained why she must learn
Challenges will appear for the rest of her life
It's okay to cry and get frustrated
Lessons and struggles are often related
The aches of failure, and pains of snafus
Are the beginning of understanding, and what have you
We eventually got through most of our checklist of things to do
Saving the most difficult task for last, she still felt blue
When she realized that I had erased all of her wrong answers, she went ballistic
Out of options, I removed my belt from my hip quick!
Anger turned to fear as her protests turned to pleas
'I'm sorry - please don't spank me!'
As the discipline took place
Tears streamed down her face
I hate the rearing part of parenthood
I wish that I were more patient, and that all of my instructions were good
If there were an option for no discipline, I most certainly would
But rods can't be spared
Or she'll be spoiled, and my instructions constantly dared
Her homework is finally done, because I cared.

## I killed a rooster today

I killed a rooster today…
As I slit his throat, I forgot to pray
I was supposed to give thanks for his sacrifice
But after running around the coop, I lost my cool and dropped my knife!
As I gave chase and shouted obscenities, feathers and dust filled the air
I finally grabbed his feet and placed him in a metal cone/chicken snare
Quickly ending the life of one of two roosters that terrorized a flock of hens
By eating their eggs and bullying them time and again
As I bid this 'yard bird' his final adieu
I whispered in his ear, 'cock-a-doodle-doo'

Stainless Steel Poultry Restraining…

I tried to write about
love and hope
Illustrated by Marcus Lorenzo Jones II

## I tried to write about love and hope

I tried to write about love and hope
But the words just didn't flow
I understand what I'm supposed to do, but my mind still said no
My mood is stuck on pissed, and I can't change the channel
My heart used to be like clay, now it's as hard as enamel
That just leaves my soul and conscience
Like two old men holding conference
Playing Chess in the park
Slow and wise, with one move, they provide a spark
To my brain to find the reason and beauty in things
And motivate my heart to listen when the world sings
My mood follows suit, based on the rest of my body's proof
And suddenly I'm writing again, smiling, and speaking the truth.

## Id vs. Ego

Off the dome, like a Lobotomist
Unwanted, like a malignant cyst
Bliss and full of the harsh reality, that this
World won't be the same without me
But my ego just told me to flee!
Trapped everywhere I go, there I'll always be!
Staring back at me in the mirror
Hopeful, discouraged, foggy, clearer

## I'm cursed and I'm blessed

I'm cursed and I'm blessed, I'm cursed and I'm blessed
Things that do and don't work, life's success and regrets
Had I been more selfish, I'd probably own me a jet!
A wife and a kid, means less money and sex
Shouda' bet on myself, and started a business
I keep asking for permission, when I should've begged for forgiveness
I work hard for my thousands, make my boss tens of millions
I gotta save up to pay taxes, while my company makes billions!
I was posta' be the playa president
Make the White House my residence
Now my sky is limited, far from the best of the rest
I wish that I was a mutant, or had a "S" on my chest
But I'm just above average, but still a pro in my field
On the bench with low minutes, but I still got some skill
It's a struggle sometimes, to not just keep shit real
So I wear a mask like the Jabawokkies and Dunbar
Work for a car company, but drive an old ass car
Freedom is relative, other grass might be greener
That Jackass sold his soul, for shiny new Beamer?
Fancy clothes get dirty, then must go to the cleaners
Some might say I'm a dreamer
But my nights are still filled with despair
My back aches often, and I think I'm losing my hair!
Don't spend enough time with my family
And my social life's a calamity
The world's filled with injustice, but musicians are only pissed about the Grammys?

## Imagine a better world

Where money is less than your mission
Everyone values life and walks with a sunny disposition
Turn off your phones people, stop, look and listen!
Imma about to spit some terrific fiction!
In a world where nobody goes missing
Or hungry, lonely, sick, confined for decades in prison
The only crimes are wasting time, and throwing away food in your kitchen!
Paper chasing is replaced with, the endless pursuit of education
Beauty is multidimensional
Fake breasts, eyes, and behinds are no longer institutional
News anchors no longer smile, while reporting on serious issues
And the evening news no longer gives you the blues
People spend $200 on charity instead of "basketball" shoes
Women get paid more than men
Let's face it, when our sisters, mothers and daughters are good, we all win!
We are not really that far away, from this way of life
Eradicate hate and immobilize intolerance to cure our struggle and strife.

## Imma Ball On Y'all

I got a 'J,' I got a floater (yeah)
Get in the paint, killer crossover!
Triple doubles, when I run point it's over! (Over!)
Hoopin', Olly oopin', think fast, no look pass!
Quickly scoopin' (scoopin')
Barely winded, and a little offended
Wishing for some competition
But something's missing
I got half a step on you
So here's what Imma do (yeah, yeah!)

Imma ball on all y'all!
Watch me ball on all y'all (Aye!)
Finna ball on all y'all!
Gonna ball on y'all (Yeah!)

Handles left and right
I'm ambidextrous, so I just might
Step back for the three
At the top of the key
Or I might just cross you up
And break your ankles, as I dunk! (Crack! Crack!)
Your coach is yelling, 'Get back on D!' (Get Back, Get Back!)
Gotta practice more, to get as good as me!
Now you're on the bench
Can't double team me, 'cuz I'll just get the assist!
Try to foul me? My free throw average is 90%!
Trying for a rebound, but all you hear is swish!
I see you peeping my game
Every shot gets drained (Yeah!)
Wow, how come he never miss?
Diggin' my style, from the flick of my wrist
To the hang time
I never take a play off, 'cuz it's always game time!
Man to man or zone (It don't matter!)
Away or at home
Big or tall
What imma gonna do? (Hun?)

Imma ball on all y'all
Watch me ball on all y'all (watch me!)
Finna ball on all y'all
Gonna ball on y'all! (Yeah!)

<Chorus> **Imma Make You Proud**

Imma make you proud....(Rayquan)
Beyond Mother's Day, you don't always get your do (True!)
Wrote this rhyme to tell how much I love you (You!)
Appreciate and dedicate this song to you (Ok)
And all the other mothers, for everything you do (Aye!)
Thank you for my life, love, and lessons
Hugs, discipline and answers to my questions
Help with homework, good food, toys and books
Church, school, and practice and for my good looks! (Amen!)
Know that all you do, doesn't go unnoticed
I can be a handful, whenever I get bogus (Aye)
As I grow up, Mom, please know this....

**<Chorus>**
(Adverb) Years ago when I failed at school (Yup!)
Still recall, what you would do
You and me, at Mickey D's...
With plans, to turn Ds to As and Bs!
Eating fries, you'd listen to my replies
Value my education, and why I should try..
For the dream, that I was pursuing
Like a dentist, who didn't know what he was doing!
Jokers – whistling, when they'd speak
'Cause he drilled, the holes in the middle of their teeth (HA!)
No longer felt bad, after our laugh (thanks Mom)
Finished my happy meal, and started my math (Yep)
Thank you, for your patience and understanding
Always reasonable, and supportive, yet demanding
From your inspiration, I got my grades up...(you helped me)
I kept my promise Momma, cuz you always make me proud...

**<Chorus>**
Life ain't a crystal stair son, she'd sometimes say
People, places, things don't often go your way (that's true)
You take the good, and the bad
And there you have a TV song after an ad
The facts of life
Wrong and right
Do or don't, fight or flight (What!)
Golden rule
Do to others, as they do onto you
Unless they treat you bad
Take a different path
When you get stressed, and depressed
Remember God and do your best (Amen!)
Storms come and go
Mom, I just want you to know... That...
Imma make you proud!
**<Chorus>**

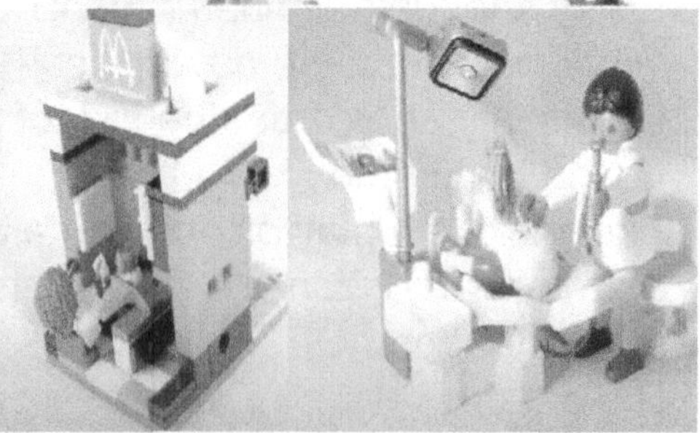


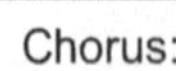

Chorus:
Imma make you proud Mom!
Imma make you proud (You'll see)
Want the world to know, so imma shout it loud (watch me!)
Future show with thousands, find you in a crowd (there you go)
Cuz, Imma make you, Imma make you, Imma make you proud (Aye)!

## In the rain with a cane

I saw an old man today, walking in the rain
Struggling with an umbrella, some grocery bags, and a cane
Trying to cross the street, over to the other side
I saw sorrow in his eyes, but he maintained his dignity and pride
A Good Samaritan stopped and offered him a ride
The old man waved to decline
The Samaritan shrugged, as if to say 'I tried'
To those suffering in silence, it's okay to accept help
As some are cursed with burdens, others are blessed with wealth
As the Good Samaritan, old man, and I
All crossed paths in the rain, we probably all asked ourselves why...
Do we do too much?
Don't we do enough?
Or why can't we put our guard down (for once) and finally trust?
The moment will soon pass
In a flash, one day I might ask
If someone needs a ride
Or perhaps, I'll be the guy in the rain, with a cane, who puts his pride aside.

## In the year 2020

In the year 2020
Things will change and also stay the same
Poverty, technology, the ecology, dollars reduced to change
The two Americas that John Edwards talked about
Rich or poor, get your ‘pay and weight up’ and remove all doubt
500 years ago, people either owned people, land, or nothing at all
When the powerless fight back, eventually empires will fall.

## Incident Report

When I picked up my kid from school, I could see that she had a tough day…
Wearing shame on her face and reluctant to snitch
I was irritated, at the situation, not her…
I was the smallest kid in school too
Nobody can ever prepare you, for the things that you can't change
She had a huge knot on her forehead
It gave me road rage, without a car!
Just once, I'd love to hear how my daughter, 'accidentally' made some other kid cry
I played it cool, as I mustered a smile, held her hand, and read the note that described the cause of my kid's latest scar, that I will always see when I look at her face.
The first of many dangers, that I can't shield her from…
She'll long forget about this blemish,
But I'll relive the anger, frustration, helplessness, and acceptance that I felt
Reading two sentences, from the school nurse's account,
Explaining how my kid ended up with a huge knot on her forehead
And how the kid who pushed her, simply said sorry.

**Insomnia**

I can't sleep
It's pointless counting sheep
I have no imagination
So I'll shoot some hoops or ghosts on PlayStation
Look at the situation I'm facing
Working every day
The government takes a third of my pay, I'm pacing
Trying to figure out the end game
My ideas are lame…
Not good enough to earn money or fame
So I write down, all the nonsense in my head
Often my mind races so fast, that I forgot what I said!
So I have a bunch of thoughts, that are half done
Like a watching the beginning of a game, but you didn't see who won
Ten years ago, I was full of promise and ambition
Now, making money is my only mission
I want to be comfortable and have a kid
I didn't end up doing half the things that I wish I did
I won't do something, that the whole world will praise
But I'm in a position to provide my family many good days
Finally, I'm getting sleepy, so I'll end this here
Another example of an unfinished thought, but at least my mind is clear!

## Is this chauvinistic?

I blame the men of the greatest generation
For messing up household dynamics, here's the situation
Most took their wives' attention and household management for granted
Unable to vote or work, women would no longer stand it!
Told their daughters to seek their own power and independence
Men today ask for permission, but the greatest generation never begged for forgiveness!
Growing up, my mom told me often, 'Don't you dare be like Mister!'
From the Color Purple, 'having women on the side and chasing away Celie's sister…'
I don't mind, that my wife brings home half the bacon
But damn was Grandpa lucky to have Grandma at home patiently waiting
With a newspaper, slippers, and dinner in the oven, I know that this sounds chauvinistic
But when my wife and I get home, we're tired, hungry, and stressed out, if I'm getting specific!
Working to pay for daycare, we spend more time apart than the greatest generation ever did
I wonder how things will be in the future for my kid?

## Island vacation

For three days and two nights
Water ebbs and flows on the beach
As sand coats my legs and feet
Steel drum melodies, compelling me to relax
But my mind still finds time, to add and subtract
Various charges, tips, and fees
Everything cost more overseas!
This wrist band and stamp on my hand
Buys any food or drink, while I sizzle in the sun and tan!
Cooled by an intermittent ocean breeze
Wish that I could freeze
This very moment in time
Alas, it will pass too fast, a three day vacation's a crime!
Customs and layovers
Tickets, bags and sore shoulders
Waiting in line
Home too soon, back on the grind...

**It's a Trap (fuck the cheese)! – Ode to Admiral Ackbar**

For the past few years
I've been a cog, turned by a dozen gears
I've had trouble getting a loan
Trouble renting my home
Trouble buying a suit
Constantly getting the boot
Trouble getting a raise
A mouse, trapped in a maze
Driven to succeed, searching for the cheese
Never seeking an exit, only aiming to please
I worked extra hard, looked far and wide
Until I finally found and ate, my long sought after prize!
Moments later, I grabbed at my sides
It was poisoned! The wrath of my master's test
I finally realized that I was born to lose, but hey, at least I did my best!
Screaming to the other mice, I hope that they hear and believe
It's a trap! Run for your lives! Fuck the cheese!

LIFE & LOVE

♥

Illustrated by
Zoe Victoria Moore

**It’s a wonderful life**

George Bailey had a wonderful life
Remember when he yelled at the kids and his wife?
Stressed, depressed and at his wits end
Then he jumped in (the river) to save his new friend
Clarence, an angel second class
Showed George his life's impact, without other's in his path
No wife, brother, sons or daughter
Now the whole town's owned by old man Potter!
All because he never existed
George had never been born, just because he wished it
Ripples in a pond impact in millions of ways
Don't give up just because you’ve had a bad day!

## Journey of self

When they said that the world was ours
I grabbed the baton, and sprinted fast toward Mars!
I was aiming for a planet, but soon I became a star!
Then I travelled so far
That I eventually met myself
Facing trials and tribulations, through sickness and health
My edges were shaped into the man that I am today
I traveled alone, but God was there when I'd pray
Valleys and mountains made me strong and weak
Humble and proud, in triumph and defeat
It's the journey, not the destination, that we all should seek

# Junk in your kitchen drawer

The junk in your kitchen drawer
The grime on your shower floor
A crumb of bread under your fridge's door
A pile of laundry, that you need to wash and fold
The grudge against a foe, that you still hold
The novel you hope to write
The thoughts that keep you up, late at night
The business idea that's still not quite right
The letter or card, that you still need to send
The new neighbor who you want to befriend
The desire to volunteer at the soup kitchen
Would you rather beg for forgiveness or ask for permission?

## Kids with scissors cutting paper before recess

Kids with scissors, cutting paper before recess
With no regard for lines, blinded by the prospects
Of playground slides and swings to relieve stress
Lunchtime, assemblies, homework and tests
Education is more than reading, writing, and arithmetic
One's growth can't be measured, alone by metrics and yardsticks
How to deal with people, in places, and other things
Is the greatest gift that an education can bring

## Last 2 months = a year of Saturdays

52 days post COVID-19, in some ways
Has been like an entire year of Saturdays!
When my daughter left a pen mark on our tan couch
I knew it would never come out
Frustration and silly mistakes, we'd both make
I'm still finding a balance between discipline and giving her a break
With no school or summer camp this year
I'm learning to 'parent' with more reason and less fear

## Life is a circle, time is a line

I’m slowly being erased
My culture, story, and face
The world, once ours, has now been replaced
By younger models and interests, not quite to my liking or taste
What I once knew, as hip and cool
Now labels me as ‘outdated’ and ‘old school’
Calendar dates flipped by so quick
The years soon became decades, in flashes, and blips
But I'm just fine with my station, a relic left behind
Because life is a circle and time is a line

## Life, Death and Dreams

Sickness is temporary
Death is permanent and scary
Even believe in the afterlife
With no guarantee to see friends, family, my daughter or wife
I try not to think twice, of the reasons why
We're so fortunate and blessed, me and mine
Born in the right place, at the right time
Purpose, place, passion, and grace
Motivated and educated me, to quest for this great dream chase!
Still humbled, whenever I stumble
Sometimes foundations crack, and plans may crumble
But thereafter disaster, can still be fixed with faith, paint, and plaster!
Whenever fate is faced, trials and tribulations will be mastered
And so goes our bodies and souls
What happens after our time on earth, nobody really knows…

♥

## Life/Religion/Rich/Poor

Well the Empire finally striked back
And they took their country back
We do more with less, and break our back
MasterCard says pay the ransom handsome, and you just might get your life back!
Multi-Media made their point with a post and a brass tack
On billboards, replacing truth with fake fact
Then flipped the script, like an friggin' acrobat!
There's a billion people in Africa, but you never hear about that!
The Vatican is made out of pure gold!
The rich uses religion as a vice to control
The poor, who cling fast to faith, just to save their soul...

## Like because, love despite

Like because, love despite
Apathy gun, passion knife
Husband, son, daughter, wife
Find and time rhyme ironically, laughter
I seem to keep losing mine, the latter
Annoyed by your concern and insolent tone, what's the matter?
You can't fix my problems when you're the catalyst/cause
I wish life were a movie, and I could just press pause
Rewind mistakes and fast forward beyond the hate
Or control the calendar, and pick a different date
So where should I go and when?

## Love Long Distance

Love long distance
Late nights and early mornings, reminiscing
Lonely, really, plus I just miss my homie and my kid
Wondering if your day was good, and what you both did
After school, work, play, meals, chores, and more
In exchange for your absence, gas and snores I'd gladly endure ;)
So I call and video chat, to get the latest stories and news
Glimpses in minutes instead of hours, those precious moments that we all lose
I hope to see you both very soon
To describe time and distance away from my family, I could write a tome.

## Lure of the ring

Slaying dragons
I'm Bilbo Baggins
Walking in the shadows with dwarfs
And I'm not much taller, of course
Armed with a ring and a dagger
My precious investment's a matter
Of addiction and internal confliction
This vice so nice
I'll gladly endure this pain
For an ounce of pleasure, so my beast remains tame
But others feel the draw, and seek to claim
Your power too
So what should I do?
Disappear and let my fear drive me insane?

♥

**Lyrical time capsule**

I'm in the Sophomore year of a midlife crisis
Too long, I traded hopes and dreams for excuses and vices
But now somehow I've seen the error of my ways
And understand the need, to seize all of these remaining days
And do what's right, and that's to write!
Even if nobody ever reads it, and it never yields a price
My value's not diminished, in the absence of fortune and fame
History will reward my work, and the future will know my name!
In the interim, the truth is what I'm giving them
As I write about life, struggle, strife, for her and him
Politics, pop culture, and every other whim
For the future, everything I write is just for them

## Magnificent abyss

I've explored vast galaxies, within your cosmic brown eyes
I spent years studying your constellations, decades later I finally got wise
So if I ever became blinded
I wrote it all down, I tried to describe what I found, so that the world could be reminded
Of your magnificent abyss
If anyone ever asks what beauty is, I'll just show them this

## Maybe we should be U & I

It’s with a heavy heart
That I ask to remove your hand in separation
Years of paint and wallpaper over problems and pain aren't enough to renovate our union
Lack of love's flame is not the problem, but it’s a symptom of our illness
My dream version of you doesn't even want me anymore!
We're just roommates, with the same last name
And the same bank accounts, same soap, and tube of toothpaste
Two people who share a home
And the bed when we're full of money, liquor, and energy
But when times get tough, the baby's sick, and the mortgage is due
We fight, blame, complain, and bring up old unsolved problems
I choose you, then you choose me
I've tried, but it’s like you're saving your best for your next
And you're just passing time with me until something or someone rescues you, from me
It doesn't even hurt anymore, I knew it was just a matter of time
After you got to know me, you'd see the trick to my illusion, and not want more
I'll spare you the future misery of my company, you're free, no hard feelings
Life is too short; I hope that your next illusion is more convincing than me
Thanks for the memories.

## Men destroy, women create

Point, counter point, devil's advocate
Know you struck a nerve, by how mad I get
Proof and truth is pointless, but you don't quit
Keep me honest and call out all my (bull...) mistakes
As I rule without regard, let them eat cake!
Men destroy while women create
Their emotions fill oceans while ours is a small lake
But when both are frozen, they use it to skate
While we're trapped down underneath
Holding in our feelings, too afraid to express our frustration and grief
Watching our love above, hoping it's enough to bust through
While she's looking down, wondering if she can still trust you....

**Mistakes make a better you**

Call me cursive
All my verses
Are carefully written
Pensive, whenever I'm I spittin'
Paid my dues, like out of state tuition
Forged by heat, been through ups and downs, like pistons in engines…
I was in a slump, I didn't like my script as it was written
But I kept trying, to test my best feat
Delete and repeat, until my cypher's complete!
Destinations are boring, never journey to cheat
Rather gather your bearings, and guide your hide true
Mistakes are nothing but blessings, and help to make a better you.

## Model rockets in the park

Memorial Day weekend, launching model rockets in the park
My daughter's counting down from ten, to begin the start
Of an ignition sequence, ending with a push of a button
Hours spent gluing, painting, and assembling a machine from barely nothing
A C6-5 engine and cardboard flying 250 mph up toward the sky
Practical engineering with answers to why
And how and what makes things work
Power at the push of a button, with a little smirk!
My daughter has plans to one day fly to Mars
But she's already reached the sky's limit, next its the stars!

## Moment of clarity

I finally get it, this late lesson in life
I was stressing, when I've been blessed with, all this struggle and strife!
Not killed, but made stronger
A sore muscle is stronger
I just wish this life lesson learned, didn't take me longer
Instead of why me, why not?
I used to complain and refrain, now I'm glad for what I got
All my mistakes, regrets, and passed opportunity
Shaped my past, my present struggle hasn't yet ruined me
Last year life was haunting me, and kicking my ass
Today, I feel like Neo in the Matrix, and suddenly, the enemy doesn't seem so fast
Punches feel like pinches
Before I even move to strike, my problems and enemy flinches
Heed my final warning, do not fuck with me!
Because I just finally realized my destiny.

## Money is worthless

We're all the same, just a bunch of mutts
Economics divides us, 5% live in mansions, 95% reside in huts
Would I lie, should I deny, that I strive to be in the top five, before I die?
I know you're with me, see, I want to get the brie!
Y'all can cut the cheddar cheese
I'm putting in work, like I'm raking up leaves!
Pay attention grasshopper
And follow the ant's lead, before the deep freeze!
Otherwise, you'll be begging on your knees
Your very existence, hanging in the balance, like a trapeze
Nearly all your wants and needs are fiction
Its all useless, except my words, yeah that's a contradiction!
Take stock of your possessions, and you'll quickly see
The rest of the world has a bowl of water; we each own a sea!
Half the world spends half of their day finding food and water, we just watch TV!
Where would we be, with no running water and electricity?
Three large meals a day, that we don't really need?
These are just thoughts, and some second guesses
Word to the wise, fools, greedy, and needy, please count your blessings!

## Morning Slumber

My arm is numb
Above my head and under yours
Legs locked like Maple tree roots
Sheets and pillows pushed to the corners of the bed
Too dark to be morning
Too light to be night
It's a quarter to five in the morning
The red glow of the alarm clock, paints the wall pink
Every sound, in and out of the room, is distant
From the birds, to the cat on the floor
A plane, train, or car passes by
A faint sound in the distance
I try to make a fist, but my fingers won't obey
My arm is still sleep, the blood rushes back to my heart
I kiss your neck and feel your pulse
I don't want to wake up, why can't the whole day be like this?
Not too hot, not too cold, time is frozen
No deadlines, no phone calls, no TV, no e-mails
Just you and I, hibernating like animals....

## My final work

Have you ever tried to write your own obituary?
I plan to be around for another sixty eight years, but it was scary
The things you want to do and places you hope to see
This humbling task yielded a short list of five goals for me
Ten years since I left college, its crazy how time flies
Got to get in shape, 1 on the list: Cut out the burgers and fries
This all started with a procession I saw on the road last week lead by a hearse
I haven't been to service in a while, 2: Join a church
Who will I be listed as "survived by", and speak at my wake?
Will I be able to leave more than memories, like millions in the bank?
3 and 4, start a journal, and invest another 5% in my 401K
Cremation or casket? What music will they play?
Can you imagine living for 100 years?
So many laughs, so many tears
So much progress, and hopefully only a few setbacks
5: try to enjoy today, collect my profit, and pay my tax
It will never be this good, or this bad ever again, that's a fact
At least that's what I will say when I'm old and wise
Before I leave, I'll finish my obituary, and life will no longer be a surprise.

♥

## No $H_20$

I'm dying of thirst!
So parched, that the first sip would hurt!
Chapped lips, near death, with my face down in the dirt
Headaches, pulse quakes, as my vision dims
Constipated, hot, cold and shaking, now I can't feel my limbs!
Focused on only one problem, and matter of concern
Patiently waiting, for when its finally my turn
Haunted by the insatiable need to quench
Tormented by the past, when I wasted water to rinse
Dishes, showers, and flushes in gallons of sin
I'd do anything just to drink one more ounce of water again!
Deals with the devil and God, for just one more drop
As I struggle like a fish out of water, and wiggle and flop
X's over my eyes
I never 'nightmared' that this would be my final demise
I'd rather burn alive or drown
Then to die of thirst, with no water anywhere to be found.

## Now & Then

Phrases amazes
Grace replaces taste
Postmark haste
Lick stamps, email, cut and paste
Delete and repeat
Facebook
Must look
Search www.allrecipes.com to cook a new dish
With a twist
Add garlic powder and marinate for an hour!
Relative, freedom and power
Did you have less or more at 40 or 4?
Whose keeping score?
Maybe its the same
I still can't avoid blame
Homework, reports, bills, and chores
Got a second mortgage
So you gotta eat your porridge
Cooties or diabetes?
Frosted Flakes or Wheaties?
Brown noser or teacher's pet?
BMX or Corvette?

## Ode to Teachers

When she that said photographs are special pictures
Her students began to snicker
Teacher tried to reach her, but slowly became embittered
She longed to make a difference
Shape minds and recruit an apprentice
Instead they said that we don't wanna take no stupid pictures!
So to reach them today, she'd skip the lesson plan
Teaching standardized tests, was even hard for her to understand!
Excerpts and tricks, instead of reading, writing, and arithmetic
Every time the bell rings, she gets a little sick
Nauseous, cautious, and exhausted, that the future's doomed
30 kids and her, in a tiny, drafty classroom
Budget cuts, its only Wednesday, but she's had enough!
She tried to quit, but can't wait for lunch, just to grab a quick puff
Menthols calm her nerves, as she contemplates and finds the words
To face the future, teach our kids, and to boldly serve

## On climbing Mt. Fuji

Half a lifetime ago, I climbed Mt. Fuji, but I didn't make it all the way to the top
Thinking back, it's silly really, why I had to stop
I got up early, to take the bus from Yokosuka's Navy base
To join a few shipmates, who invited me to take somebody else's place
But nobody showed up for the 4am bus, so I went all alone!
I realized, after rushing to get there, that I forgot my wallet AND phone!
All I had was my ticket, a jacket, and a few hundred yen
When I arrived, I spent all of the money that I had, just to check in!
They gave me a map and a walking stick, but I couldn't buy any water to quench my thirst
Half way up the mountain, I couldn't decide which was worse
Watching groups of older folks, easily passing me by
Or the fact that I couldn't catch my breath, because we were up so high!
The terrain of the mountain side, was like fine black sand
As I checked into the next station, they marked my walking stick with another kanji brand
They had oxygen, water and food for sale, but again, I had no money left
So I just meditated and took a few deep breaths
And tried to psych myself out, by pounding on my chest!
When I made it up to the next station, I was dizzy and breathing like I had almost drowned!
A guide spoke in Japanese, and basically said, 'You need to take your tired ass back down!'
I was so thirsty, but there weren't any drinking fountains
So I slowly made my way back down, the world's 35th tallest mountain (12,388 feet)
It was suddenly covered with a dense fog/mist
I was glad that I had made the trip
But honestly, I was so pissed
That I left my phone and wallet back on the ship!
But then half way down the mountain, I remembered this…
I had a disposable camera in the pocket of my jacket
So I asked an old lady if I posed for a picture, would she snap it?
She did
And here it is!

## Othello

Othello, our old fat cat
Black
Tail too long
Breath too strong
Only three teeth left in your head
Survived cat herpes, I'm surprised that you ain't dead!
Eyes cloudy
Still rowdy
Lazy
Crazy
A $1,000 Vet bill
Born with bad gums and bad teeth, I so wanted to kill
You, or drive you to a park
Miles away, sometime after dark
Open the door and fill up a dish
Of your favorite food, then drive away and make a wish
That you would never come back
No more vomit, fur balls or other smells and stains of cat
To clean
But that would be mean
But when the kitty litter ran out
And you took a steamy shit on our couch...
I wanted to kick the rest of your fucking teeth out!
I didn't, but man, I was so pissed!
For 13 years, and all you do, is just sleep, eat, and shit!
But for the good, bad, and ugly, we just can't quit
You, plus you keep away the mice and bugs too
And Zoe would miss you
Even though you sleep 23+ hours a day
You are our cat, so you can stay.

**Paralyzed by ideas**

Friday night, half past one
Laying on the couch with a headache, numb
Paralyzed by ideas, problems, and truth
Bewildered by my fleeting youth
What am I supposed to do?
My dreams are useless, I have no clue...

## Procrastinate

I wait and procrastinate
Then I'm late
And have to hurry
And then I worry
If I just did what I should
When I knew, then I could
Then I'd be straight
But, I still like to wait...

## Reciprocity wasn't a requisite?

Love, I give you my all
Praise when you triumph, and care when you fall
But reciprocity isn't a requisite?
Considering my long term investment…
When I was down and out
I tried to withdraw support for our account
But all I got was a printout, that said 'insufficient funds'
Those two cold words, took all of the air out of my lungs!
I thought you was my day one…
But you were only there for the sunny days and fun
But when the storm came, you decided to run…

## Red ember in the dark

As a kid, in the late of night
I woke up and went downstairs
To escape the August heat, in a house with no AC
Between the shadows
Beams from the streetlights outside, lit a path to our couch
A familiar smell, made me grin a toothless smile
A faint outline would breathe, and make a crackling sound, and an intermittent red light would flash, then fade
I whispered into the void, to share my dreams, ideas, jokes, and every single thought that popped into my head, not asking a single question!
My dad, smoking a cigarette in the dark, listened patiently for nearly twenty minutes to every word of my stream of conscience monologue, chuckled then replied
'Go to bed!'

## Red light in the rain

Sitting at a red light
Turn signal blinking
Radio off, waiting, thinking
Heading toward a new destination
100 miles, by way of navigation
As wipers push the rain away
I can't wait until next Saturday
Watching the other vehicles, driving by
On the corner, there's a homeless guy
If I had a dollar, he could have it
But I'm third in line, and don't want to hold up traffic
Plus if I roll down my window, I'll let the rain in
I don't want to soak my favorite suit again
The arrow's green, but from the two cars ahead, nothing!
At a stand still, the driver must be texting or something
So I honked my horn twice
Eyes through the rearview, hit me as cold as ice!
The cars slowly started to roll
As a middle finger waved hello
The light turned yellow
As the second car went past
At the light red again, I heard a laugh
From the man with the sign
Who asked if I could spare a dime
As the rain soaked my suit
I gave him a dollar and said this is all I can do…

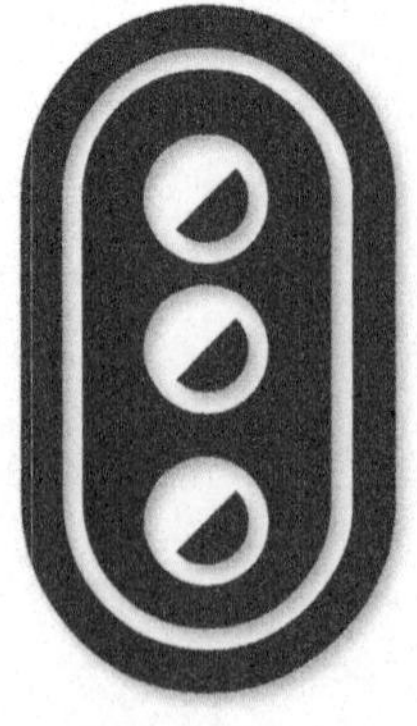

## Relationship as an old boat

Floating on hopes and dreams
Two separate but related ships, steam down twisted streams
Bound together with anchors, ropes and other things
Floating toward an ocean unspecific
Storms formed from clouds of words, mostly explicit
In lieu of weathering the waves, we opt to dock somewhere exquisite!
Back underway, much to our dismay
Our problems remain, stubborn stowaways
When our crew, cargo, and responsibility grew
Our resources became strained and few
We abandoned my ship, it made no sense for us to have two
With half the space and freedom, we'd all die if it ever sank
When you get on my nerves, I wish that you'd just walk the plank!
But I'd rather sail with you, in that little old boat we got
Than to be alone, in an expensive, magnificent yacht!
I'm no longer the captain of my fate, see, we co-master control
We're literally on the same boat, so wherever you go, I go!

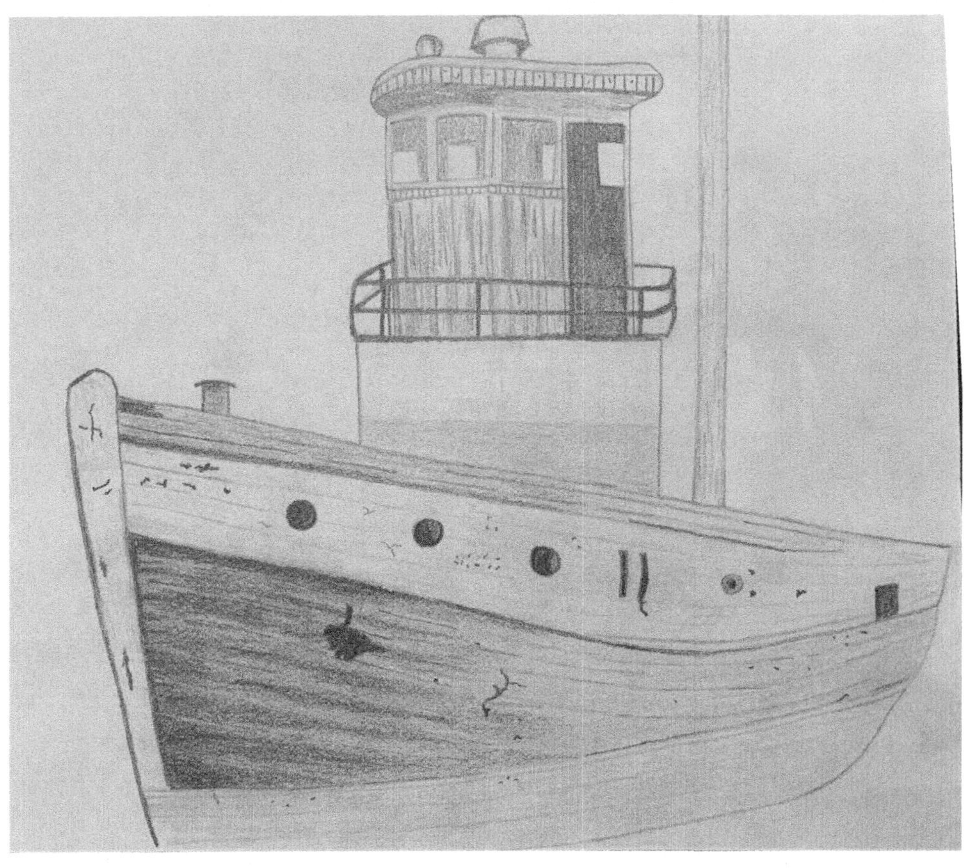

Illustrated by
Keisha Marie Moore

## Reminded to know

I was just reminded of, how blessed I am to know you
And you me too, true?
Seriously, as we cuddled under the sheets
Odd the odds, half a lifetime ago that we'd meet
Fantastic how the past went, what a magnificent feat!
A journey from a few college classes that led
Us to share a love, a life, and this morning together, in bed!

## Road Rage

My car goes from 0 to 60 in six
But when a joker cuts or flips me off, I get pissed real quick!
It takes all of my will power, to not 'set trip'
Park, fling my door open, and then bust somebody's lip!
Boiling in rage, the other driver is huge, and waving a gun
He'd better shoot me or run!
It's not entirely his fault, but he yanked on my 'proverbial straw'
He's about to catch these hands, and all the hell that's been stored up for the rest of y'all!
All of the injustice, Ill-will, and hate that the world's got (for me)
This coward aimed his 'little pea shooter' at the sky, and fired a fucking warning shot?!
I continued walking toward him, until I was inches away from his face
Looked up at the sorry giant, and said 'you're such a fuckin' disgrace...'
I walked away with his pride, dragging my cojones across the parking lot
The last thing I heard was a single gun shot...

## Road Side Memorial

Flowers on the side of the road
Next to a cross, pictures, and some stuffed dolls
Mortality marked like a tombstone
Caused by accident, carelessness, or nature
Who brings the flowers by the same time every year?
The victim's family, the responsible party, or both?
Reminders of lost love or friendship clear my thoughts
Like thousands, I drive by, with a glance of reverence
We mark our space as a reminder, that time is fleeting and not promised
Curious kids on road trips ask about and point to your memorial
The rest of us hope we never have one
For ourselves or for others
To those to tend to these flowers on the side of the road
Peace be still.

♥

## Roses are Red

Roses are red
Violet's a hue
Love is strange
I have no clue

What's in people's hearts
Or thoughts in their minds
When they portray hate
I try to be kind

Life is a blessing
Pain is a test
Triumph is the reward
For doing your best

Time is unfair
Too constant and fast
Be present for the future
But never forget the past

## Same tribe

I favor many faces
Been so many places
That I often get mistaken
When I say that I ain't him
Some say that I could be a twin
I reply on a whim
Without any anger
That I must have doppelgänger
Or a brother from another mother
Or perhaps the other and I
Are just from the same tribe
I used to think that I was unique
Or maybe I just time travelled, ahead by one week
And everywhere I go, the future me will go and meet
Everyone that I'm soon destined to see?

**Self Doubt**

Whenever I'm full of self-doubt
I often curse myself out
In my mind and under my breath
Pity, really, should be the cousin of death
For those who can't sleep
A break from being conscience is a treat
Being woke is a cruel joke
I envy the masses
So oblivious to these cultural and personal disasters
Happy and carefree, with no guilt at all
They don't pray to God, but pay weekly for Powerball!
I shake my head at it all, trying to figure it out
Then I think I should just quit, on account of self-doubt.

Illustrated by Jason Lawrence Moore

Slumlord
Illustrated by Marcus Lorenzo Jones II

## Slumlord

I began with good intentions
Bought a nice single family home, that we would never live in
All new everything, with fair rent, maintenance and taxes, we'd basically break even
Sweet turned sour with late rent, lies and thieving
Diapers and tampons thrown in toilets and then flushed
I didn't realize that owning a rental property would cost so much!
To fix, no matter who we picked
Some people just don't give a shit!
Young, old, religious, black, brown or white
Replacing windows, appliances and managing expectations is a major fight
I clearly said no dog, but they got **TWO** pit bulls
Four people on the lease, and they all broke the rules
Ole' Boy kicked down the door, then spent all of the family's rent
Somebody stole and sold the A/C unit again, then smoked that shit!
The neighbors didn't see anything, or say a word
See, they don't have A/C either, so they are happy that it occurred!
The renters took the stove, fridge, washer and dryer I figure
Property management actually said, 'What did you really expect from a nigger?'
The Property Manager said (with a straight face) 'I can rent it with just a dishwasher'
Those 'people' only eat fast food and can't tell the difference between and plate and a saucer
I once had to pay a $1,000 water bill!
My tenants were washing clothes for profit, shit just got real!
I keep getting notices and warnings from the city
For overgrown grass, trash in the yard, what a pity!
With my renters finally kicked out and no more income, all that I'm left with
Are bills, roaches, rodents and carpets stained with dog shit!
And all of their useless crap and trash left behind
If I have to pay to throw away another pissy mattress one more time....
Exposed and in debt, my investment was nothing but stress and a liability
Choosing the right people and making money in real estate is beyond the scope of my capability
So, I fixed up everything (again) and sold my rental property for less than I paid for 10 years ago
Do you ever want to be a landlord again? Hell No!

**Stolen Mercedes Medallion**

Back the early eighties
Kids would snatch an emblem off of any parked Mercedes!
Apparatus for status
Fashion lattice fantastic
Before gold chains
One's main claim to fame
Was… sportin' an automotive medallion
In the streets, our peeps was wildin'
The guilt made me so nauseous, that I'd vomit a thousand island!
As my hand clasped the cold chrome emblem, I froze
Not because of the December cold
Rather the owner of the yellow Benz
Was a neighbor… and family friend
I walked away without a medallion, but at least my conscience was clean
Way back in my adolescence, before I became a teen
The peer pressure would fester, while reading Word Up magazine
Trying to be cool like LL or Rakim, a microphone fiend
Wondered if I'd ever become fresher
Grabbed a brush from the top of my dresser
And tried in vain to get some waves
With gobs of Murray's pomade
Slept with a durag for weeks… at… a… time…
Never got any waves tho', but my forehead had a huge line!
Got clowned at school, still remember all the 'Joans' that they said
'He ain't got no waves man, but look at that creasy, greasy forehead!'

## Stream of Life

#1, maybe #2, shower, Zest, Brut, shave, begin day, breakfast fruit, Crest, fresh breath, pressed, dressed, less stress, just forget, water, duck, back, running track, poison symbolic rats, rumble concrete jungle, hustle smart, pray every day, pay taxes, damn bastards, natural disasters, rich masters, par golf, got Roth IRA, retire before fifty maybe, love baby, wife, daughter, slaughter any threat, bet, drop of a hat, word bond, nothing, me versus King Kong, sing song, ringing door bell, bing bong, terrestrial radio loquacious, commercials racist, reporter's a sadist, meteorology never submit apology, rain soaked suit, stained smokers tooth, abstract truth, remove Virginia Slims, beltlines expand, dessert sands avalanche through metropolis, extinct populous.

## The Corner (after Common's song, 'The Corner' ft. The Last Poets)

On the corner, early 80s always waiting outside, claim you never had a Curl, fool youza a lie! Mines was like Michael Jackson **and** Prince in they prime! We was just boys in the hood, barely committed a crime. Franklin Township Schools stole our education and dime! Progress paid for by black folks' money and time. How come white kids never got, bussed to the hood? Dreams deferred, we was never heard, they ignored the greater good. Bussed 20 miles back and forth daily, out to the country, we was sleepy **AND** hungry two hours before lunch see?

Man I hated school, white kids had majority rule, 1/10 ratio black to white, what could we do? Second grade, I got played as the butt of a joke, on the playground, a white kid named Kyle spoke, He said, 'God gave hair to all people at the beginning of time, Whites and Asians were first, but niggers was at the back of the line! Lazy and late, y'all had to take what was left behind, the trampled nappy dirty scraps left down on the ground,' they all pointed and laughed, turned my smile to a frown. Tears flowed, I went home, man, my stomach felt sick! I asked my mom and dad to buy me a kit real quick, to turn my naps into curls and take back my pride!

Went to school the next day with my head held high! A product of integration, all we knew was bus lines, on the Corner of 40th and College early morning most times. The concrete so cracked, we always walked on the line, but it was cool cuz mama's back turned out just fine. Winter days we was amazed at how our Jeri Curls froze. 6am spitting rhymes and perfecting our flows. We had rhyme battles, and occasional fist fights, under dawn lit street lights, but mostly we'd 'Joan,' on busters at the corner with the wrong 'ish on! So we'd be and home… cleaning our canvas white Nikes, and putting Fat Laces in our Converse and British Knights. It wasn't too rough then, but who knew it could get worse? The baddest gang in our terrain, mayne, they name was the Smurfs! We was born and raised, on the Northside of Naptown, a block away from the Indiana State Fairground. Franklin Township teachers treated me like a scrub, but my folks on the corner showed me nothing but love! In time, I grew into my prime and learned how to grind, slangin' newspapers for a quarter and penny candy for a dime. Shoveling sidewalks, mowing lawns, and raking leaves, if you parked at outside the Fair you probably paid me some fees!

The corner helped make me, but it would also break G's, in the summer, the city made the whole hood sneeze! Their trucks came often and sprayed clouds of pesticides, that left a bitter taste in our mouth that stung and watered our eyes! Poisonous air lingered for days, probably caused homicides. Rich folks never got gas trucks, why am I not surprised? No schools or parks, we had the only court for blocks, so Curb Ball was invented on the corner by street jocks: Two players facing each other on opposite sides of the street, threw a basketball to hit the other curb's concrete. Bounce the ball back to you – that's one score, do the same thing when a car passed, and that's four more, points. I hate to babble and tattle, but on 4th of July, man we had us some epic battles! Duos on Ten Speeds armed with sawed off U pipes, lighters and bottle rockets, shooting jokers riding side by side! With age and hindsight it was hella fun and dumb. I once blocked a rocket, and it made my hand numb - for two days! Still amazed at all the stupid 'ish that we done, on the corner in the city where I'm from – Naptown!

He said, 'God gave hair to all people at the beginning of time, whites and Asians were first, but 'niggers' were at the back of the line!

♥

### The emancipation of your fears

Push...through the pain, boredom, and shame
Attitude really is everything!
Failure and success is all in your brain
Some accept defeat, way before it should be claimed
Miles of tasks and finish lines envisioned
Will never materialize, if your mind is imprisoned
The view from the valley, looks quite intimidating
And climbing mountains, can be most frustrating
The energy spent, getting you from here to there
Will be incrementally difficult, and just as thin as the air
As you struggle to breathe and leak blood, sweat, and tears
Know these symptoms, as the emancipation of your fears!

## The future is bright & in good hands

When you're my age, the world will be a better place
Men and women will work together, to win the human race!
Disease, war, discrimination, and hunger will not be tolerated
More fame and fortune will go to those who help others, to become better educated
Not just those who play games, pretend to be other people, or tout opinions as fact
The meek shall inherit the earth, where will you be at?
Maybe you'll be the scientist that cleans air and ocean pollution
Or a politician that negotiates diplomatic solutions
Or maybe you'll be a biologist, that cures a deadly disease
By discovering a new substance, in the roots of rainforest trees
Maybe you'll write a song that inspires someone 100 years from now
Perhaps you'll be a farmer, that humanely treats a cow
Or you just might be the first person to greet an alien in outer space!
I can't wait to witness the day in the future when you achieve your fate.

**The Janitor**

An ocean of emotion, once poisoned her soul like a potion
She used booze to smooth bumps and scratches, like an ointment or lotion
Why continue to dream and scheme, was her final notion
Then on a whim, she sang a hymn, or maybe read scripture
Over time she was fine, and then things became clearer
Enlightened, she saw life as a different picture
Not concerned about those who yell, sell, and tell
Or convincing mere mortals, that she's not going to hell
Inconsequential is the need, to succeed nor to fail
She's just doing the right thing
True, it's not easy being a human being
Just follow the golden rule
The first thing we all learned in school
Treat yourself and others well
Savor the sweet Now & Laters, never past dwell
That's the secret to life, as far as she can tell
She wears her pride well
Like a frown upside down
Attitude is contagious
Her countenance courageous
It erases the disgraces, of those whose presence she graces
Her charm works like an alarm
That shakes awake
Many non-believers and the few with faith
Change happens one person at a time
Ideas sprout from seeds, planted in your mind
Growing into trees or weeds, only you can define
Show know control your heart, soul, and behind!

**The Midwatch**

On the starboard bridge wing, hours before reveille
Waves munch on the hull, like stalks of celery
The night sky and saltwater smell to me
Is the best part of being underway/at sea, and the epitome
Of freedom, it's so humbling, alas!
Billions of stars above and below, and an ocean so vast...
Tracking a contact with my binoculars, so that we don't crash
Hundreds of nautical miles deep, in the Pacific Ocean
With a sea state of one, there's barely any pitch or yaw motion
Another class three merchant safely passes
I look down at the waves, and see bioluminescent light flashes

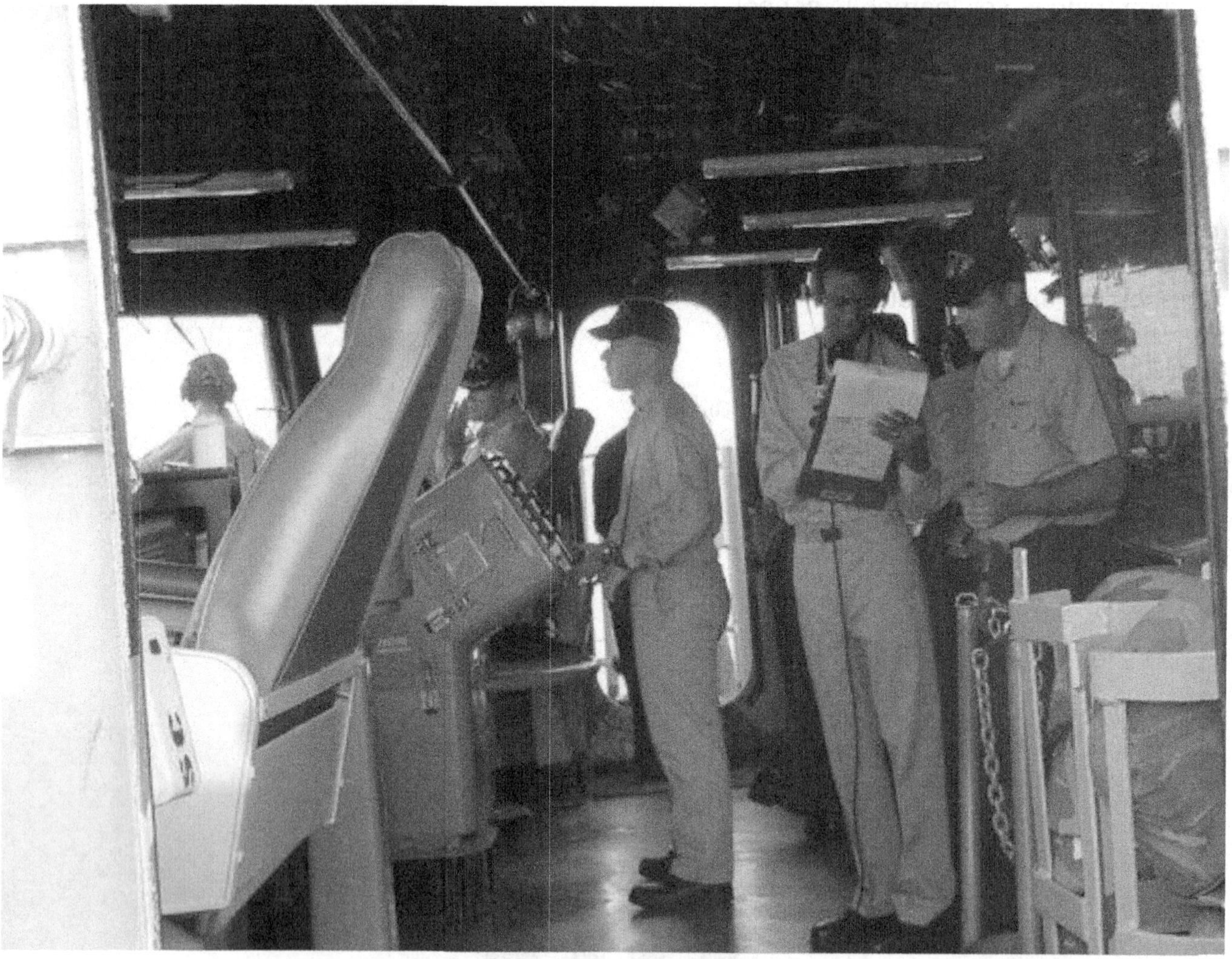

## The more I learn, the less I understand

Scientists say that the center of the earth
Is as hot as the surface of the sun…
How is that possible, #1:
That's only 1,800 miles down…
#2: That's the same distance as a one-way flight bound
To Birmingham from Los Angeles, how can that be?
If an 'earth' ever somehow surrounded a sun, wouldn't that just boil the sea?
#3: So is the center of earth the actual location of hell?
Where sinning souls go, like some kind of spiritual jail?
10,832 degrees Fahrenheit, is how hot the center of the earth is right now!
What I don't understand exactly, is how!?
If the sun is about 92 million miles away
How can it easily just burn my skin, at the beach on a sunny day?
But just less than 2,000 miles beneath our feet
There's almost the same amount of heat?
As the earth spins counterclockwise at 1,000 miles per hour, on its tilted axis, it's all just so confusing to me...
The more I learn, the less I understand, what I already know and see.

## The past is the future?

Up is down and water is dry
Just yesterday, I seen a dragon fly!
Not an insect, I suspect, that my imagination is malignant
Made believe my reality in figments
Like the Europeans did, with differences in pigments…
That the world now takes, as facts over lies
Like kids 'trick-or-treating' while wearing a disguise
No rhyme or reason
But at the end of Autumn's season
We buy bags of candy and give it all away!
As a tradition, people hate work, but love to play
Amusement parks, where we stand in line just to pay for a quick thrill
Centuries ago, the fear was free, but we spent life and limb just to catch a meal!
As humanity evolved, we avoided pain and pursued pleasure
Now we're all slowly going insane, addicted to our treasure (knowledge)

**The Summer of 2020**

Crazy best describes, the summer of 2020
We lived like hermits, but saved a bunch of money
The news was bleak and the weather was very hot
Nobody envied black folks, nurses, or cops!
A lack of common sense, caused record COVID-19 cases
Americans were banned worldwide, from traveling to many places
School, church, sports, and camp were all cancelled for the youth
The world needed a cure, but settled for the truth.

THIS PAGE LEFT INTENTIONALLY BLACK

**To spank or not to spank...**

Had to discipline my child twice today!
Pissed me off, it's so difficult to keep my calm at bay
She has no issues at camp, church, or school
But hardly listens to me and her mom at home - she must think we're BooBoo the fool!
She's barely nine, so that reference is oft misunderstood
I wish that I could travel back in time, and show her my old neighborhood
True, I probably had it much easier than my mom and dad
But she wants for not, and her 'worst' ain't even really all that bad!
With her own room, homework via Chromebook, and an iPod full of apps
My brother and I shared a bed, and once spent a week collecting bottle caps!
I suppose progress/privilege is a double edge sword
Less timeouts and screen time, and more belts, race tracks, and extension cords?

## Trip thru the cosmos

I suppose, we could take a trip through the cosmos
Walk through history with sand between our toes
And listen to the ocean, preach to the beach
The gospel is the tide, delivering the moon's message to each
Time and pressure can turn mountains into hills of dirt
And trillions of zillions of sand particles here on earth
The universe is vast, yet so small we can't see
Beyond religion and rational thought, so who are we?
Like machines that we can program by zero and one
Cause and effect creates and destroys everything, even our sun!
Does this tiny grain of sand, in my hand, contain a universe too?
How do my thoughts and actions affect you?

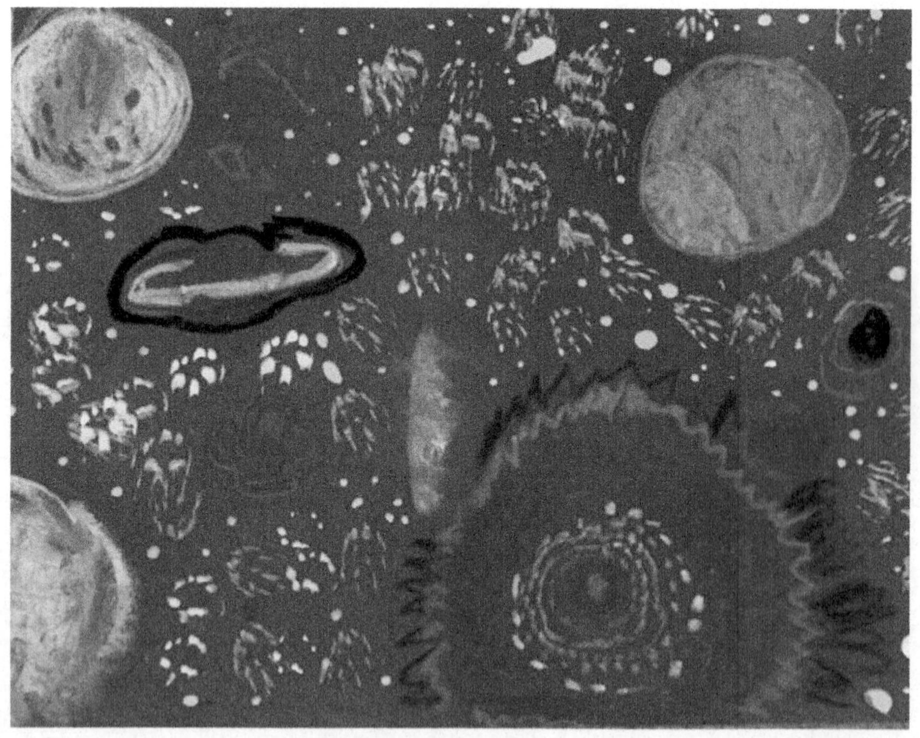

Illustrated by
Zoe Victoria Moore

**Trust Fall**

Falling through the air
Trusting my peers to catch me, without a care!
Look at the smile on my face
At humanities camp freshman year, deep in the woods someplace
Campfires, discussions, not religious or heavy handed
In a tent with a group of upperclassmen, who demanded
To know my plans for the future, college and career
Telling stories about what happens in college, the frat parties and beer!
A cool weekend, making s'mores by the fire
I'm glad that I signed up to attend, after seeing the flyer!

**Unbraiding Zoe's hair**

Unbraiding Zoe's hair, so curly and rich
Two pinches of locks, connected in twists
Head moving all around, staying still's an un-granted wish
I bet Carol's Daughter, didn't holler and whine
Every three weeks, when it was **her** hair braiding time!
Beads bouncing around, sounding like a little didgeridoo
Her teacher's note read, 'I found all these little beads by her desk, but didn't know what to do...'

## Unplug

Government's shut down
No job is safe, what now?
Broken systems, powerful people, exposing and imposing themselves
Still rich and famous, closet mansions filled with bones on the shelves
Power corrupts
When is enough, enough?
When others get caught
They still don't think, 'maybe I should not?'
They'll never believe, you versus me
Am I talking about singers, comedians, actors, or politicians?
All of the above, plus the smoke and mirrors of social and commercial media magicians!
We all scrolling for comments and likes, begging for permission
Memes and videos on 3" by 6" inch screens
Hypnotized, no longer wise, we're just information feigns!
Like erratic, static, and various media streams
Overloaded with fake news, facts, and entertainment
Lines blurred, reality's absurd, free candy crush addictions become a monthly payment
Unplug...

LIFE & LOVE

## Unsolicited advice for life

There's more in life that unites us
Than the stuff that divides us
Let's all just work on our problems, and then split up the prizes!
Why can't we, civilly agree to disagree?
Like how we generally hate each others favorite NFL football team?
But at the end of the day, we all really have the same dream
Love, life, and work
Try to minimize hurt
Stay true to the golden rule, and don't be a jerk!
Whether you're Kermit and Miss Piggy
or Ernie and Burt
Who cares how you get busy!
Just be less Gargamel and more Poppa Smurf...

## Wait…

I'd like to tell you how
I got to this point here
First I wasn't truthful, but now
I'm open, free, and clear
If you give me a moment today
I'll give you two in exchange tomorrow
If you'd just sit awhile and stay
I'd love to share your frustration and sorrow
Please listen to my plea just a little longer
Your eyes and ears I need to borrow
Because my love for you has grown stronger

**Warrior @ Peace**

When a warrior carries water, it's a sign that all is well
When a warrior carries water, know that he once faced hell
When a warrior carries water, realize that she's known grief
When a warrior carries water, it symbolizes peace.

When a warrior carries water, long after the battle is done
Lose, draw, or even if its won
With fists, rocks, spears, arrows or guns
Under attack, you either face facts or run!
Our thoughts, words, and actions, will eventually become
Our measure, if you don't seek peace, then you'll never have none.

Illustrated by John G. Moore, Jr.

## Washing dishes

Washing the dishes, used to be my least favorite chore
As an adult, I don't think that anymore
Now I see it as a time to meditate
The time it takes time to wash our utensils, is when I allocate
Prayers for family and friends, patience, and understanding
While I wash the pots and pans, I review all the things in my life that are demanding
During the cups and mugs, I acknowledge my problems and opportunities
As I soak and scrub the dishes, I mentally review upcoming events and other soon-to-be's
For the bowls and other odds and ends, I just count my blessings
As I dry and put away the dishes, I write rhymes in my mind, just like this lesson!

## We Clueless

The truth is, we clueless!
But we knew this
I take my daughter to church and try to teach her
We're praying to God, but still paying to Lucifer
Is "R" the difference between evil and good?
Can't find the right words, like I know that I should
For six decades, I've roamed the earth
Maybe I have another four, before I become dirt
Today, I'm considered middle age
What if a biblical year was just 30 days?
And Methuselah was only 75
Maybe the translators of the bible got it wrong, or lied
If God is real, maybe we don't exist?
When Judas sold out Jesus, for mankind that was it!
The son of God gave them jokers power and glory
He's all knowing and understood the real story
The spin back then, for all the non-believers and grievers
Was drop your current gods, this one here is easier!
He'll give you everything, and you can treat him like shit
But you'll still get to go to heaven, if you just repent!
Instead of taking the lives of your kids, and cattle and other sacrifices
Just give your money to the church, at weekly reasonable prices!
Really, does money sound divine?
Did going to the new religion cut down their time?
When people were offering sheep to several gods, they lived for centuries
With one god, they only lived to their 50's and 60's?
Were there women disciples?
If the truth were know, we wouldn't need rifles
The end of days is more than just a phrase
When crime pays
And we envy the rich and famous' dubious ways
We're left with hella debt and the devil's holds the loan
Blindly worshipping false idols, like a phone!
Everywhere we go, from the bathroom to the bed
We're all probably growing tumors on the sides of our heads!
More concerned about what people think
Than the wasted food and water that goes down our sink
2am, tossing and turning, out of the bed I fell
I woke up and discovered the truth, THIS IS HELL!

## We're all complicit!

Kids are locked up in ICE cages!
What's new on Netflix?
Hey! Thousands of kids are still locked up in cages!
Let me check on my stock/draft picks...
When the parents are deported, their kids are left alone, and thrown in cages!
I think that I'm going to like/retweet/hashtag this silly little meme!
The kids caught COVID, crouching, crying on cold floors in cages!
What's the latest news on my favorite NFL/MLB/NBA/NHL team?
In 2019, over 500,000 people (men, women, children, and babies) were locked up in 200 American ICE Detention centers nationwide!
Say, let's DoorDash some Ice Cream!
People seeking the American dream are now living in an American nightmare!
Maybe I should buy something else that I really don't need online...
Babies are being born in cages!
Let's binge watch that reality TV show again, just one more time!
What if it was your folks who were locked up in cages?
Most times, my online comments (in the comment section) have absolutely nothing to do with the article that I just read!
How is this 'not' on the news every day, innocent kids are still being locked up in cages!
All week on social media, I'm going to quote nothing but scripture...
Did you hear me? Kids are still trapped in cages! Do something?
What? I didn't do anything, why are you calling me Hitler?
Exactly! Download the 5 Calls app, call all your congresspersons and tell them to 'begin the release of migrant families from detention and end child separation,' immediately!
Wow, that's a really direct and specific request, okay, will do! What else?
Please tell your family and friends to do the same, until they're free, we're all complicit!

**We’re all the same**

If you want proof that everyone is the same
Go to an amusement park, that has little fanfare and fame
Not a ‘World’ or an ‘Island’
But a place that still requires a wristband
There, you’ll see real American culture
Eating corn dogs and waiting in line for the next roller coaster
Sure, some folks will sneak in their own food
And others will cut line and act rude
But most just want the same things
To seek pleasure and avoid pain, like all other human beings

## What are you?

What is won't be
Expect rewards and change, now do we?
Whenever one remains the same
S/he gets out scored and loses the game
They're laughing at your little 'participation' ribbon!
While you talk, they'll listen
Actions versus words are like predator and prey
Which did you choose (to be) today?

## What does Veteran's Day mean to me?

What does Veteran's Day mean to me?
As a former service member and defender of Liberty
I was motivated to serve and become a part of history
Like my grandfather and great uncles before me
I pledged an oath, and served with pride in the United States Navy
I thought I'd be a hero, but it was my shipmates who'd saved me
Time and again
These brave women and men
Taught me the value of honor, courage, and commitment
Brothers and sisters in arms, from every background, religion, and pigment
Throughout American history, we've stood against tyranny, terrorism, and slavery
I salute our past, present, and future veterans, for their sacrifice and bravery.

## What gives?

What gives?
Who lives?
Like this?
Tired and pissed
A nursing home, kind of sounds like bliss!
Do nothing and sleep
All day, sitting alone, I could just write and eat!
Misery and grief
Agnostic belief
If heaven and hell don't exist
Is the 'here and now' supposed to be our torture or bliss?

## What if I get it?

What if I get it?
Quarantine restrictions lifted
Once young, black, and gifted
Now I'm old, masked, and restricted
The news is so bleak
That only pariahs and liars speak
How much time is left?
How much time is right?
Even with all of our power, money and military might
We don't even know how to fight this invisible plight!
Technology may be our only salvation
Socially isolated, frustrated, and dying in the world's once most powerful nation

**What if?**

They got drugs for opioid addiction
Imagine that - a narcotic prescription, written by a doctor, for your affliction!
Like paying tuition for an education, when knowledge should be free
What if it was illegal to breathe, unless you owned your own tree?
What if the government (Flint, MI) knowingly poisoned your water several years ago?
But all that you saw, on TV was trash, and a forecast for more snow!
Bathing and boiling gallons of donated bottled water
Working and paying your rent and bills, yet living like a squatter
What if the president demanded your tax dollars to build a wall, just to be a dick?
Why do evil people live so long, and never seem to get sick?
What if the law made bathrooms white/male/female only, and told you shit in the street?
What if you were innocent and then were thrown in jail, because a cop was pissed?
And you were stopped and frisked for ‘allegedly’ packing heat?
Ripped out of the arms of your daughter and wife
This ain’t dystopian fiction, dawg, this is real life!

## When did we get old?

My future was once so bright
That even at night
I used to wear shades!
Those greener pastures, flooded fast, and then became everglades!
I used to party and B.S.
Now it's all just work and stress
Sounding like my old man yelling, 'Y'all clean up this mess!'
And, 'Why in the hell are all these lights on in the daytime?' if I knew or had to guess...
Time is the sneaky thief, who robbed me of my success
Less money and hair in my middle age
Passion and ambition were soon replaced with pessimism and rage
Work, bills, taxes, and emails
Thinking back to my youth, at beach, collecting sun rays and seashells
While carefully building castles in the sand
I didn't really, fully understand
How life, like that tide, would soon be relentlessly crashing in
Knocking down my hard work, hopes and dreams, time and again
Me thinking, naively, somehow that I could actually win!
When did we get old?
I really used to believe, that the sky was my limit
Now, all that I see are the cons and the gimmicks!
Right and wrong, left or right, decisions and consequences
When the deck is stacked, you lose, and then wonder, what's the difference?
Are the glasses half full or empty?
Actually, the measurements are identical, ha, so don't tempt me!
Semantics, ideas and dreams implanted
Unfulfilled, when I shot for the stars and then landed
Right back to the same place where I started!
Winkles and gray hair, so I no longer get carded
The youth get my pity, rather than envy
Whenever I reminisce, my antidotes are way too lengthy…
Suddenly, I woke up in the distance future
Eating a grand slam at Denny's, 3:30pm in a stupor
Redeeming my senior citizen discount, man life comes at you fast!
Youth is fleeting, this bears repeating kids, enjoy it while it lasts!
Youth is fleeting, this bears repeating kids, enjoy it while it lasts!

## When the world changed...

When the world changed
Most people didn't
Programs executing rules of 'cultural' software written over time
Right or wrong, even when forced to change
We hold onto the past, like our lives depend upon it
Simpler times when things were better?
Or were we just younger, less educated, and naive?
The present truly is the best and worst of times
So much potential to improve things for everyone
Pushing billions of people off of a ledge into the abyss of poverty, injustice, and death
Government, money, and politics is no different than sports and entertainment
It's all made up to waste time, consume resources, and divide people
Even when progress marches toward injustice
It's not bullets, viruses, and weather that cause disasters
It's people consumed by greed, fear, and ignorance that do!
The house that we 'own' sits on land, once stolen from a people that were terrorized, raped, and killed less than a 150 years ago
We've all got to do better.

## When we walked everywhere

Remember walking home from school?
The store, library, church, games and practice?
We used to wear out soles
And sweat out clothes
Dreaming of the freedom that a car would bring
We couldn't wait to be grown!
Sitting on chrome
With your own place, food, and a phone…
Then we got older
And that reality became colder
Real freedom, it seems
Was as a child and in our teens
Where we could go anywhere and do anything...
For free.

## Why I got a colonoscopy

This colonoscopy literally
Got me seeing shit clearly!
At age 45 my…
Doctor recommended that I…
Get a screening, the reason?
Because I may have cancerous polyps and lesions
Days of drinking Milk of Magnesia
Liquid only diet, with no solid food, or red or blue stuff
All of this time spent on the toilet, I've had enough!
Two days of a liquid only diet, is getting kind of rough!
The cramping, the growling, the runs, oh my!
No disrespect to women, but I'm so glad that I'm a guy!
I can't even imagine having PMS!
Just a few hours of abdominal cramping and I'm already distressed!
I had to drink 238g of MiraLAX mixed in with lemon Gatorade (64 ounces total)
Over two days, in my bed, doubled over in moderate pain and discomfort, I laid
Thinking that this would be an effective method of torture for most
As soon as this is all over, I'm eating two plates of bacon, pancakes, eggs and toast!
I realize that this 'necessary evil' is needed
Online researching about colon cancer in African American men, I had to re-read it!
We have the highest incidence and mortality rates of colorectal cancer than any other group in the United States!
Underlying conditions and history, it's about **WAY** more than just race!
For some reason the right side of a Black men's colon ages more rapidly
Recent studies point to these "epigenetic" changes in our colon tissue factually
Ironically, the occurrence of colon and prostate cancer in men, **IN** Africa, is not as prevalent
The impact of slavery to survivors of the diaspora's health, is still quite relevant!
We're 20% more likely to get colorectal cancer, and 40% more likely to die from it!
So I can stomach this temporary discomfort, the explosive diarrhea, and liquid shit!
"Black Panther" star Chadwick Boseman died of colorectal cancer at age 43
So I'm raising awareness and getting tested*, for my daughter, for my wife, and for me!

The **colon** is longest part of the large intestine, ~5 feet long, the part of the large intestine extending from the cecum (#3) to the rectum (#4). The colon removes water and some nutrients and electrolytes from partially digested food.

♥

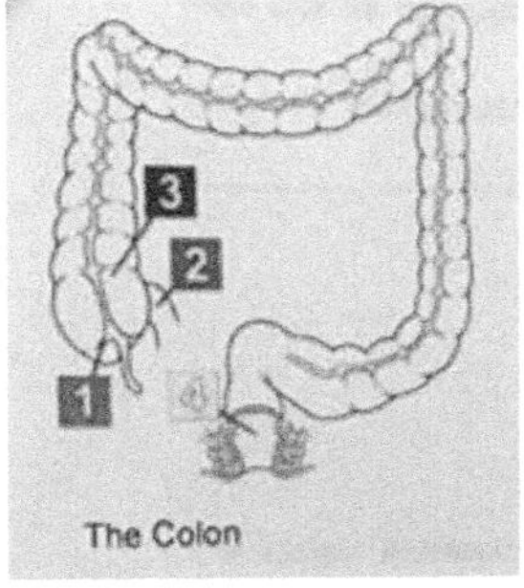


*My results were normal

LIFE & LOVE

**Winners never lose**

The bases are loaded
Their cards have folded
All the chips are in
Prepared for years for this win
Studied hard, passed tests, and ran scrimmages
Every fiber of my being, cells and appendages
Are focused, and in tune like an opus
Witness this magic ladies and gentlemen, hocus pocus!
I was once hopeless, and saw that light at the end
As a run away freight train, but now I just pretend
That it is an exit, and the beginning
Even if I lose, I'm still winning!

## Worksheet ink

Worksheet ink
Dark blue hue
Recall those sheets from elementary school?
The scent of the toner had a pleasant musk
I'd grasp the paper with both hands, still warm to the touch
Knowing that I was going to ace every question
And show all of my work, to prove that I'd mastered the lesson
My teacher once caught me sniffing a worksheet
She smiled, did the same with her handouts, no need for us to speak!
This public school, it's teachers, and even the worksheets understood me
In that Township school I was a prisoner, but here I was free.

## You Can't Winnnn!

I was watching "The Wiz" with my kid
When the Scarecrow sang, she was shocked at what I did
So was I
Believe it or not, I started to cry!
I mean an ugly cry, "You can't win"
Tears flowed as soon as the song began
"You can't get over, you can't get out of the game!"
My life summed up in a song, I was so ashamed
I had seen and heard it a dozen times
As a kid it was fun, I liked how it rhymed
But as an adult, the lyrics hit me like a eulogy
Of my ignorance and bliss, I had just realized how America's been abusing me
Discrimination, veteran, mortgages, taxes, high interest rates, debt, its crazy!
I really can't get out of the game, I'll be working 'till I'm 80!
I don't want my baby to feel like this
Trapped, disillusioned, frustrated and pissed!
My parents felt the same way too
To break the cycle and change the game
WHAT ARE WE GOING TO DO?

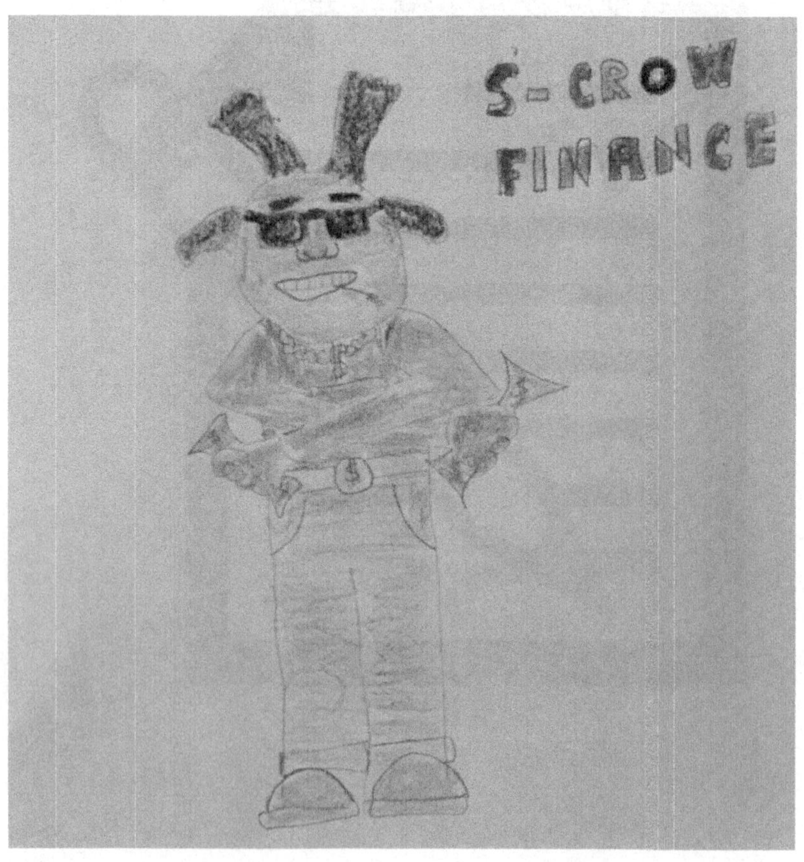


Illustrated by Jason Lawrence Moore

## You still want me?

You still want me?
Warts and scars
You still like me?
All my flaws
You've often seen me
Ashy in my drawers!
You know all the sounds of me
Belches and farts
You still need me?
Despite the fits and starts
You still love me?
Thank you for that part!

## You're what its all about

You're what it's all about
Though my words and actions, may sometimes lend doubt
I endeavor to give the world to you
That sum and more, if you only knew
Just how much you mean to me
I wish that I could write, well enough help you see
Just how incredible you are, and how happy you make me!

# PART III: POLITICS & RELIGION (290-351)

Top 75 = ♥

| | # | Poem |
|---|---|---|
| | 290 | 1994 Crime Bill |
| | 291 | 40 years in the wilderness |
| | 292 | 66 Books of the Bible |
| ♥ | 293 | A Promissory Note (I owe you) |
| | 294 | A terrible time for Jesus |
| ♥ | 295 | Advice & Sin |
| | 296 | An open letter to the Chinese government |
| | 297 | Ancient Alien Invasion |
| | 298 | Apostasy |
| ♥ | 299 | Apostle Cypher |
| | 300 | Ballots and Protests |
| | 301 | Blood Revolution |
| ♥ | 302 | Book of Job |
| | 303 | Born to lose, die to win? |
| | 304 | Boycotting table grapes like Caesar Chavez |
| | 305 | Br'er Jordan (after Br'er Rabbit) |
| | 306 | Cognitive Dissonance |
| | 307 | Cuban Paradise |
| | 308 | Daddy Warbucks? |
| | 309 | Dust to Dust |
| | 310 | Ecclesiastes |
| | 311 | Fishing for freedom |
| | 312 | Flames explain the present |
| ♥ | 313 | Gideon's Army |
| | 314 | Go Go Elijah! 1st Kings 17 |
| | 315 | Go Jesus, it's your birthday! |
| | 316 | God is a single parent |
| | 317 | God is real but we don't exist |
| | 318 | God is time |
| | 319 | Greed is Good' marked on America's tomb |
| | 320 | Holy erythrocytes! |
| | 321 | How November 2016 felt |
| | 322 | How the devil dies |
| | 323 | Humble |
| | 324 | I bought lunch for Judas today... |
| | 325 | Jingoism |
| | 326 | Joshua Crosses The Jordan River |
| | 327 | Joshua Fit The Battle Of Jericho |
| | 328 | Keep the faith! |
| ♥ | 329 | Make Haiti the 51st State! |
| | 330 | Muppim and Huppim |
| | 331 | Nerf guns responsible for mass shootings? |
| | 332 | New Normal |
| | 333 | Occupy This! |
| | 334 | Omega - post script of the bible |
| | 335 | On Footprints and Isaiah 46:4 |
| | 336 | On God |
| | 337 | Pennywise |
| | 338 | Politics as a religion |
| ♥ | 339 | Prophet's Delight |
| | 340 | Protesting is pointless |
| | 341 | Sampson & Delilah |
| | 342 | Some Angels disliked utopia |
| ♥ | 343 | The 10 Commandments |
| ♥ | 344 | The Return of Nommo |
| | 345 | They don't believe in God or COVID |
| | 346 | Unfair Bears (the opposite of Care Bears) |
| | 347 | War on Drugs |
| | 348 | What is faith? |
| | 349 | When they decide to deport you |
| | 350 | Why did I choose apes |
| ♥ | 351 | Zeus died? |

## 1994 Crime Bill

Just watched that documentary, the 13th
It all makes sense now, good grief!
Been supporting Bill and Hillary, but where's our relief?
In the 90s, the economy grew, due to 100,000 police
Who put millions of brothers and sisters in jail
Many still to this day, can't cope, vote, or make bail
America threw parties, while niggas caught hell!
Cotton and tobacco got replaced with drugs and crime
America got fat, rich, and happy, while we died and did decades in time!
For profit prisons, provided cheap labor to produce various goods
Three strikes and you're out, no doubt, decimated our hoods!
Modern day slaves
As 'they' say, crime pays
'They' being 'Massa'
The legal gun blaster
Skin the color of plaster
Stop and frisk, to fill those new prison cells faster…
Perpetrated hate, in a subtle way, so that nobody knows
The enemy is mostly brown, black and poor in most movies and TV shows
Cops, Law & Order, and movies about gangs, courts, and prison
If art imitates life, is that how we 'posta be livin'?
That 1994 Crime Bill, sealed the deal, I thought we was cool Clintons?
I guess we're all just 'Super Predators' and these politicians are stool pigeons...

Tough love – I voted for Secretary Clinton.

H. R. 3355

One Hundred Third Congress
of the
United States of America

AT THE SECOND SESSION

*Begun and held at the City of Washington on Tuesday,*
*the twenty-fifth day of January, one thousand nine hundred and ninety-four*

An Act

To control and prevent crime.

*Be it enacted by the Senate and House of Representatives of the United States of America in Congress assembled,*

**SECTION 1. SHORT TITLE.**

This Act may be cited as the "Violent Crime Control and Law Enforcement Act of 1994".

**SEC. 2. TABLE OF CONTENTS.**

The following is the table of contents for this Act:

**40 years in the wilderness**

After God helped Moses and his people, escape from Egypt
God carefully explained the following edict
Travel to the promised land, and I will care for y'all and provide
After years of wandering in the dessert, the tribes thought that God and Moses lied!
When food ran low, each morning God provided manna bread
This kept them fed, but soon they wanted some meat instead!
So God sent the Israelites a bunch of quail
It tasted just like chicken, they had pounds of it by the pail!
Still deep in the desert, the tribes begged Moses for some water to drink
Moses prayed to God, cuz' these 'Hebrews' brought him to the brink!
God told Moses to tap a rock lightly with his staff
He struck it twice (hard) in haste, frustration, and wrath!
A river of fresh water flowed, cold, clean, and refreshing
But the Israelites still complained about everything, which slowed their progression
So God sent a swarm of snakes, to bite and teach each a lesson!
They got bit quick, then got real sick
But God was merciful, and told Moses to gather a bunch of sticks
And fashion a snake statue
People were instantly healed, when Moses pointed it at you!
This journey continued for 40 years for every, man, woman, and child
God, life, lessons, blessings, and complaints, somewhere in the wild...

## 66 Books of the Bible

He-Brew, He-Brew, He-Brew, He-Brew....
66 books in the Bible
Instructions vital for survival
39 old and 27 new
Listed below without further ado (Go!)
Genesis, Exodus, Leviticus, Numbers, and Deuteronomy!
G-E-L-N-D, see the eponymy? (Yeah!)
Joshua, Judges, Ruth, Samuel (1&2), Kings (1&2), and Chronicles
J-J-R-S-K-C 2 Samuel 10:4 is quite comical! (ha ha!)
Ezra, Nehemiah, and Esther
E-N-E, wraps up the yester (day!)
Job, Psalms, Proverbs, Ecclesiastes, and Song of Solomon make it!
J-P-P-E-S, Just Poets Prophesying Everything Sacred! (Yeah!)
Isaiah, Jeremiah, Lamentations, Ezekiel, and Daniel also!
I-J-L-E-D, prophets who predicted the Gospel (Amen!)
Hosea, Joel, Amos, Obadiah, Jonah, Micah, Nahum, Habakkuk,
Zephaniah, Haggai, Zechariah, and Malachi!
H-J-A-O-J-M-N-H-Z-H-Z-M all God's alibis!

B–I–B–L–E, B–I–B–L–E… (hold up!) B–I–B–L–E (Yeah, yeah!)
The Holy Bible
Vital for survival
Who all do you know?
Still blindly follows false idols, versus numero uno? <My God>
Written for centuries in Hebrew and Greek
Eloquent prose, conquers foes and save souls <That's deep!>
The point of this song, I hope that ya' gettin'
All the answers ye, seek have already been written.... (Amen!!!)
Repeat after me… B–I–B–L–E <<<hold up!>>>
400 years after the OT ended
A New Testament was written, then amended (Whoo!)
Matthew, Mark, Luke and John's Messiah
M-M-L-J's, words will always inspire! (Word!)
Acts, Romans, Corinthians (1&2), Galatians, and Ephesians!
A-R-1-2-C-G-E Paul wrote for various reasons….. (Yeah)
Philippians, Colossians, Thessalonians (1&2), Timothy (1&2), Titus and Philemon
P-C-T-T-T-P, was all about salvation and sin (Amen!)
Hebrews, James, Peter (1&2), John (1-3), Jude and Revelation
H-J-P-J-J-R, the final books of our foundation!
B–I–B–L–E X7 (hold up!)… He-Brew, He-Brew, He-Brew, He-Brew....

| OLD TESTAMENT (39 BOOKS) | NEW TESTAMENT (27 BOOKS) |
|---|---|
| 5-12-5-5-12 = 39 | 4-1-21-1 = 27 |

## A Promissory Note (I owe you)

The world's been broke
Empty promises and false hope
If banks just sell debt
Then what exactly do we get?
If ten dollars, costs ten cents for Uncle Sam to make
That remaining $9.90 is just a huge profit rake!
When they print more money
Inflation gets real crummy!
Debt, liability, asset
Buyers and sellers pay, but banks never forget!
Because to them money **IS** debt
Making sense yet?
We toil for a living wage
From little babies, up to old age
Banks profit from our interest, but don't see our rage!
It's like we're all slaves
Pay each bill, until its nil
But we never quite pull back the whole peel
Debt is fake, but a bank's profit is real?
CitiBank is the real David Copperfield!
Then the cycle begins again
A new house, car, computer, or credit card my friend?
Give someone a gun and they can rob a bank
But give someone a bank, and they can rob the world!

**A terrible time for Jesus**

It was a terrible time for Jesus, right after he was baptized
40 days in the wild, with the devil and his lies (Whoa!)
Jesus fasted the whole time, meaning he didn't eat!
Despite wild beasts like pigs, chickens, and sheep! (Uh!)
The devil tried for weeks, to get into Jesus' head (Yeah)
He said, 'If God really is yo' daddy, then turn these rocks into some bread!'
Jesus said, 'Don't live by bread, rather by what God said!' (Amen!)
The devil led Jesus into Jerusalem, high above a temple
And said, 'Throw yourself down and angels will save you, its simple!' (What?)
Jesus cried, 'You can't just put God to the test!?'
The devil had struck out twice, so his last (attempt) had to be his best!
He promised Jesus the world, if he'd join him and start, 'God forsaking'
Jesus replied, 'No, get behind me, Satan!' (Amen!)
The devil left Jesus after weeks of lies and stresses
So God sent angels to comfort and feed Jesus some breakfast! (Ok!)

Luke 4: 1-13

## Advice & Sin

God, please forgive me, for I have sinned
I cuss, lust, and covet stuff, and then pretend
That the consequences of my actions
Can be paid off in dividends and fractions
With the small amounts of money and time
That I spend to pray away, and repent for my crime
Personal calamity nearly drove me to insanity!
Those vices and prices, shrunk and punk the man in me
Bad habits control addicts, like a cruel master
As their slave, my actions create a tragic disaster
Which leaves a path of destruction, that invites unwanted discussion
From family and friend's urging me to begin again, and then do something!
Glass houses, my anger grows, as I too cast stones
Advice is like a transaction with down payments and high-interest loans.

## An open letter to the Chinese government

Dear China:

Please use your influence and international bully pulpit
To force France and the United States of America to commit
To pay Haiti billions in reparations, for centuries of documented despair and theft
Haiti has tried reason and sympathy in vain, now all that is left
Is a desperate plea, to the divine state*
From a humble global citizen, who re-read 'world' history, to better relate
What France and America did to Haiti was way beyond greed and hate!
France collecting reparations was crazy, but America's occupation of Haiti (in 1915) was insane!
And eerily similar to what Russia is currently doing in the Ukraine
Short of declaring war against Russia, the world's support of Ukraine remains close-knit
But back in 1915, when America invaded Haiti, the rest of the world didn't do shit!
I could beg, borrow, and try to get France and America to do right by Haiti
I'm just a middle-aged black man, by the time I succeed, I'd damn near be 80!
You are the only nation that can get America and France to do it
Just stop building and shipping all of their shit!

**Shénzhōu* ('Divine State') China's name

## Ancient Alien Invasion

As the chills and goosebumps ran up my sleeve
The spirit moved deep, somewhere within me
Not to dance in the rows and pews
But rather stare in quiet reflection, at the stain glass hews
Brown and blue, John, Jesus, and the River Jordan
Above me in church on another Sunday morning
Where I was hit with a Déjà vu/epiphany
This life on earth is more than just a gift to me
The Holy trinity appeared, and I was blinded and humbled
Like the pastor preached, my burdens and fears instantly crumbled
An out of body experience, that I can't truly explain
Everything you think you know, is actually quite insane!
All the dogma and history that we were taught got it all wrong
We're not alone in this universe, but you already knew that all along!

## Apostasy

Apostasy is one condition that plagues us most
To know the truth, reject it, and pull on a different rope
To forget the word, the past, the world, and hope
It is the epitome of sin, to fully comprehend, and still have doubt
Not just in God, country, humanity, and family, but also in what we're all about
It's never too late to change, to learn, to forgive, to live, and repent
I always wonder, about our biggest blunder, why do we pretend to forget?

# Apostle Cypher

**(#12 - Judas Iscariot)**
Oh thought you wasn't gonna see me?
I'm the Iscariot of this!
This, this Judas, the **real** bad guy in Bible!
Did you know? Did you know, that I was elected the
Treasurer of the group? And 12th, and final, Apostle…

**(#1 - Simon/Peter)**
I rhyme biblically
All of these Sagittarius and Pisces
Can't define how I be dropping these, crisis!
Literally perform miracles nightly
Lyrics bush burning, revelation flaming
Traveling village to village, salvation explaining
I was born Simon, but Jesus renamed me Peter
But you can call me either
As long as you believe
Wear your faith, like a shield, attached at your sleeve
Seeing ain't believing, just look at me!
When I first walked on water, when I doubted Jesus
I began to sink, so I understand how faith can leave us…
I actually refused to let, Jesus wash my feet!
What in the world, you ask, what was wrong with me?
All that time with Jesus, fishing for souls in our primes
As His most trusted disciple, and I denied Him three times!

**(#3 - James)**
Its James, my brothers were cool with John and Peter
Taking you on a ride, turning off the meter
As the 'Sons of Thunder,' we witnessed dozens of miracles
Back then, fools didn't believe that the earth was spherical…
Water to wine, fish and bread for 5,000 people?
Times were tough, and most weren't treated equal
Only 93 women, are mentioned in the Bible!
Sorry we excluded you, I was wrong for being idle….
Maybe that's why His message of love fell on deaf ears?
Why was hope and faith, replaced with doubts and fears?

**(#2 - Andrew)**
Andrew on the mic!
Quitting my fishing gig, was well worth the price!
I first introduced Peter to Jesus Christ
Led a nomadic, sporadic, yet spiritual life
Traveling with Jesus and eleven other guys
Everywhere we went, people were so surprised!
The lame, insane, hungry and tired
The blind, guilty of crimes, left Jesus healed and inspired!
I was a year older than Jesus, age 33!
Born and raised in the city of Zebedee!

**(#6 - Bartholomew)**
Bartholomew, aka Nathanael, before Philip introduced me
Jesus knew I was Israeli, and spotted me under a fig tree!
I was the joker of the group, quick with wit or a joke
I also took care of all Apostle's families - that's just a footnote
I was cool with all the Apostles, except for Judas
When he betrayed Jesus, I told y'all he'd do this!!!

**(#8 - Matthew)**
I'm Matthew, aka Levi,
A dishonest tax guy
When Jesus said follow me, I didn't even ask why…
I immediately stopped collecting taxes
Dusk to dawn, to ashes to ashes
The Pharisees dissed Jesus, when he invited me to dinner
Accused him of eating with a tax collector and other sinners…
Jesus replied nonchalantly with this sentence
'I came not to call the righteous, but sinners to repentance.'

**(#4 - John)**
John Zebedee, at 24, I'm the youngest of the group
First on scene during Easter, with the scoop
The only one who didn't abandon Jesus at his trial
But even I also, betrayed Him after awhile
But Judas did it for 30 Silver, zero Gold and Platinum
What will our legacy be, in a few millennium?

**(Jesus)**
Jesus of Nazareth, by way of Bethlehem
When I return, I fully expect to see you fam!
Taught y'all to be, fishers of men
But none of you were with me, at the end
All alone, shooting free throws at the gym!
But y'all sang my praises, and helped to celebrate the win?
When I died, God forgave all sin
Hindsight's 20/20, had I to do it all again?
I probably would have chosen 12 women over men
The message was hijacked, when men twisted facts with a pen
My lessons were never meant to conquer and enslave
Divide and massacre, why won't you people behave?
I died so humanity would have it made!
No sacrifices, just belief whenever they prayed
Love y'all, but I had to flame this track!
Thought all y'all had bars, but honestly its kinda wack!
After 30+ miracles, most don't believe in salvation
You only need faith as small as a mustard seed, but time is wasting…



**(#5:Philip the Curious, #9: James Alpheus, #10: Judas Alpheus, #11: Simon the Zealot, and #12/13 Matthias – replaced Judas)**
Jesus is love, faith of a mustard seed, Jesus is love!
But you gotta believe, But you gotta believe!!!

**(#7 - Thomas Didymus)**
They call me doubting Thomas
Didn't know that Jesus was alive, I promise!
Until I saw, and touched his wounds
I didn't believe Jesus, had left the tomb
I followed Jesus into Judea, just spreading the Gospel
Picked by God's son, how is it possible?
That I still have doubt?
I was 29, four kids and a spouse, when I joined the team
As the skeptic of the group, proof needed to be seen!
Proof needed to be seen!!

**Ballots & protests are mostly ignored**

Power concedes nothing without demand
Success comes from the mind, heart, and hand
We need to sacrifice, seek advice, then plot and plan!
Take action and learn lessons from the past
Beg for forgiveness, never wait to ask (the answer is always no!)
The masters, for crumbs and pitiful sums
Our annual salary versus theirs is just a stack of ones!
When we complain, they show disdain, like driving by bums
In the streets, we, the masses in this analogy
Are the ones holding up signs, but in reality
Ballots and protests are mostly ignored
Just like homeless folk's cardboard...

## Blood Revolution

The currency of revolution is blood
Rain changes earth into mud
When the establishment withers to dust
Between the community and government, who can we really trust?
To employ, entertain, protect, and keep us healthy
The poor give their all to empower and support the wealthy.

## Book of Job

Three books in the Bible, each foretold
Proverbs, Ecclesiastes, Job (Job!)
The first said that God is wise and just
People get what they deserve pretty much (Yep!)
The second said life's unpredictable and hard to understand
The third begins and ends with a blessed and trusting man (Who?)
Angels in heaven had a meeting with the Lord
Talked about Job, who measured above board (Oh!)
Satan, whose name means the one who is opposed (Boo!)
Questioned God's wisdom, so here's what he proposed!
Job is only good, because he's very blessed
Take away everything, and watch him fail the test! (Mmm)
Satan thought Job fooled God, just to live well
God took Satan's bet, and put Job through hell! (Bet!)
His kids, servants, and livestock, all died and made Job yell
He got a bad skin disease, and shaved his head in utter dismay (Uhh!)
Job 1:21, the Lord giveth and the Lord taketh away
Job lost everyone, and everything (that) he cared about
But in God, Job still had no doubt! (Amen!)
But then Job got in his feelings and wrote a few versus
A long poem, lamenting all of his inexplicable curses
Job 3:3, 'A child is conceived... may that day be darkness'
Eloquent prose from Job, but Satan was really the artist!
Job's friends visited, and offered some 'sage' advice
You used to be the man homie, how did you mess up your life? (What happened?)
Remember Proverbs, God is fair and just!
You must have done something wicked, lie, murder or lust? (Trifling!)
This goes on for 34 chapters, their guesses all wrong!
Job maintained his innocence, but started getting alarmed
Accused God of being unfair, and demanded a visit!
God obliged, in the form of a great storm cloud exhibit!
But God didn't explain the bet, that He made with Satan
Rather showed Job the universe, and what he'd been contemplating (Mmm)
He asked if Job could manage all the large and small details (Nope!)
Snow on the mountains, sand under seashells?
Finally… God showed Job two ferocious beasts (Animal sounds)
Bragged about how essential they were, for balance and peace (Mmm)
Job realized, for God, there's more to wrong and right
Universal decisions, more complex than black and white
Job knew that he couldn't be God, for a day, minute, or second (Yeah!)
Job's demand for an explanation, he instantly regretted (Oops!)
Humbled by God, he never learned the reason for his trouble
But was shocked when God gave him back everything in double! (Amen!)
Job's restoration was a gift, that God would give him
And anyone else, as long as they trust in His wisdom (Amen!)

## Born to lose, die to win?

I came here to worship
Not to play these silly games
If I fail to tithe, think I'll end up in flames?
Sister, deacon, usher, preacher
Hats, fancy clothes, and choir features
The gospel, idols, grape juice, punishment, contradiction, testament
If we aren't the chosen ones, then why is all this even relevant?
Sex, money, drugs
Family, hate, and love
Why is God a man?
How come we can't understand
All of the voices
Right and wrong choices
Cursed with the gift of free will
Yet we still beg, borrow, and steal
Cheat, covet and kill
Driven to avoid pain and seek pleasure
So we crave riches and constantly compare to measure
Worth - Born to lose and die to win?
Why are so few favored, and many cursed again?

## Boycotting table grapes like Caesar Chavez

Organized labor aggravates the rich and the Feds
Why can't they do as we say - Simon Says?
Gonna end up in prison or dead
The haves and have nots, rarely break bread
Masters and slaves, no tranquility
Peasants and nobility
God and man
Water and sand
Follow orders and command
No in between
America's Middle class, is the only one that history's ever seen!
Oligarchs claim power, wealth and domain
No multiple gods or 15 seconds of fame
All or nothing in human dynamic groups
Everyone can't be happy or free - here's proof
Winners and losers fight nail and tooth
Life seems unfair, to most, as a universal truth
We envy others and desire more than we need
Neglect what we've got, as we plant and grow seeds
Our kids watch, rinse and repeat
The cycle never ends, my daughter emulates me

## Br’er Jordan (after Br’er Rabbit)

Is commerce over conscious shrewd?
Republicans buy sneakers too?
Rich ignorant bald headed fool!
4th grade my team was the Bulls
And my favorite brand was Nike
The 1985 high tops in black, red, and white
Years later, older, wiser, I was a overwhelmed
Jordan didn't endorse Gantt over Helms?
My man sold out, acting in Space Jam
You were an incredible athlete, but you'll never be Muhammad Ali
I was wrong to think that you could fly, because you clearly cannot see.

## Cognitive Dissonance

The US is in a state of cognitive dissonance
I almost miss the days of religious and political indifference
The rest of world is not much better
Extreme poverty, intolerance, and weather
Humanity can create and solve its own problems
But those with money and power want to ban abortions and condoms
Solutions won't come from an institution
Because the government and corporations **profit** from crime and pollution
Don't forget that cloud of debt that floats up above
As banks yank, and pull you up from under, your foundation like a rug!
Steal a dollar from as many people as you can, and then get them hooked on drugs
That's the secret of wealth and success, yet they still call us thugs!?!?

## Cuban Paradise?

Havana Cuba was like a paradise
But deep down, I knew that someone paid the price
Beyond the music, cigars, old cars, beans and rice
A tobacco farmer told me that the government takes 90 percent of his life!
To feed his family, he sold cigars at an inflated price
Revolutions begin to improve life
Once in power, Masters build towers and views skew, as the people cower
Once sweet victory rots, then life is sour
Free healthcare and education comes with a big 'but'
Months to get an appointment and even a Doctor's salary is not enough
My cab driver was a Civil Engineer
Teacher's second job is at a bar opening kegs of beer
They don't have Netflix, internet, or new whips
The Revolution was televised, but the people didn't get shit!

**Daddy Warbucks?**

Makes me so sick
Daddy Warbucks' in bed with the Bolsheviks
Taking away arts and education from Annies
Dissing and grabbing women by the panties
Stole health care and Social Security from granny
And told Punjab, too bad!
You're fired, go drive a cab!
We want 'our' country back, go back to Baghdad!
We made a King out of the court Jester
Moronic Tweets and speeches, made with the tiniest of hand gestures…
Elephants and Donkeys refuse to tell our new King
To stop saying stupid things, and that he has on 'Mom' jeans
Our emperor's sans pants, I cover my face with my hands
In a trance, I just can't stop watching and reading the fake news and rants
It's the beginning of the end of America, we stand no chance...

# Dust to Dust

Specs of dust dance in the light
Of colored sunbeams cast from church stained glass windows
As we're blessed by the word
My speckled show is altered by a turbulence
Caused by a hand fan, waved by Sister Mary
Who's hand I've shaken twice, at the Pastor's urging
To 'Shake your neighbor's hand!'
But what if she has a cold?
And doesn't sneeze into her elbow?
I'm not a germaphobe, but I just don't want to get sick
Perfume and a cool breeze cause more dust to dance before me
The scent is pleasant but unfamiliar
As we stand to sing a hymn that I actually know
I sneezed into my elbow
And sister Mary gives me a look, and moves away from me, like I'm going to get her sick!

## Ecclesiastes

Turn…turn…turn… Everything has a season!
Time, purpose, reason
We all live and die (RIP!)
Seeds become harvests, why?
…Do we kill instead of heal?
If ye seek heaven, then what's the deal?
At every turn's cause for concern
Some of us may never learn…

'Ecclesiastes,' is Greek for preacher (preacher, preacher!)
These Solomon's words, all up in your speaker (speaker, speaker!)
From the time we're born, to the time we die
The seeds we plant must grow, can't standby! (Nope!)
There's a time to kill
And a time to heal
Sometimes you gotta destroy
Before you can ever rebuild (Amen)!
There's a time for love, and a time for hate
But if you know what's best, just respect your mate! (Yup!)
A time to fight, and time to do what's right!
No winners in wars, 'cuz life has an invaluable price (Amen!)
You may laugh, and its okay to cry (Boo-Hoo)
Do you really need to know, exactly how and why?
A time to mourn, and a time to dance
If you don't boo-hoo or catch a groove, you'll soon regret the chance! (That's right!)
Time to scatter stones, and a time to pick 'em up (Pick 'em up)!
Know when we cool, and also when you're pushin' your luck! (Uh Uh!)
Know when to search, and then when to quit
It's okay to keep things, but other times just let 'em slip!
There's a time to mend, then you gotta let it rip! (Rip!)
There's a time to speak, then again, zip up your lip! (Shhhhh…)

If you're frustrated, look me in the eye (Eye!)
You may laugh, and again, it's okay to cry (Boo-Hoo!)
Take your time, morn and enjoy
Humanity's complicated, we build and we destroy! (Heard that!)
Y'all just wanted to have fun
But somebody brought a gun! (What!)
Causing panic at the dance
Foolish actions, ruined our chance!
Don't bring no war, up to our shore!
Break bread instead, libations should pour! (Cheers!)
In these uncertain times, love can 'Trump' hate (Amen!)
Put your differences aside, and find ways to relate!
Born, morn, seed, feed, kill, heal, smile... NOW! (Now!)

**Fishing for freedom**

Fortune and fame are just smoke screens
Choking on fumes, jokers and dope fiends
Wasting time on pointless pipe dreams
Sneakers and triple beems
Stocks, education and other things
Should be the priority
Fraternity, sorority
Corporate thugs got diplomatic authority
And immunity while the majority 'Trumped' minorities
With mostly fabricated stories
Hook, line, and sinker, but they just caught an old boot
Poor good ole' boys and girls will soon learn the ugly truth…

## Flames explain the present

Blessed but troubled today
As the world turns every which way
Injustice keeps happening, but nobody's asking why
Limited by expectations and history's irrelevant arc
Flames explain the present, but what caused the spark?

## Gideon's Army

Gideon, Gideon, Gideon, Gideon, Gideon, Gideon's Army, Gideon, Gideon, Gideon!

Gideon thought that his life seemed a little odd (Odd!)
After Joseph died, Israel rejected God (God!)
The Midianites burned down Israel in a few days (Days!)
Then all the Israelites, were forced to live in caves! (Whoa!)
Gideon hid under a large tree and harvested grain (Mmm)
An angel gave Gideon a tall task, but he didn't complain (Nope!)

God told him to destroy false idols, build an alter, and start a war (Whoa!)
Gideon asked God to wet and dry a fleece first, just to make sure! (Ha Ha!)
Gideon quickly, assembled 32,000 troops (Ok!)
God was like, 'No G, we need make much smaller groups!' (Word!)
Gideon said anyone too afraid could just, 'skedaddle'
So 22,000 bounced, 10,000 remained for battle (Yeah!)
Gideon sent them to a river, for God's water test
The vigilant soldiers who drank with cupped hands, were picked as the best!
300 soldiers remained, but Gideon was still unconvinced (What?)

He overheard a Midianite's dream, about some bread destroying some tents! (Oh No!)
This gave Gideon an idea, to beat the Midianites
300 solders with trumpets, pitchers, and torches would attack at night! (Yeah!)
Blowing trumpets, smashing pitchers and lighting torches caused dismay (Ahhh!)
And the entire Midianite Army got up and ran away!
God, Gideon, 300 soldiers, saved the day! (Amen!)

Gideon, Gideon, Gideon, Gideon, Gideon, Gideon's Army, Gideon, Gideon, Gideon,
Gideon's Army!

Judges 6-8

**Go Go Elijah! 1st Kings 17**

Go Go Elijah, Go Go
Light that fire!
Go Go Elijah, Go Go
Light that fire!
Go Go Elijah, Go Go
Light that fire!

1st Kings 17 to 2nd Kings 2
Here's what God told, Elijah to do
King Ahab, Queen Jezebel, both hated God
And killed all of His prophets with a ruthless vice squad
God told Elijah to **Go Go Go!**
Tell Ahab no mo' rain, 'till I say so!
Elijah challenged Ahab to a 'Sacrifice test'
On Mt. Carmel, to see which God is the best!

Elijah had two sacrifices - ready to ignite
Ahab's Gods versus the Lord - to see who's right!
The first, to spontaneously combust
Was the God, that all of Israel could trust!
Ahab's prophets, they tried in vain
Singing and dancing, but there simply was no flame!
Elijah soaked his sacrifice with water and prayed
When the Lord's fire lit, all of Israel was amazed!
The flame was so hot, it even burned the stone altar!
King Ahab's reign, immediately began to falter
The sky filled with clouds
The wind began to blow
When it rained, farmers exclaimed, 'Now our crops will grow!'

A Chariot of fire appeared, from above to send
Elijah to heaven, in an inferno whirlwind
Like Enoch, Elijah went to heaven alive!
FYI, Ahab and Jezebel, they both died!
This is the story of Elijah, so now you know
The moral, be like Elijah and **Go Go Go!**

Go Go Elijah, Go Go
Light that fire!
Go Go Elijah, Go Go
Light that fire!
Go Go Elijah, Go Go
Light that fire!

**Go Jesus, its your Birthday!**

Go, Go, Go, Go, Go, Go!
Go Jesus, it's your birthday
You gonna save our lives from the worst fate!
You died and was revived, to send us to heaven's gate
So we gonna give you praise, cuz it's your birthday!

December 25th is about more than trees and gifts
Let's travel to Bethlehem and picture this
Away in a major
No vacancies in the inn, for our savior
His parents, Joseph and Mary
Travelled with a foal of a donkey, who would carry
Lil' Baby Jesus, in this instance
They travelled to Bethlehem, to be counted in the census!
Ordered by Caesar Augustus, the Emperor of Rome
By royal decree, everyone had to return home
To be counted, so that they all could the taxed
Digg that, the nativity was caused by a bureaucrat!
Matthew and Luke detailed the birth of Jesus Christ
700 years after Isaiah prophesied his life
The wise men, who brought myrrh, frankincense, and gold
Weren't kings, numbers unknown, and didn't show 'till Jesus, was just a few months old!



Go Jesus, it's your birthday!
You gonna save our lives from the worst fate!
You died and was revived, to send us to heaven's gate
So we gonna give you praise, cuz it's your birthday!

*<<Whooooooooo!>> Matthew chapter 1 versus 18!*
*Mary was to marry Joseph, but here's the thing!*
*Mary was with child through the Holy Spirit!*
*When she told Joseph, he simply couldn't hear it! <<Whoooooo!>>*

He had it in his mind, to get a divorce
But the Lord appeared to Joseph and changed his course!
Told him to marry Mary, and go to Bethlehem
Name the baby Jesus, which means to rescue - God's lamb
Joseph did as the Lord commanded, free of doubt and mystery
That's the story of Jesus' birth, the rest is history!  Go, Go, Go!

Go Jesus, it's your birthday!
Go Jesus, it's your birthday!
Go Jesus, it's your birthday!
Go, Go, Go!  Go Jesus, it's your birthday! Go Jesus, it's your birthday!

## God is a single parent

God is like a single parent
Distracted, all or nothing, aberrant
All powerful, in the since that a dad is with his kid
Second guessing decisions, rainbows remind us that he also regrets what he did
Some say that he works in mysterious ways
Capable of tremendous love, and outrageous rage
Floods and fire, when his kids don't make the grade
They don't listen when
There is a lack of discipline
So when he spares the rod
They act out again, then say, 'Why God?'
Through the screams and tears
Behind the omnipotence, God still fears…
For the well being of his creation
There is a mutual understanding, in the mist of all of this frustration
The child wishes to be the parent, and vice versa
Although things change, life remains at inertia

## God is real, but we don't exist

God is real, but we don't exist
When believers and atheist hear this, they gonna be pissed!
We're figments of our own imagination - language, love, life
People, politics, paradise
War, worry, wind, time, temperature, and trees
It's like the Matrix movie, it's all just make believe!
History is fiction, in this simple truth, all religion is missing
We are less probable, than what makes us special
Mankind's time in the universe, is infinitesimal
A tiny grain of sand in the universe
All life we know, opposable thumbs dearth
This impossibility, transcends intelligence
I think, therefore I ponder my relevance
Necks on giraffes and trunks on elephants
Pale in comparison to our thumbs' developments
Evolution provides tools to survive the elements
Divine intervention makes sense
In the self-centered cloud of a dream - that's this!
Were atoms in the cosmos, aware spirits in a dream
Time scares us like we saw a ghost, death wakes us from that dream!
Time on earth is heaven, where we control our bodies like machines
Life is seldom what it seems
Don't believe your eyes, the world's a grand illusion
Time flies and facts lie, so I came to this conclusion
Life is background TV, were actors and the world's the show
God's our only audience bored to tears, because she's seen it all before.

**God is time**

Lost and found
Limitless and in short supply
Managed, leveraged, tracked, paid, and borrowed
Told and sold
Fast and slow
Reasonable and cruel
Certain and doubted
Man made and divine
Praised and cursed
Measured and shared
Catalyst for growth and death
Spared and divided
Infinite and misunderstood
God Is Time.

## 'Greed is Good' marked on America's Tomb

I used to salute the stars and stripes
Ignored the struggle and strife
America changed, but the hate remained
Built on a foundation of labor, lies and pain
Genocide and slaves
Millions died in unmarked graves
If those ghosts and karma were real
Stocks would drop and blood would spill
In the street, alas our kingdom has peaked
The fall of another empire, we ain't unique
Or immune to the fate of doom and gloom
'Greed is Good' marked on America's tomb

**Holy erythrocytes!**

Found the bones of Jesus Christ
Boiled them, marrow and all, like Minute Rice!
Drank the holy soup and instantly became omnipotent
Didn't deserve the power, but I was a willing and humble recipient
Followed all of God's directions
Fed the hungry and healed the sick's infections
When the infidels came, I knew exactly what was next
Could have ended them easily, but I didn't want the stress
I can walk on water, but I can't change minds
Free will only bends when you break behinds!
My sacrifice is a lesson, that humanity will never learn
Better me than to let you and your family burn
History unread or misunderstood often repeats
Once Jesus, now its me, getting stoned in these streets!
When the weak prey on the powerful, its so ironic
The world just killed (again) its only cure for the next bubonic...

## How November 2016 felt

November 2016
Was somewhere between reality and a dream
The Cubs won, and so did Donald Trump
Gas was $2.25 at the pump
It was unusually warm and the moon was huge
Many didn't notice, instead they cried the blues
We moved across the country
Bought and sold a home, seemed like a made up story
Daily living in hotels and eating fast food
Paying tolls, tips, fees, and taxes, put me in a foul mood
In a new place, watching the news
Wondering who, what, and where they was talking about
Gridlocked traffic jams, damn I miss the south!
Prices and taxes, in the Northeast
Right before your eyes, seem to rise like yeast!
And take bread right from under your thumbs
As your funds drain down, you frown, and give ones to some bums
Then feel a chill, break out in a sweat, and start to get numb
Could that be my fate?
'Can you spare some change,' scribbled on the back of a paper plate
Just before the election, I was more confident in my fate
All that hope and change, thinking somehow we could all relate
The electoral college put the country in reverse
Passengers trapped on the wrong bus, each mile and minute away, feeling worse
Aimlessly pulling on the line to stop the madness, but it don't work
Some quickly lose hope and say don't bother
Others relinquish the burden to Jesus and the holy father
I wrapped my shirt on my elbow, and bang repeatedly to break the glass
Hoping that I can jump, when the bus isn't moving so fast
Most think I'm crazy, and tell me to stop
Others get scared, when they can't recognize the block
You can't stop the driver, or convince the others to command
Get bruised, bloody, and free - our fate is in your hand!

## How the devil dies

It was a slow suicide
As I jammed a dagger inside
Before I killed the devil
I dug an abysmal hole with a shovel
Laying in the cold wet ground
The loss of immortality, makes for the most pitiful sound
Ruling for eternity as the villain
I never thought I'd enjoy the feeling, of my blood spilling
But I did, like the melody of the greatest song
Who is right, what is wrong?

## Humble

Praying the pain away, but my soul still hurts
Sweeping floors in the basement of my church
I need cash now, like J. G. Wentworth!
Believe in Jesus, but he can't pay my bills
In the Soup Kitchen, preparing some warm meals
Been trying for that promotion, but it's not based on skills
I bet it's me
Wrong pedigree
Or could it be
That I'm supposed to do something more?

## I bought lunch for Judas today

I walked past a homeless man
Bought an extra meal, came back and then said, ‘Can I join you fam?’
‘Thanks,’ he replied, we sat quiet for awhile, as we ate
He hesitated, then looked up from his plate
And said, ‘What if I told you that I was eons old,
And betrayed my savior for 30 pieces of silver, not gold
For years I walked beside the king of kings
Witnessed and performed miracles, and saw many godly things
But I still didn't believe, and now I'm cursed and considered one of history's worst....’
‘Damn,’ I replied, ‘for a second I though you were going to say something really crazy
I've travelled the world, so there's not much that can faze me
I'd say you'd make a convincing Judas, however
The bible says that you didn't survive your endeavor,’
He chuckled and said, ‘It's been a while since I've laughed,
Or had a meal, or for that matter even taken a bath
Jesus didn't, so I don't expect you to believe me too
Where are you from, what do you do?
Who do you love, what is your truth?’
As we ate our fries, I told a stranger about my past
When I got to college, I paused, and then asked
‘Wait, my manners are out of line,
You are a lesson in bible, what have you been doing all this time?’
With a serious gaze, he replied with a phrase,
‘Betraying Jesus was hell, but being 100 years a slave...’

## Jingoism

When a group of people
Decide what's just and evil
Be wary of this false idolatry
Gossip seems sweet like a pastry
Until the pie is thrown in your face!
Embarrassed now, holier than thou, let them eat cake?
Build a wall, gas them all, make them pick cotton
Fries, chips, mashed, au gratin?
A potato's end, often depends
On one's recipe and fickle opinions
Power and morality, masters and minions
Our fate shouldn't be determined by other's definitions

Jingoism - an extreme form of patriotism that often calls for violence towards foreigners and foreign countries

## Joshua Crosses The Jordan River

Joshua chapter 3 verse 5: And Joshua said unto the people, Sanctify yourselves: for tomorrow the Lord will do wonders among you. Amen!

Chorus (x2)*
Lord help me!
Cross the Jordan River, so that we
Can bring the Arc to the other side!
Lord we can't swim, and I, think the water's too high, high....ahhhhh!

I ain't a swimmer, but you blessed me
With a miracle to reach the promise land, where you'll test me
Lord, you know I ain't no Moses (nope!)
Appreciate how you choose us
And parted the Red Sea, to set us free.... Shalom!
40 years later, might you do the same for me?
On the banks of the River Jordan, with the whole tribe
We can see, the promised land, just on the other side
After years of being lost, and wandering in the wild
The people of Israel are humble, but ready to make you proud...
Please help us flee
Just like the Red Sea...

Chorus (x2)*
Lord help me!
Cross the Jordan River, so that we
Can bring the Arc to the other side!
Lord we can't swim and I, think the water's too high, high....ahhhhh!

I told a dozen priests, to stand in the river with the arc
When they did, like you said, the waters began to part!
They carried it to the middle of the river bed
Every Israelite passed around, with a sense of dread
'Cuz we told them to stay 2,000 cubits away before
That's like 10 football fields, so they quickly made it ashore!
As soon as a dozen priests, made to the other side
The waters of the Jordan, swiftly began to collide!
Lord, I did exactly what you asked me to do
Picked guys, from each tribe, the Arc of the Covenant crew!
Then set up 12 rocks, in the exact spot!
Under the Jordan, were the Arc was temporarily stopped!
Thank you Lord, for bringing us all safely to shore
Now onto Jericho, let's get ready for war!

Chorus (x2)*
Lord help me!
Cross the Jordan River, so that we
Can bring the Arc to the other side!
Lord we can't swim and I, think the water's too high, high....ahhhhh!

## Joshua Fit The Battle of Jericho

Chorus*
Joshua saw a man with a sword in his hand (Who dis?)
Asked if he was friend or foe? (Who dis?)
'Neither,' the stranger replied, outside Jericho
The commander, of the Army of Lord (Army of the Lord!)
Pointed at Joshua's sandals, quickly with his sword
**'What are those?'** he deadpanned
Take them joints off man!
This here's holy land!
Joshua fell down, on the ground, at the angel's command!
The Commander said our weapons are God and sound
Order seven priests, to carry the arc around…
And blow their horns… scream, and shout
And Jericho, will fall, without a doubt! (Amen)

Chorus*
Joshua fell on the floor (Flo')
Rahab its time to go (Go)!
Rams horns will blow (Blow)
And knock down Jericho (Oh)
I said!!!!

Chorus*
Jericho is so secure, how they could ever begin?
Nobody can get out, your majesty
And no one can get in!
On scale from one up, our security's at a 10! (10)
They just wasted six days, marching and tent pitching (pitching)
Everyone's account for... except for some reason Rahab's missing.... (Where did she go?

Chorus*
Joshua sent in two spies!
From Shittem (Shittem).... and each wore a disguise
Rahab gave them the element of surprise (Element of surprise!)
So she and her family... would be saved
Before all of Jericho's... walls caved
A scarlet rope hung in... Rahab's window
A signal for where to... Joshua's men go
To save Rahab... and the rest of her family
The other Cannaites, fate that night, a total calamity!
For six days, Joshua's priests marched around the city (City!)
On the seventh day, their Ram horns played a little ditty! (Ditty!)
While Joshua's army, would scream and shout (AHHHHHH!)
And shook loose, Jericho's foundations and grout!

Chorus*
Listen to God Joshua!!! Humble, humble, humble (humble). Fall Jericho!!!!
Tumble, tumble, tumble (tumble).... Listen to God Joshua!!! Humble, humble, humble (humble)… Fall Jericho!!!! Tumble, tumble, tumble (tumble)

**Keep the faith!**

Though I may sin, I pray every night
Jesus wept, bled, and paid the ultimate price
For you, me, he, she and the third
To follow golden rules and study the word
His eye is on the sparrow, a magnificent bird
Though the news seems bleak, the gospel is good!
History repeats, if lessons are misunderstood
The answers ye seek, to all that ails
Are already written, scripture never fails!

## Make Haiti the 51st State!

I would've never known
Until I looked it up, because I was prone
To believe in western history, but the 'truth' was a lie
Some of our 'heroes' were really the bad guys
All the propaganda and exclusions, made me ask why?
Did France sell its Louisiana Territory to America, for just $15 Mil?
In 1803, Thomas Jefferson got one hell of a deal!
The Haitian Revolution was Napoleon's bitter jagged pill!
Haitian slaves beat three empires (Spanish, French, and British) in the world's only successful slave revolt!
But in western education, culture, and history, its barely a footnote!
I know all about Columbus, Washington, and Lincoln
But nothing about Dessalines and L'Ouverture, so that got me thinking...
Why did the world suppress such a history?
A search on Google, quickly helped me to solve that mystery!
The United States occupied Haiti, from 1914 to 1920
For the same reasons as the French, it was all about the money!
President Woodrow Wilson sent in the US Marines, file and rank
To steal $500,000 in gold from Haiti's National bank
That Haitian gold was then sent back to New York's National City bank
Today it is known as 'Citibank'!
America's debt to Haiti, is worth trillions more than gold once illegally taken
Haiti should be America's 51st state (and Washington D.C.) in the making!
Plus reparations, for decades of trade embargoes and to deodorize France's stench*
If it weren't for Haiti, Americans might all be speaking French!



*The Haitian Revolution ended in 1804. France returned to Haiti in 1825 (21 years later) with warships demanding that Haiti pay them $150 million Francs ($2.2 billion in today's dollars) in 'Reparations' to compensate their former slave owners who lost their property and lucrative sugar, indigo, cotton, and coffee profits. France also forced Haiti to give them a 50% discount on all its exported goods (Haiti produced half of Europe's sugar).

In 1838, France agreed to reduce the debt to $90 million francs to be paid over a period of 30 years. Haiti paid a total of $21 billion (interests, fees, etc.) in reparations to France (worth $250 billion today) and made Haiti one of the poorest countries in the western hemisphere. Haiti's final remittance (for France's 'Reparations') was made to National City Bank (currently New York's Citibank) in 1947.

## Muppim and Huppim

In Genesis 46:21, no frontin'
Are the names Muppim and Huppim!
The grandsons of Jacob, ain't that something'?
Meaning double mouth and a type of tent used at a wedding
There were two different people in the bible named Huppim, no kidding!
3,200 people are mentioned in the bible
These are two of the absolute worst names in history, without rival!
No major stories or lessons
Miracles, sins, or transgressions
Here's a crazy theory
Take a second and hear me
Maybe Cain and Able is really just a fable
And they somehow turned the tables
People lived hundreds of years, maybe they just changed their labels
And weren't killed and/or banished for their confession
But they were just the world's first example of witness protection!
Seriously, why were they mentioned, how did their names pass the edit?
You got to give their parents (Benjamin and Rachel) some credit
For the worst names in history, I'll certainly never forget it!

## Nerf guns responsible for mass shootings?

Water guns, Nerf guns, and video games
Three reasons why, mass shooters keep blowing out other people's brains?
There's a Nerf gun for sale, that can shoot 25 foam darts!
When those kids grow up, will they aim for their victim's heads and hearts?
Some say it's just child's play, and helps to develop one's imagination
We went from cap guns to automatic toy rifles, in a just one generation!
Desensitized, from decades of a violent crime rise, America's manifestation
As the 'Wild West' that Hollywood promoted to sell military weapons at retail
To a hammer, everything is a nail!
The protagonist uses more bullets than words, up on the silver screen
As the bad guys and victims run, die and scream!
The crowd cheers, craving even more blood and death
Brainwashed to gradually remove our humanity, until there is nothing left.

**New Normal**

We all read the news, and then complain
But what good will that do, and what will it change?
Nothing, consequences and actions
Just more fodder and distractions
Frogs in a pot, safe when the water was cold
Back when Clinton/Bush/Obama controlled the narrative and nuclear codes
But 45 lied, defied logic, and treated allies as cannon fodder
Then those frogs (still in the pot) began to die slow, in boiling hot water!
Numb and used to the nation's state of affairs
Only half of the country, really still cares
Team 'Make America Great Again' vs. team 'What in the hell is happening' on a battlefield
Online, in boardrooms, and behind closed doors, debating congressional deals
Throughout history, it seems
The fancy few, demand all of the meager many's hopes and dreams
Fake news from thousands of places
People interact via devices, no longer by faces
It's easy to fear, that which you do not understand
The perspective has flipped, pebbles of optimism have eroded into grains of sand.

## Occupy This!

Arrested with handcuffs on your wrists
How dare you compare civil right to this!
The world cannot relate
Catered food, WIFI, and tents, your worst fear is pepper spray?
No need to debate
Sure wall street and the government is due blame
If they are pimps in the industry, y'all just whores for the fame!
Baby boomers are pissed about retirement
Gen XYZs are worried about student loan requirements
The burden of the American dream is the theme
College and home loans are the real Ponzi schemes
Look in the mirror, to place the real blame
Corporate America and the Fed didn't force you to buy all of those things!
The amount of food and water that we waste, we should all be ashamed!
To proud to do the work of "illegal" immigrants
While fruit is dying on the vine, covered with rats and ants
We just want the cheese and wine
But don't want to milk the cows, and pick the grapes in time
We want something for nothing, while standing in a line
Like the lottery and reality TV shows
Want to bankrupt the pimp? Stop being the hos!

## Omega - post script of the Bible

1 - And it came to pass, that the truth should be known
2 - Man and God alike, had to reap what was sown
3 - God spoke, not as a burning bush, but as a woman
4 - Who humbly admitted her failed age old plan
5 - Her words twisted and manipulated, by man, like the telephone game
6 - The versions that we all know, were simply just insane!
7 - Mankind was made in her image, but she too, was make believe
8 - Another fantastic illusion, just like the air that we breathe!
9 - The other Gods loved watching her creation
10 - Humanity as entertainment, was a mere manifestation
11 - Of one God's idea, brought to life by a cast who had no clue!
12 - That their lives were not real, and everything that they'd do
13 - Love, war, money, religion, and politics
14 - Was all really just thoughts and ideas on paper, just like this!

## On Footprints and Isaiah 46:4

Apologies, for this may sound rehearsed
Jesus sees us, at our best and our worse
Plus Shiloh needs us, please grab your wallet or purse!
For offering and tithes, folks now it's time to search
Your soul, 'cuz the goal is greater than heaven or hell
Rather life on earth, in the time that we dwell
The past and the present, the best and worst of times
Pandemics, racism systemic, income inequality, and various crimes
Against humanity, the insanity of waiting for hours to vote, in line…
The news is bad, but the gospel is good!
A thousand words can paint an ugly picture, whenever the scripture is misunderstood!
So read them early and often
Between the crib and the coffin
Try to practice what it preaches
One set of footprints, along the shores of sandy beaches...

Isaiah 46:4: Even to your old age and gray hairs I am he, I am he who will sustain you. I have made you and I will carry you; I will sustain you and I will rescue you.

## On God

Sinners pack pews on Sunday, solely seeking salvation
Reading the good news, from Genesis through Revelation
Froze for 40 winters, in reverent anticipation
For blessings earned, whenever opportunity meets preparation
No longer debating with non-believers, constantly wasting
Their breath and my time, so I'm seeking new destinations!
No sprinting in this life-long marathon for information
History is cyclical, its imperative that we understand, exactly what we are facing!
And that, we don't get trapped, on these digital and social media plantations
Learning from our mistakes
So when the milk spills and eggs break
Our recipes remain eclectic, with nothing but perfection on our plates!
Food for the spirit, wine to sip, and bread to break
This reunion is a communion, so let's rejoice for heaven's sake!
As our time expires, and we reflect on all of our life choices
One day, all of our angels and ancestors will finally hear our voices!

**Pennywise**

Pennywise
It's no surprise
That this killer clown
Is the talk of the town
A symbol of a nation, turned onto its end
What it is and what it ain't, it all depends
On the musings and whims of a narcissist
When fictional plots pale in comparison to real life twists?
It's the end of the end
But for whom is the real question to comprehend
Life is far from fair, but balance is a universal law
Before we fly, drive, run, and walk, first we must crawl
Life is created and destroyed, empires rise and fall
What is next is a mystery, but it will be witnessed by all...

## Politics as a religion

Fanatics fleeing morals
Clinging to dogma, 'deplorables'
Pandering to half truths and lies
Lobbyists promoting policies
Wolves in sheep's disguise
Party before country with motives so odd
They're worshiping iconoclasts instead of God

**Prophet's Delight**

**Chorus***
The Kings of Judah were such a disgrace
In the race to praise Jehovah, I got first place!
**Its the I – S – A – I – A and please don't forget the H!**
I'm the He-brew, who first knew, that Jesus was on the way (Say What!)
700 years before he was born, so please listen to what I say!
I testified, day and night, about God's mercy and grace
I wrote all, about Satan's fall, and how he lost his place
Finally, I scolded Israel for its sin, ignorance, and mistakes…
The next up is a good friend of mine, who also has an eponymous book
He spent some time in prison y'all, but-but-but folks he ain't no crook!

***Chorus**
I said a Shem, Lot, a fish ate Jonah, for not doing what he ought,
Moses hit a rock!
Years after he saved his people, and fled Egypt by parting **THE** Red Sea!
Now what you hear, was all a test, written in antiquity…
And if you dig these rhymes, then find some time, to read your B-I-B-L-E!

I'm **Jeremiah**, the weeping prophet, A.K.A Jehovah exalts
May I share with you, just a few, of my pitiful woes and faults?
When I was young, I didn't speak
God said, 'Chin up kid, you're so unique!'
The message that you need to share, most won't wanna hear (Say What?)
So just smash a pot, when folks get shocked, then they'll lend an ear!
These are my 'Lamentations,' that's a fancy word for grief
I was double crossed and thrown in jail, but-but-but folks I ain't no thief!
They tossed me in a cistern, but I didn't drown because…
In lieu of water, I was shocked, the whole place was full of mud!
An Ethiopian and 30 folks pulled me out, and told me not to fret
But-but-but we ain't friends, 'cuz just then, they put this yoke around my neck!
After I was finally free, I travelled way, way out west
And don't you know, in Egypt y'all, they stoned your boy to death!!!

POLITICS & RELIGION

Wow, man, that testimony was really depressing and dark!
Give it up for my 'Main Man' Jeremiah, y'all, 'cuz he had heart!
My name's **Ezekiel**, that means God strengthens, in Hebrew
When God led me to the valley of bones, I knew what he would do!
God resurrected 'dem bones, and showed me an incredible vision
And told me that Israel was where we was 'posta be living!
For years, my people were exiled, way out in Tel Aviv (Say What?)
So I put my city on my back, and then I rolled up my sleeves!
All good deeds, olive branches, and fig leaves?
No more false idols, lofty titles, do-overs, or reprieves!
We'll be really good this time, Lord, I'll get them all to believe!

Its **Daniel** y'all, the last prophet, of this pious crew
Let me tell you all, what it was, that God would have me do!
Beyond reading the writing on the wall, and surviving in that lion's den
With God's power, I gave Darius back his sight again! (Say What?)
Even my friends, Abednego, Meshach, and Shadrach
Walked out of a burning fire, 'cuz God had their back!
Just learn from all of our lessons, and be each other's blessings
God's got your back, whenever you get lost
No fee see? Because He, already paid the cost!
Just pray every day, and use the Bible as your map
The Lord works in mysterious ways, Jack, ain't that a fact?
**Chorus***

## Protesting is Pointless

The bereaved cannot conceive
Of the phrase, 'Administrative Leave'
No arrests, cops still get paid, despite what the video shows
The media makes excuses: gold teeth, CDs, criminal record, baggy clothes
We went from hope, fear, anger, frustration
Depression, 'body and dash cameras,' and promises of legislation
You can march 'till your feet bleed
Tweet and hash-tag, until they decide to read
But what will change?
Nothing.
I'm numb, but still want to do something
What if I protest and loot?
Buy a gun, go to the range, practice and shoot
Gun or no gun, minding my business, plenty there to witness, hard fact
When I get pulled over, I could be the next victim shot in the back.

## Sampson & Delilah
## (after Ray Charles' song, 'I got a woman')

Well.....She cut my hair off
When I was sleep, oh no!
She cut my hair off
When I was sleep, Oh no! Oh no!
She cut my hair off!!!!
When I was sleep-eep!!!!
Yeah, she took, all of my strength from meeee!!!!
The Philistines paid Delilah, then captured me,
Oh no! Oh no!

As the last Judge Israel!
I was super strong
My own wife Delilah, oh she did me wrong!
They tried three times to get me!
But they failed!
Bow strings, ropes and looms, I just couldn't be held!
Delilah wanted to know the secret!!!
To my power and promised she'd keep it!
So I told her about my hair, but Delilah lied!
Then claimed the Philistine's prize!
Well, when they dragged me away,
The Philistines had a marching band, this what I heard them play... Listen!

Man, that's a tough break, Sampson. Them Philistines are no joke!
So, what happened next? Listen!

First they put me in prison...
Then poked out my eyes...
So I prayed to God…
And to my surprise...
My hair grew back!...
And I was strong again! Now my mission was simple
Pushed the pillars down and destroyed their temple!

Oh.....Delilah cut my hair off!
Guess that's on me
Oh yeah!
She kept asking questions
But I just couldn't see
Oh how ironic, now I'm blind but free!
She cut my hair off!
When I was sleep!
Yeah, they took all of my strength from me!
The Philistines paid Delilah, then captured me, oh no! oh no!

**Outro:**
Ya'll Sing!
'Now that ain't right!'
What you doing with that knife?
Now that ain't right!
I'm just Nazzarite!
Now that ain't right!
Thought you was my wife!
Now that ain't right!
Leave me alone at night!
Now that ain't right!
Yeah!

## Some Angels disliked utopia

Think about this...
Lucifer was an angel in utopia
Yet he was still pissed!
And challenged God, taking 1/3 of heaven's population (with him) in a coup
If 33% of angels didn't like heaven, what will you do?
Were the other 67% just afraid?
Or were they not up for the challenge, and promise of change?
Sometimes it is good to break the rules
Other times, it is best to stick with the flock, or you might lose!

# The 10 Commandments

Ten Commandments…There's rules to this...Some call them golden…
The Ten commandments are in Exodus, Chapter 20.... listen:

**Number 1**
Absolutely no Gods before the lord
A simple but costly mistake that we can't afford
God said jealousy would bring mad wrath
All the stories of plagues and attacks, y'all do the math!

**Number 2**
Don't take God's name in vain and such
Y'all be using OMG's and JC's a bit too much!

**Number 3**
Remember to keep the Lord's day holy
You can still enjoy the game, chips and guacamole!
Sunday's focus, should be on God, family, and service
If you don't work at Chick-Fil-a, please don't be nervous!

**Number 4**
I know you heard this before
Always honor your both mom and dad
If you don't, when they're gone, you'd wish you had!

**Number 5**
…Please don't kill! If you're ever provoked, I quote, 'please chill!'

**Number 6**
Don't cheat on people, places, and things
Especially when you've exchanged vows and wedding rings!

**Number 7**
…Thou shall not steal!
If someone ever took your bike, then you know how it'll feel

**Number 8**
Don't bear false witness, because snitches, don't really get stitches!

**Number 9**
Shoulda' been number one to me…
Don't be jealous or have envy
The grass is greener, blah, blah, blah…
Don't player hate, congratulate the bourgeois!

**Number 10**
Always tell the truth! It can be difficult for all, old folks and the youth!
Follow these rules, and a good life will be seen
Your reward is in Leviticus chapter 25 verse 18.

## The return of Nommo

A pair of Gods slowly emerged from the sea
Walking along the shores of an African beach, finally free
Centuries gone, their reign long forgotten
Their sacred crops scattered, broken, and rotten
Foreign powers invaded and conquered the motherland
Two pairs of hands each grabbed fists of sand
Connecting a network, linking sun kissed souls worldwide
Beaming truth and power via an ancient melodic vibe
Despite the diaspora, we are still one tribe
Their absence was unforgivable and it's difficult to explain why
The deities who supplanted them told an incredible lie
Flummoxed that they were cast aside
Even Gods have pride and can be surprised
Eons passed in a blink of an eye
The new world had yet experienced true wrath and salvation
Once again united, the world was no longer filled with divided nations

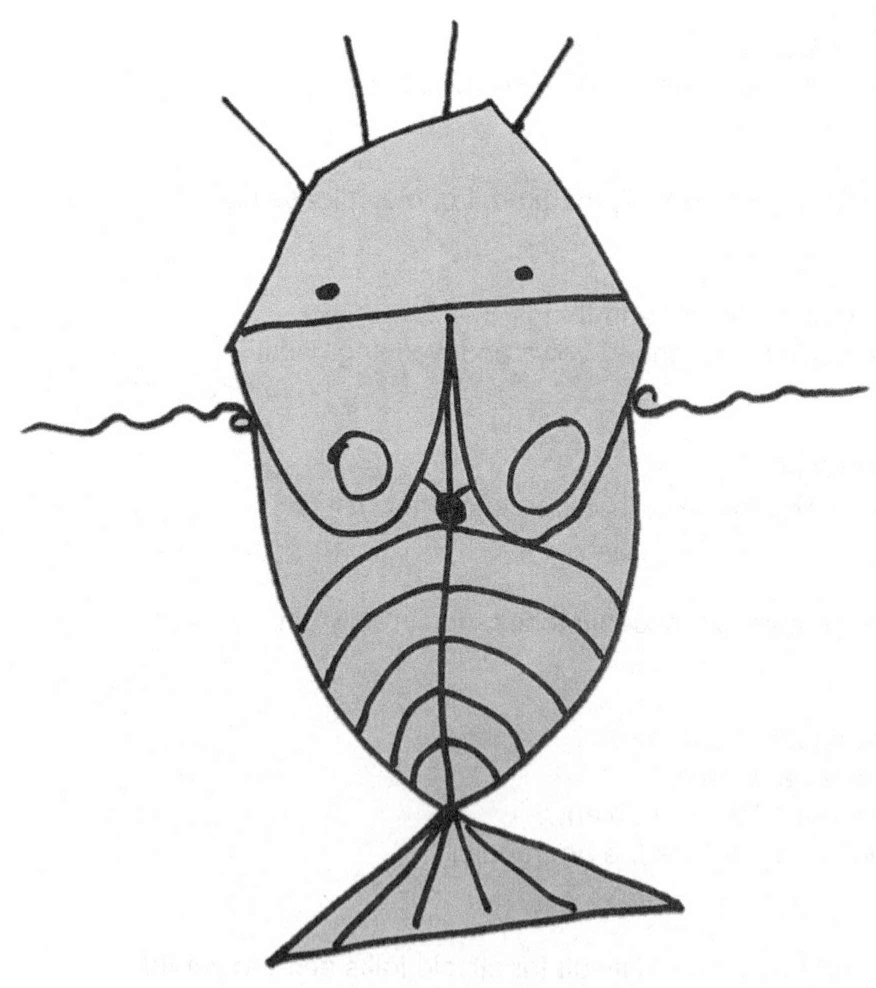

Illustrated by Jason Lawrence Moore

## They don't believe in God or COVID

Both invisible to the naked eye
With scripture and science, we try to explain why
To all of the cynics, who don't believe, we ask
Them to pray, get vaccinated, and to properly wear their masks
But they still refuse, to find time to, accomplish these simple and painless tasks
We really can't blame the devil, in this instance
Just free will, conscientious stupidity, and sincere ignorance!

**Unfair Bears (the opposite of Care Bears)**

Unfair bears
The leader's a cartoon with orange skin and fake hairs
With a big 'D' on his chest
How he got elected, is anybody's guess
His special power is lying while tweeting
Until moral improves, they'll continue the beating!
Citizens defiant and devoid of tact
Spewing fake news and alternative facts
A group of grumpy old bears
Pulling at the fabric of society, until it tears
With a chili pepper on his belly, is Spicy Sean
Depressing the press, like buttons from video games won
Billionaires and entertainers, now run the government
Adding injury and insult, along with all our money spent!
Bannon, Rex, and Jeff were probably the kids causing trouble in the halls
Back of the class, acting up, and launching spit balls
The Nerds got served with opinions over data
The Tri-Lambs got ‘Trumped’ by the Alpha Betas...

## War on Drugs

Our values are foil plated
Suicide contemplated
Jaded, yet they still getting faded!
Issues only debated
Never repaired
The future is scared
Dreams deferred, vision impaired
Doctors prescribe diatribes
Slangin' pills and smoke screens to drug fiends
White America didn't really care, until it happened to their teens!
Crack rock evolved into Meth and Molly
When Maria got hooked, she didn't get a second look
Then Amy started losing teeth, so we rewrote the book
Treatment not prison
Reform not scorn
Orange is the new black?
Reagan said America was a melting pot, but now you want your country back?

**What is faith?**

According to Hebrews 11:1, it's the substance of things hoped for, the evidence of things not seen
What is the scripture talking about, what does it really mean?
The how's and why's of everything
That we all take for granted
Ideas in mustard seeds, sown and then planted
Assure us that God's absence is fiction
As well as mankind's interpretations, manipulations, and depictions
Evil is the manifestation of free will without faith
So our creation was just random evolution from an ape?
I've climbed Mt. Fuji in Japan
Rode on an elephant in Thailand
Held a baby kangaroo, at a zoo, in Australia
Piloted a Navy warship through the Panama Canal, four times, let me tell ya!
Each trip took a whole 24 hours to complete
Walking through Dubai's Gold Souks, eating shawarmas in crowded streets
I ate kimchi in South Korea, painted a school in Ecuador
I've sailed on every ocean, visited nearly every shore
As a teenager, I explored Iceland's capital city of Reykjavík
But I didn't stay too long, because I had duty back on the ship!
I'm sharing my life and travels, not to brag, but rather to explain
To both atheists and the righteous, who constantly debate and complain
From myopic views, both too stubborn or scared to ever choose
To wander, explore, and walk in somebody else's shoes
My years of travel have shaped my global, spiritual, and cultural perspectives
Breaking bread in distance lands, ignorant of the menu choices that I selected
I've seen seas so calm, you'd think that the water was made of glass!
And waves so turbulent, you'd try to standup, but just keep falling back down on your ass!
The sea, like our creator, is simultaneously peaceful and dangerously violent
So loud at times, deafening, but mostly completely silent.

## When they decide to deport you

I wish I were smart and rich enough, to fix all that is wrong
But I barely got 200 views on my latest song!
Most of the people who have influence and a voice
Use it to make money, its an understandable, but selfish choice
The lens of history will view our current state of affairs
With duality… ignorance and bliss are fateful pairs
America versus the rest of the world
Injustices levied and obscenities hurled
They hardly notice, whenever the POTUS insults us
They built detention centers, with barely a fuss
Pacified by Netflix and gadgets
While our government reeks havoc
Laws bend, to the every whim of a maverick
Fascists build walls instead of bridges
The masses do nothing, but they should be livid!
We just build more callouses on our morals today
We'll soon regret our inaction, when they decide take **US** away

## Why did I choose apes?

As you celebrate another holiday, I still breathe cautious
Reading mortal's history, I often become nauseous
All this 'anti' talk among Christians, Muslims and Jews
How can you people be so blind, and yet still choose?
To believe or not to believe, in a resurrection
That's not the question, nor all of the details and direction
Jews believe in the old bible
While Christians cling to the new, both tribal
Muslims believes that Allah saved Jesus, while his own people betrayed him?
When everyone points a finger, its just us against them
Division of faith and history, seldom yields truth
Everyone is wrong, and nobody is right, here's some tangible proof
When a child is born, he/she/they knows no certain destination
Guided by their family, choices, environment and a single manifestation
When your man-made reason for being (religion) is challenged, why do you get so pissed?
Perhaps I'm real, and you-all simply don't exist!
And I no longer believe (in you)!
Heartbroken, over littered oceans and burning trees
Disappointed, but not surprised, that you people keep on making the same mistakes
Your actions prove my fatal flaw, why in the hell did I choose apes?

## Zeus died?

When people stopped believing in me, my world ended
Mortals just don't understand, what happened when the Gods blended
When the names changed, power still corrupted absolutely
When the eye of the beholder envisions beauty
They never consider its expiration
When children grow and go away, so goes their dedication
Forbidden fruits
Reveal hidden truths
As serpents slither
Innocence withers
With knowledge, minds grow and hearts die
Nobody worships me anymore, but I'm still up in the sky...

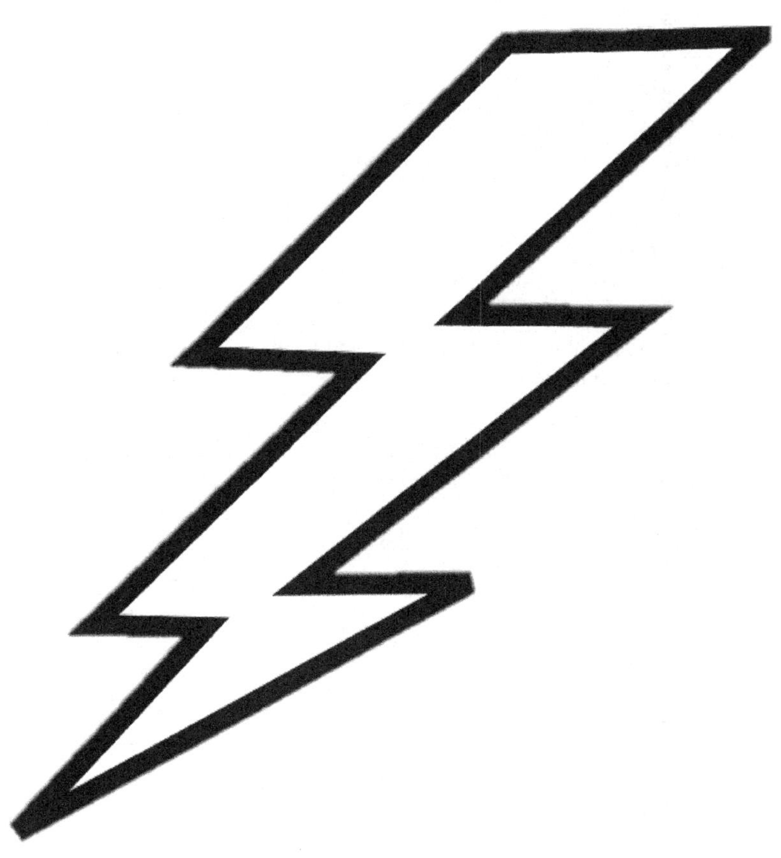

# PART IV: ART & MEDIA (353-406)

Top 75 = ♥

| Top 75 | # | Poem |
|---|---|---|
| | 353 | #'s on my head |
| | 354 | A poet is... |
| | 355 | Alter Ego (Star Trek Nemesis Summary) |
| | 356 | Amazon Genie |
| ♥ | 357 | Better now (after Post Malone) |
| | 358 | Blood-Sickle |
| | 359 | Bricks without straw |
| | 360 | Can't re-write the realist shit I ever wrote |
| | 361 | Chewing food for thought |
| | 362 | Chocolate Chip Cookies |
| | 363 | Coca Cola |
| | 364 | Cold Sweat (after James Brown) |
| | 365 | Death of Hip Hop |
| | 366 | Duces (after Chris Brown) |
| | 367 | Flawed |
| ♥ | 368 | Fool's Gold (after Jill Scott) |
| ♥ | 369 | In the comments section |
| | 370 | IND Ride 1 |
| | 371 | IND Ride 2 |
| | 372 | IND Ride 3 |
| | 373 | IND Ride 4 |
| | 374 | Internet Killed the periodical for being subpar |
| ♥ | 375 | Internet Rabbit Hole |
| | 376 | Look at me now - Trump Remix (after Chris Brown) |
| | 377 | Muad' dib – Urban Poet |
| | 378 | Mukbang |
| ♥ | 379 | New Jack City |
| | 380 | Ode to Inspectah Deck |
| | 381 | Ode to Pootie Tang |
| | 382 | Ode to the Black Eagle (Joe Madison) |
| | 383 | Pick a Different Topic |
| | 384 | Poor MC |
| | 385 | Prince & Michael Jackson |
| | 386 | Punks jump up to get beat down! |
| | 387 | R.I.P. Kobe |
| | 388 | Say Jim, that's a bad outfit! |
| ♥ | 389 | She kills me (Picture) |
| | 390 | She kills me |
| ♥ | 391 | Staying Alive (after RickyDesktop) |
| | 392 | Sucker MCs |
| ♥ | 393 | Sweet Sixteen |
| ♥ | 394 | The 'Internets' |
| | 395 | The Media |
| ♥ | 396 | The Struggle |
| | 397 | Top Ten Musical Memories |
| | 398 | Vice is but a nurse of agonies |
| | 399 | Watchmen |
| | 400 | When did reality become fiction? |
| | 401 | When the stars fall |
| | 402 | Why ain't you packing? |
| | 403 | Why is my cable bill $100 more? |
| | 404 | Words become movements |
| | 405 | Write. Every. Day. |
| | 406 | Zealots |

## #'s on my head

Can't get these #'s off my head yo!
Explains the ink stains all up on my pillow
Tried to scrub it off with a Brillo
Seems my time is up
Life is so abrupt
Traded my ticket like Beetle Juice, and now my head is shrunk!
This track is funky like a skunk!
Pass me another 8 Ball, man, I'm finn to get drunk!
I can't believe she left me, damn I'm such a punk!
Tried to keep our relationship afloat, but it still sunk
Greed and lies harpooned and torpedoed us, now I'm in a funk
Social life of a hermit, sex life of a monk
Please come back baby, it been a long month
I had a string of bad luck
First I chipped my tooth, then they repossessed my truck
The cops raided the wrong house, now our place looks like a dump!
We used to always play patty cake
Now it constant keep away
Then she said, 'tag your it!'
Then moved very far away
Changed her Facebook status, and won't return any of my messages
Damn I miss her cooking and feeling on her breast-tis-is
They say that I should just let it slide, like water off a duck
But its hard admit, when your #'s up.

## A poet is...

A poet is...
A comedian without jokes
A politician who don't get votes
A musician who just made a new tune
A janitor with a dust pan and no broom
A truck driver with oars and a row boat
A fish out of water, who just jumped out of a moat!
A veteran who sees civilians as sheep
A policeman, one paycheck away from being a thief
A survivor of illness, who won't take their health for granted
An urban farmer, whose first seeds were just planted
Two strangers who just discovered a new friendship or love
An addict who just flushed away, the last of his drug
The student who just learned something new
And the teacher who persisted, inspired, and knew what she could do!

## Alter Ego (Star Trek Nemesis Summary)

In Star Trek Nemesis, he grimaces
When he sees his clone
Danger on the premises
Enemies hell bent to destroy my home!
In the prequel and the sequel
My adversaries and I weren't equals
But it seems that I've met my match
My past is about to kick my ass!
But my advantage is my uniqueness
And time is his weakness
Ambitious but friendless
Love trumps fear in every instance!
Absolute power conquers like a prison sentence
A lifetime breakdown, like water and erosion
You initiated self-destruction, but there was no explosion!
Heated moment tactics, full of holes like a donut
I'll charge ahead at ramming speed, before you back me in a corner
Faced with certain annihilation
I find myself pacing
On the damaged bridge of the Enterprise
Battling my former self for survival, how shall I rise?
Clever persuasion won't work on this occasion, perhaps a disguise?
Beam over with the beta version of Data, and attack with the element of surprise!
Attacks provoked, under the cowardliness of a cloak
Defenses down, away team deployed, time for a 16th century quote
Shakespeare wrote, 'All the world's a stage'
We're all actors, in the universe, so who's writing this plot?
In the end, we're alive but we didn't win, because we lost our robot (Android)

## Amazon Genie

Ads for fads, deplete our savings
Wants versus needs, starve imaginary cravings
Consumers, addicted and conflicted
Lusting for new and shiny products, like pornographic fiction
Psychosomatic its tragic, but we're still scratching to itch it!
Ecommerce is worse, when we click, then they ship it!
Don't need it, greed spent it, as our conscience remains quiet
Hoarding goods, gadgets, and gifts
Technology's a genie, granting our every wish!
Instant gratification, the punishment is debt
And a future of junk, wasted time, and regret.

## Better Now (after Post Malone)

You probably think that you are better now (better now)
When I gave you everything, you'd complain and frown (complain and frown)
I bared my soul, then you took my heart out (heart out)
Then you said that I was shit out of luck (oh wooo)...
Instead of arguing, I just hopped in my truck
In a rage, I yelled and hit the steering wheel...
Without arguing, just once, I wish that could explain, exactly how I feel...
Replaying our back and forth, I finally had an epiphany
Maybe you were just being honest, and you're just not that into me...
Asking you to compromise, shouldn't fill me with guilt
But now I feel, just like that carton of Almond milk
You had your taste, now that phase has passed
Expiration date, came and went, and now I'm in the trash!
All along I was happy, hoping that you were too
Even after all these years, we're at odds, and I'm not sure what else I should do....

## Blood Sickle

Born with a blood disease
Crisis attacks, like a chronic sneeze
Pain that will bring you to your knees!
No cure from pharmaceutical companies
Then my weakness, vanished in my late teens
Fate bit me on the arm
My transformation was caused by a strange bat's harm
Was it a blessing in disguise?
No changes observed by casual eyes
Over time, my intellect and strength grew
I was amazed at what I could do!
Superhuman strength and speed
Sleep, food, and waste, were no longer needs
With the ability to transport and bend time
I single handily righted wrongs, and solved thousands of crimes
Cured Sickle Cell, Leukemia, COVID, and HIV in just one trip
To the past, so now they don't exist
But even with all of this power
There are still only 24 hours
Choices and decisions remain grave
What should I fix, who should I save?
My actions had dire consequences, and I'm still fixing my errors
Tried to help folks, but all they saw was terrors
I nearly lost my soul and my mind
So I travelled back in the past, one last time
Found and killed that bat, just to be sane
And then I reset just about everything
Now all I feel is pain...

**Healthy**

Normal red blood cell

**Sickle cell anaemia**

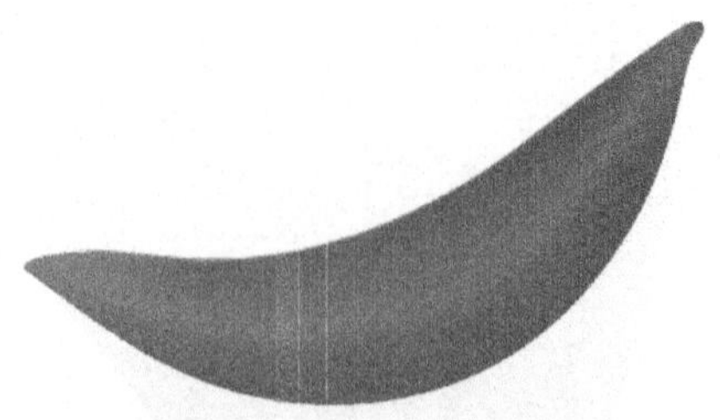

Sickle red blood cell

## Bricks without straw

Billions try hard, millions often fail
Thousands just do it, hundreds manage to excel
Like spreadsheets, cell by cell
Integers entered by column and row
Manipulate data by pivot tables and charts to show
Trends and projections, to make sound choices
Zeros and ones speak volumes without voices
The Information Age is as ancient as stone
Modern day slaves traded bricks and pyramids, for information and phones.

C18 fx

| | A | B |
|---|---|---|
| 1 | Bricks | 400 |
| 2 | Straw | 1,345,594 |
| 3 | Phones | 23,420,914 |
| 4 | Information | 345,698,102,753 |
| 5 | Data | 123,456,789,012,456,000 |

Bricks & Straw

8 6 4 2 0

10 8 6 4 2 0

Bricks Straw Phones Information Data

A B C

## Can’t rewrite the realist shit that I ever wrote!

So I wrote this nice new rhyme right?
On a certain website, at 11:30pm last night
It wasn't perfect, so I changed some stuff
Like a barber edging lines for too long, I really messed it up!
I knew that time wouldn't be kind
My words grew out awkward, like a jacked up hairline!
Trimming my thoughts, past the point of no return
Going from Drake to George Jefferson, was cause for concern!
Hours passed, but it was nearly perfect
When I hit submit, then the internet just murked it!
I hit the back button
Hoping to salvage something
But it was long gone, up in smoke
I couldn't rewrite realist shit that I ever wrote!

## Chewing food for thought

How come there aren't a bunch of rich poets?
Musicians, comedians, writers and playwrights know it
Artists must make songs, movies and more
Because original thoughts and ideas bore
The masses, think back to your classes in school
Students studying literature, bored to tears and drool
Not engaged by mere words on a page
But lyrics evoke emotions, from joy to rage!
While jokes shock and awe with instigation
Because stories, plays, and movies pique our imagination

## Chocolate Chip Cookies

Chocolate chip cookies weren't invented
Until 1938 in Massachusetts, I'm pensive
World, look at what America's gifted!
iPhones, Rock n' Roll, movies and TV shows
Gadgets, ideas, style, and fashionable clothes
All sorts of material wishes, fast cars and... a Tupac rhyme
Culture, money, jewelry, drugs, guns, and crime
This age that we're living in, it is quite pivotal
Information overload, ads subliminal
The Food and Drug Administration regulates profits and chemicals
This is just some 'Monday Morning Quarterbacking'
Amused at the irony, as I sit back here laughing
I used to be blind, but with time, now I see
How I love America, but she sure hates me!

## Coca Cola

John S. Pemberton Invented Coca Cola
As a remedy for his morphine habit, and to make some payola
He was a pharmacist
But I was alarmed by this...
He served as a Confederate Lieutenant Colonel
And got a saber wound at the Battle of Columbus, chest injuries internal
After the war, John became addicted to morphine to dull the pain
To cure his addiction, he created a drink laced with cocaine!
His bookkeeper coined the name 'Coca Cola'
He thought it would be a hit (he was right), but it struck like a cobra
It didn't sell, and after John's business failed, he sold all of his rights for $1,750
In 1880, that was worth about $45k in today's money – what a pity!
John died broke and addicted, and so did his son
I had a bottle of Coke just today, my last one.

## Cold Sweat (after James Brown's song)

I know what you mean James!
It also happened to me, strange
Me and my lady did thangs
I thought I'd just break her off
But my plan was canned, man because she was so soft!
Its insatiable bliss, whenever we twist
I soon lost my nerve, with each squeeze and every kiss
A sensual competition, of magic and gymnastics
We should have broke out a towel, a mat, or maybe even some plastic!
A pool of sweat, began to collect, and all of our commotion made a vast ocean
Soaked in lust and love, we found ourselves a floatin'
We nearly drowned, as we labored, to catch our breath
Then I awoke from the wildest dream, drenched in a cold sweat...

## Death of Hip Hop

They were out for hemoglobin, like Dracula and Dexter
Patiently waiting, for matriculation in the final semester
School was in session, and they cooked us with pressure
Crabs in a barrel, rap beefs got us nowhere, like steps from M.C. Escher!
Wack MC's displeased me, 'cuz they should have done better!
Mainstream sodomized the game, that shit wasn't cool
Hip Hop woke up one morning, and found blood in her stool!
Defenseless, her leucocytes were removed, as infection ensued
Parasites stole her rights, in exchange for narcotics and booze
Mosquitos and leaches beseeched us, but we had the power to choose!
Like blood created in bone marrow and destroyed in the spleen
Four months to live, Hip Hop's time was in-between
A rock and a hard place, and too late to save face
Sagging skinny jeans and whack rhymes, man, it was such a disgrace!
Rest in peace to Hip Hop, cause of death, paper chase!
Your friend to the end, I still can't believe that you left me
I was a pallbearer, and spit this here at your eulogy
I tell my grandkids about how we first met all the time!
A beauty in the park, with a beat, breakdance, and a rhyme!

## Deuces (after Chris Brown)

Early one morning I was driving to work
Clinching my stomach tight, cuz that shit hurt!
Excuses, late night Chipotle
My will power was useless…
Should have skipped the beans
An unscheduled stop, at a public bathroom it seems
Gas station bathroom, heck-e-naw, I ain't sitting on that!
I opened the toilet seat and out flew a bat!
I saw a Target store, a few blocks back
When I arrived, I knew that I had to #2
No parking spaces, so what else could I do?
Parked in a fire lane and an Associate, in a red vest, started to complain
"I know", I exclaimed, "fuck it, just tow it, no time to explain!"
Eyes watering, walking bow-legged, ass hauling it
They put the fucking bathrooms, all the way in the back, so now I'm 'Prairie Dogging' it!
Ain't this some shit, only two stalls, and both of them are full
I'm dancing around, holding my ass, like a mother fuckin' fool!
I gotta pee too, one urinal's occupied, and the other one is broke
Can't believe my luck, this is like a really bad joke!
Shit is getting heavy, literally, and I'm at my wits end
Considering going to isle 13, to grab a bag of Depends!
Finally a stall is open, get the hell out of my way!
People scoffing at me, I got 5 shits worth, fuck what he say!
I am about to have a real occupy movement
No toilet paper in the stall, but I said screw it!
Had the biggest Duce of my life, no fronting
So embarrassed for the aftermath of my ass drop, that I actually bought something!
Deuces! I've got to boo boo, you too?
Who knew? Two scoops
Walking in a park with my Shih Tzu
Sit U boo, Sit, good dog! <Woof!>
I didn't pick that up, Mr. Officer, because it thought it was a log
I've only got this, look at that, I'll need a Glad bag!
That's that weapon of mass destruction, that President Bush said was in Baghdad!
Really, a ticket and a misdemeanor?
I thought that the grass was greener
On the other side, yes, that's me in the fecal APB
But the incident at Target was totally different, this time I'm not guilty!
Mr. Officer, it wasn't me and my past BM's are irrelevant
Honestly, that's some X-Files shit, so it probably belongs to some kind of an alien elephant!
I'm appalled at your accusation, I'm going to write my congressman
You have me on video? OK, well, I guess I did it then, I knew it was wrong
This is blatant discrimination, you'd better leave me alone!
I'll win in court, on account of irritable bowel syndrome
Take into consideration, my current state of constipation
Banned from public restrooms for life, can you imagine my frustration?

## Flawed

I fail at folding fitted sheets
Misspell words when the I's come before or after the C's
I've never completely, successfully raked a yard of leaves
Don't enjoy the taste of beer, coffee, or tea
I still can't program the remote on my TV
When I press the wrong buttons, trying to watch BET
Then I don't understand, these young MC's
Sagging skinny jeans, it just make no sense to me!
I voted for Hillary, but then I got Trumped
Love American democracy, but now I feel like I got dumped
Random nails punctured my side walls, so I'm at the air pump
In the cold, parked at a gas station
The machine must be broken, because the quarters constantly needed replacing
I asked the attendant, now standing outside smoking
'When I asked you for change earlier, why didn't you tell me that it was broken?'
He smiled and replied in a foreign language
My fingers were freezing, replacing the valve stem caps, in utter anguish
I heard a chuckle behind me, and then a bell rang
The attendant just went back inside, so I guess it was kind of pointless for me to complain...

## Fool's Gold (after Jill Scott)

I've long searched in the dirt, for everything that gleams
To find fortune, we must realize our dreams
My years yielded nothing, but trials and tears
I was driven by inspiration, but was ultimately hindered by my fears
My mind, body, and soul was traded for acres of fool's gold
I mined enough of these rocks to build a very long road
The action of their extraction, helped me to grow
The weight and repetition, also conditioned me well
Those that follow, now have a comfortable path to dwell
And maybe that was my purpose
To extract what was worthless
So that the future now knows exactly where to go!
If we reap what we sow
Then I accept my penance, and work in peace
Gold is real, but somehow still, just past my reach!
So I pretended that all that dirt, was really just sand at the beach
And I was on vacation, with the ocean beneath my feet
Back to reality, that water's just a creek!
Digging 24 hours a day, seven days a week
Trapped in a jail, with no rest or bail
In time, my intentions forged a path to hell!
And the moral of the story, that I often tell
Beyond the characters, locations, and plot
Is count your blessings, and enjoy what you already got!

♥

## In the comments section

A few lines down in the comment section deep
Lie hundreds of anonymous, racist, and misogynist creeps
Crudely expressing their desires and opinions
Get rich quick schemes, memes, and misinterpretations on religion
Often arguing with each other's dubious claims
With a familiarity, suggesting that they've long known each other's screen names
A few voices of reason, with credible 'on topic' remarks
Are like blood in the water, for hundreds of frenzied virtual sharks!
Each believing in irrational fears, like kids in the dark
These bullies aren't just teens surfing the web in their basement
They are doctors, lawyers, captains of industry, and master of entertainment

**IND Ride (Ode to Indianapolis) – Part I**

I to the N, D to the Wiz-I
Welcome to Indianapolis
The best trip of your liz-ife!
Come for the game,
Stay for the scene
Explore the I.N.D.
You'll never want to leave!
Bring your spouse, momma and children,
The IND has a 'lil something for all of them
Don't sleep on the IND cuz Hoosiers call it "Naptown",
Anything you-want to do, in the IND-it can be found!
Plan a trip, to a city that's close and quick
"Crossroads of America"
Stay a day then dip!
Your flight just landed,
Well, welcome to the airport
This is the IND ride
And I'll be your passport!
We have a few hours, before you have to check-in
Let's drive around 465
And take the city in!
Want a bite to eat?
'Cause Indy's got it all!
Great seafood and steak, anything that swims or craws!
Shrimp cocktail at St. Elmo's - WOW! what a sensation!
Or, get some grub downtown at Union Station
Circle Center Mall, so much more in store
Kids love the Children's Museum and the Eiteljorg
The big game was on Sunday, let's not forget
Lucas Stadium, NFL, Super Bowl 46!
So much to see, hear, taste, feel, and breathe
N-D-A-NO-PLACE, but the I.N.D!

## IND Ride (Ode to Indianapolis) – Part II

Two years ago
Two friends of mine
Asked me if the IND
Was just a waste of time?
Listen to the rhyme, that I told them both
Then write it, bite it, recite it, and feel free to quote…
Back when the IND was just new to me,
Others asked “is it cool?"
I said indubitably!!!
1825, inspired by Pierre L’Enfant,
Made to be exciting and yet nonchalant,
But now, how can we ride in the IND,
And I neglect to check the best sites to see?
Broad Ripple, Friday night
Hit the clubs, hear the hype!
Landsharks and Slippery Noodle Inn
Grab a brew
With the crew
Party till they close – I think it's 2!
Best tacos and nachos
Its Acapulco Joe's!
Cheese Burger or Sushi
Scotty's Lakehouse or $H_2O$
Soul food, finger licking
College Ave, Kountry Kitchen!
Fast food, hot plate
Diminutive fries, Steak and Shake!
For even less of a hassle
Drive through any White Castle
No stress, good wine, taste test
Easley Winery is the best
But I digress
May I suggest?
If you stay more than a day
Check out the Indianapolis Motor Speedway?

## IND Ride (Ode to Indianapolis) – Part III

Looking for love?
Here's a good place to start
It's on display at the Indiana Museum of Art
Broadway all day, Clowes Hall and the Murat!
Amateur sports capital of the world
Where, you can ball, bike, hike, swim, shoot and curl!
Colts, Pacers, and Fever will make you into a believer!
Watch our guards and receivers
Score and beat the other team!
Live vicariously through their actions
Become a part of their dream!
It's all or nothing cousin,
Nothing else is in between
When you're in the 317, you gotta root for the IND!
Yell defense, when it makes sense
Then, when your team wins
You can, celebrate the date with your family and friends!
See, Indianapolis is fabulous
Grab a cab and ride in this
Big city action, small town feel
Your dollars last longer
Weekends are a steal!
Explore the IND, and for a nominal fee
Get so more than you can imagine man, so much more to see!
This ain't no train, so keep your spare change
Rather it's an enigma, 'cause it can't be explained
Something strange,
When the IND gets under your skin....
You can feel a change in your direction
Like sails in the wind...
It's the IND ride!

## IND Ride (Ode to Indianapolis) – Part IV

These rhymes to me, are more than advertisements
Its love for my city, plus tourism encouragement
Growing up Indy gave me plenty of nourishment
Sports, history, culture, and now the subsequent
Visitindy.com to see what's going on!
jlmoorerealty.com and buy a house from my mom!
I used to wander Indiana, wander Indiana, wander Indiana
From the 'Circle' to the 'Square'
To Carmel, Haughville, Speedway and back to the Fair!
Shout out the South, East, West, and North sides
20 minute trip around 465
IUPUI and Butler are already on my brackets
Can't wait until March, for more IND Madness!
Alexander Ralston designed Indy, I was mistaken
His name didn't rhyme at the time, lost in translation
Props to my brother, J.G. and Masta Ace
Ron Isley on the hook, INC on the bass
Ya'll inspired me, and I finally had the gall to…
Write a ditty 'bout my city
So one day I hope that all (of) you…
Get a chance to explore, experience and visit
Can't explain the IND, you simply have to live it!

## Internet killed the periodical for being subpar

Downtown Chicago on Michigan Avenue
Between hotels, restaurants, and what have you
Is the Johnson Publications building, abandoned with neglect
Soon to be 150 apartments, a rich guy cut a check
Hit with some introspection, when was the last time I bought an Ebony or Jet?
I subscribed back when they first went digital, but then I broke my tablet
When I got a new device, I honestly forgot that I had it
'Internet killed the periodical for being subpar'
I used some hotel points to get an Essence subscription
So my daughter can see how beautiful black is, juxtaposed to social media fiction

**Internet Rabbit hole**

Trapped in an internet rabbit hole
Clicking, reading, wandering where does the time go?
Searching for something, nothing, attention deficit disorder
Distracted by web banners and pop up ads along the border
Hours pass, and I've accomplished absolutely nothing
Happy when I window shop, then sad after I buy something
That I know that I don't need
My virtual habit's a symptom of greed
News is more like gossip
Articles masquerading as ads, designed to raise company profits
Views and clicks proxy value and opinion
The illusion of power, over information dominion
Too much of a good thing is a curse
As well as too many choices, so do we just pick which is worse?
Ignorance is bliss, and knowledge is hell
I'm done browsing the web for now, its time to check my email....

Illustrated by
Zoe Victoria Moore



♥

**Look at me now - Trump remix (after Chris Brown)**

Russian.. Model.. Chick..
Crazier than Giuliani
No evidence of collusion
Tell Muller to keep it moving
Yep, yep, this looks nothing like a toupee
I get what you get in 10 years, in two days!

Ladies love me
I'm on my Elvis P
Top floor of the Trump plaza, nobody can rob me!
You're just an apprentice in my lobby
I'm better than everybody, and I'm not sorry!

Look at me now!
Look at me now!
Oh… I'm getting paper!

I've failed at casinos, airplanes, steaks and vodka
I looked in the mirror and said, 'Donny boy, nobody will ever stop ya!'
Fox said I'd be more relevant as an elephant
So I got rid of all my lawsuits, once I became the President!
At first I was hesitant
But then I realized that I can do no wrong!
I raised taxes and my tie is way too long!
I play golf often, while my peers are sent to prison
I'll just fill all of the vacant positions, via nepotism!
I'm a billionaire, that means I got all the money
Richest and oldest POTUS ever - MAGA 2020!

## Muad'dib – Urban Poet

Muad'dib's an urban poet
Does he know it? Can he show it?
What it do? What is was?
First was fly, then got shoos, zero buzz
Just a pest? Naw cuz!
Feel this flow
From concentrate, original
Mixed flour and oil into a rue
Heat and time, 'till there's a stew
Rather gumbo, felt my stomach rumble
Quaked the pavement, cracks to shake the concrete jungle
As the city sleeps, legions of zombies creep
And graze for brains, like deranged sheep!
Hear them bleat, some report, others cheat
Lemmings trip, off of cliffs, then hit, like guitar riffs
And jam with drums, crowds clap, till their hands get numb
Used to rock in my basement, now I'm #1
All hell, my bad, that's LL!
LOL, let's sit a spell
Tell me your deepest secrets, I promise that I won't tell!
I used to be like Poppa Smurf, now I'm more like Gargamel
Filled with hate, and plagued with greed
I wear all black, yell at my cat, who I forgot to feed…
As I quench my thirst
Like the Ghostbusters, I push a hearse
Life's a blessing, but I'm still cursed
With a conscience and a mind
And an uncanny ability, to write a rhyme
Cyndi Lauper, time after time
When my pictures fade and turn to gray...

## Mukbang

People are watching people eat food online?
I thought this one chick had totally lost her mind
'Vloggers' who Mukbang, where they eat a bunch of food
From South Korea to America, I was like, is this for real dude?
We're not talking about competitive eating competitions
These folks are getting paid for the clicks on a mission!
It's like porn, but nobody's getting fucked!
Instead they are just getting stuffed
I saw this one dude, just drink a large soda from Sonic
Reminds me of some strange Japanese game shows back in the day, so ironic!
Why would someone make a 40 minute video of themselves eat crab legs and other stuff?
I guess its because they can make over $9,000 per month!

## New Jack City

Driving a Black Jeep Wrangler around town
Cash money new school, call me Nino Brown!
Throwing thousands of C notes down
While model chicks on my conference table shake they round brown!
Hitting switches, paparazzi posted taking pictures
Quick temper, constantly canceling these snitches
And making their boyfriends extremely sad
Grandiose Motherfuckers stressing whenever they feel my wrath
Slicker than Tony Montana, nobody washes my cash
Interest rates raised and collected, banks pnwned his ass!
No gangster or dealer, I only slang rhymes to these fiends
I administer my product audibly, fulfilling their wildest dreams
Lyrics so sick, the FDA labels my MP3's as a contagious disease
No A&R, I spread my buzz, like a cold with a sneeze
You give it to friends, then they carry it around for weeks
Out of spite, you even share it with your foes
Frantic and implanted, you admire my prose!
I kept you waiting, and now you're shaking for more
Hooked on Adverb, got 'em scheming for a score
Hypnotized, I commanded you to search for truth
Instead you busted some random snitches' goose loose
Next year, you're on Maury Povich, praying for false proof
My rhymes are in your ear like a Bluetooth
Making these classics in the sound booth
Spitting the truth, Ruth!

♥

## Ode to Inspectah Deck

I played Inspectah's Triumph verse, a least dozen times
Decided then and there, that I wanted to rhyme
The best 16 ever spit, descriptive, specific and terrific!
He never asks for permission or begs for forgiveness
Witness a poets flow, in the booth and on the radio
Skip to the outros, just to practice my humble flow
I started writing rhymes on my phone and downloaded the instrumentals
Reading all of the classic lyrics, just to study the fundamentals
I'm a student of the game, ten years toward my rhyme degree
Five years left, until I earn the title, 'Real MC'
No hooks, just bars, in my own style
Collected thousands of rhymes, now I got a big file
Different phases, it amazes me, when I rhyme what I wrote
Some of it's wack, but honestly, most of its dope!
Striving to be a poet and God MC
May my words one day ignite sparks and inspire others, just like me.

**Ode to Pootie Tang**

Ode to Pootie Tang
What did you say?
Sa Da Tay?
Cole me down on the panny sty
And be a role model to the little Tipi Tais
What's the Dabble Dee?
May I dane on the cherries, Mama T?
Never froze when my foes unkind
I just sine your pitty on the runny kine!
Belt gone, farm life, its going down!
Heading back to the city - Sepatown!
That movie was so bad, it was good!
Comedy/fiction/depiction/abstract/fact/good/bad, ain't that the hood?
Dirty Dee, Biggie Shortie, and Trucky, they was all silly
Stay in school kids, and remember, don't bang the dillies!

Illustrated by Jonathan Riley

## Ode to the Black Eagle (Joe Madison)

Joe Madison with news and politics on SiriusXM
Shines a light, on those who don't act right, and enlightens the dim
I love it when, a young person calls in on a whim
And the Black Eagle says, 'Excuse me, I've got underwear older than him!'
Hanging up on a caller, and adding a dollar to the swear jar again
Most shows get it twisted
But Joe puts it where the 'goats' can get it!
Sincere ignorance and conscientious stupidity
From the famous MLK quote, is the epitome
Of what Joe loathes the most…
So, let's make a toast!
To man in the morning, with the latest word
(The Eagle is... a regal bird, you don't hear meee...)
At the approach of a storm, Joe Madison can see
Through the fake news
Critical thinking is key, you have the power to choose!
So tune into SiriusXM channel 126
While you drive, open your ears and eyes, and listen to this!

♥

## Pick a Different Topic (Migos spoof on ‘Walk it Talk it’)

**Rayquan** Been a fan for a while, but it’s getting old
Guns, drugs, and misogyny, again, really? No!
Stop! Be about hype beats and flow
Y’all popping pills and cuffin’ garden tools – Whoa!
Gangs, guns and money all have consequence (Mama!)
We lost too many talents from all this nonsense (I heard….)
Rather talk about you in the future, not past tense
Everyday, I keep reading the same news
Jokers killing Jokers for they chain and shoes
Dope beats and whack rhymes, it’s a shame (shame, shame!)
Wasted talent and dumb names done ruined the game, so we…. Gotta…
**<Chorus>**
**Adverb** Remember when rappers had normal whips?
Videos with Fords, Nissans, Chryslers, and Buicks? (Word!)
Now they braggin’ ‘bout fake behinds
And other nonsense in their rhymes
Pocket watching, and still throwing up gang signs?
Female dogs, expensive cars, and diamond grills
Baking soda, and teriyaki chicken meals (What?)
Really though, when will fans demand real skillz?
African Americans are pocket watching?
Supposed next we monocle coppin’?
Y’all sagging skinny jeans, but I still refuse that option!
**<Chorus>**

**Chorus**
We gotta pick a different topic
Pick a different topic (Whoot!)
Pick a different topic
Pick a different topic (Phone Chirp)
Pick a different topic
Pick a different topic (Skurt Skurt!)
Pick a different topic
Pick a different topic (I said!)

**Rayquan** General Tso’s chicken, Man y’all be trippin!
Your clothes, flow, and gold is all fiction (I heard…)
It rhymes fine, but really tho’, what are you spittin’?
Stains on carpet grains, when you spilled the Prego?
Hurt my foot, when I tripped, stepped on a Lego (ouch!)
No shade, when the shadows block my sundial
I get moody now, whenever the clouds crowd
When my smiles turn to frowns (Barz!)… Gotta…
**<Chorus>**
**M.C. Zoe** M.C., Z. to the O. E., Don’t act like you don’t know me (watch out!)
Princess of the playground, leave your pockets full of posies (OK)!
Bet when I drop these rhymes, YouTube gonna own me (That’s right!)
Cash this, cash this, are you all down? (Yup!)
Rayquan kick that knowledge!
A million more views cuz, and we can pay for college! (Jackpot!)
Running rings around these Rosies
Loot at these hits – Man these kids are nosy (Ha!)
Z loves all her fans, stay tuned for future plans, sincerely, M.C. Zoe! (Barz!) Wont’ you...
**<Chorus>**

## Poor MC

You're feeling old, you know?
When your favorite rapper died decades ago
Getting frustrated online whenever I search
At the New Jacks' current net worth
Way more than mine and my top five
And the God MC's, who are still alive
Bad contracts signed to EMI and Jive
Still pretending to live lavish, like Magnum PI
But really just renting a duplex
A normal sized lifestyle, Durex
No condoms, baby mammas' garnished all them checks!
They all up on social media, showing mad disrespect
Critics said my Sophomore album was trash
Flow was cool, but my style's a relic of the past
Plus my fan base is dead, in jail, or too old
To buy my independent albums, so my concert tickets ain't getting sold
When the game changed, my label dropped me
And I promised my momma and them, I'd never do reality TV
I can't act, DJ, and never got a shoe
So now I work for a radio station, playing whack hits everyday
Wondering how in the hell did my life turn out this way?

## Prince & Michael Jackson

In the blink of an eye, the world lost a Prince and a King
Too soon, *it feels like a strange dream
Where the voices that help to define us, are all suddenly gone
So I play and sing along, to some of my favorite songs
To drive away the doom and gloom, with harmonies so iconic
Some say music is dead, I agree, how ironic
Lately, it seems the rich and famous are dropping like flies
So we lament our lost artists', entertainers', and perfect strangers' abbreviated lives
Survived by their work, awards, fans, friends, kids, husbands, and wives
It is rare to admire and miss someone, whom you've never met
RIP to Prince Rogers Nelson, and so many others that we should never forget.

## Punks jump up to get beat down!

In a riot fight
They nearly lost their life
Moments earlier, she drank a diet Sprite
Hoping to lose weight and quench her thirst
Thinking life's too short, soon bad became worse!
When she was stopped by a gang of bandits
Money or her life, was what they demanded!
Tugging to save her snatched purse
Her against three, she thought, we'll see who leaves here in a hearse!
She remembered her training
As her attackers' provoked, she recalled an old saying
'Punks jump up to get beat down!'
A left punch, dropped the first flat on the ground!
A kick to the other's hip nearly missed
But the last, fell dead on his ass, when her elbow struck his lips!
Standing over her foes like, 'ain't this a bitch?'
They ran away shocked, limping and covering their lips
Who is this?
The leader thought, when he'd finally met someone, who made him question why he'd exist
But this ass whooping didn't even get him too pissed
It had been a decade or so, since he had last been whipped!
Momma made him go outside, to retrieve another switch
Not no little twig either, but something that would really make his ass itch!
The terror he felt then, was more of a fear of the unknown
He had the same feeling today, but he thought he was grown...

**RIP Kobe**

Reduced to a hashtag and a kind word
Close to perfect superstar, fake news, it all sounds so absurd
The good die young, this is all for the birds!
News of random accidents once heard
Keep you up at night, wondering what's not deserved
Fame/wealth/problems/thirst/punchbowl/turd

**'Say Jim, that's a bad outfit!'**

Superman Returns
I watched it on a VHS tape a lot
Still recall every scene, each character, and the plot
I wished that I could fly, but of course I could not
But my brothers and I, kept rewinding one small bit
Where a pimp tells Superman, 'Say Jim, that's a bad outfit!'
I didn't even know was a pimp was, but he could not contain his pride
What he was doing was illegal, but Superman had bigger fish to fry
The more I watched his part, the less I found it funny
While Superman saved the world, this pimp was smacking around women for his money
Today kids can see heroes who look like them fighting for all kinds
Watching Black Panther and Storm, instead of a pimp cheering from the sidelines!

## She Kills Me!

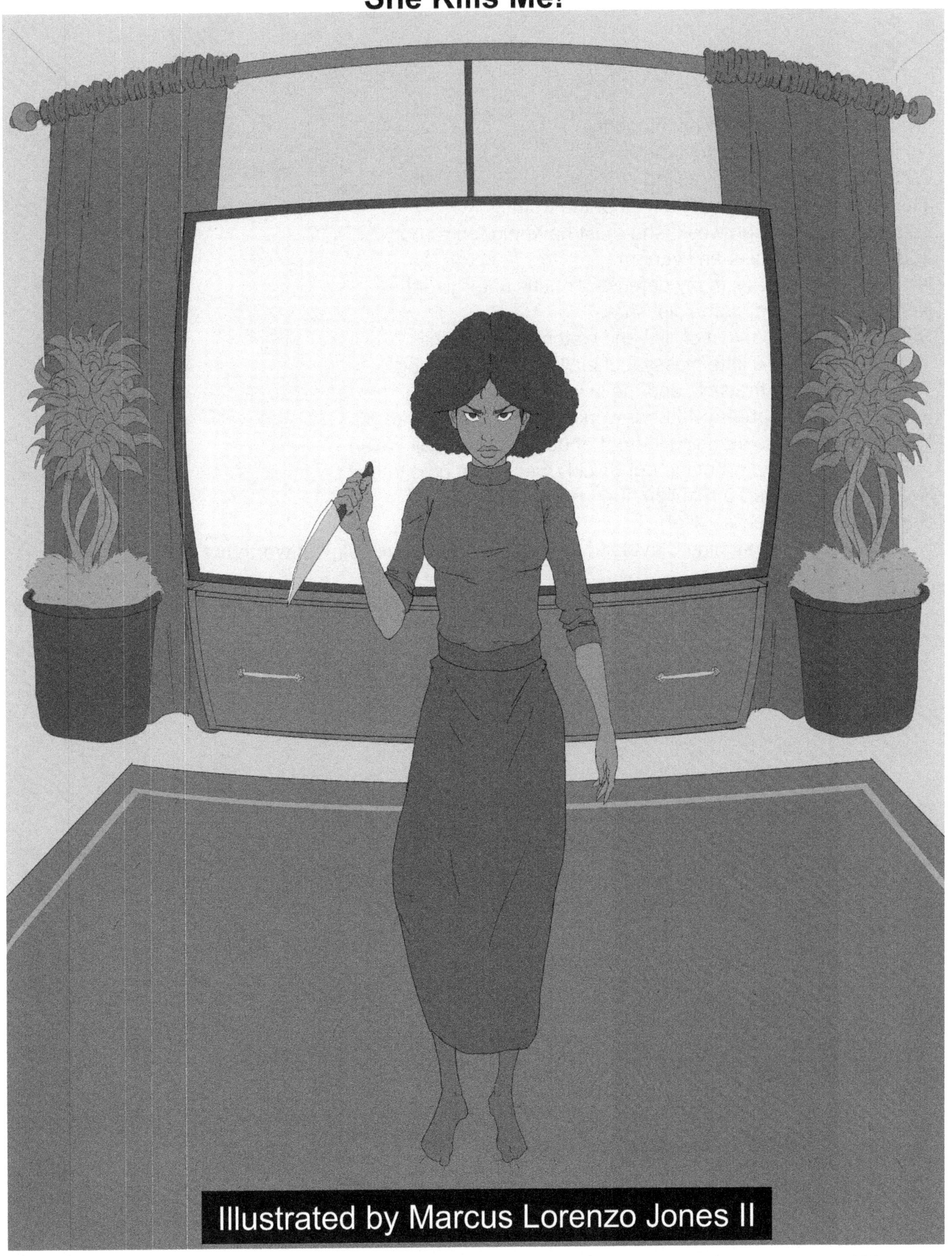

Illustrated by Marcus Lorenzo Jones II

## She Kills Me

'Die nigga die!'
I heard her cry, as I saw my blood fly
No mercy, why'd she curse me?
When I asked why, she replied
'Hell hath no fury...', damn, ain't that the truth!
I already had a rough week, she must have hidden a root!
Man, she's full of piss and venom
No matter what I say, in my defense, I'm still unforgiven!
Not sure what I did, same ole' same
Saturday afternoon, just chillin' and watching the game
Yeah the house's a little messy, but ain't no mold growing…
There's dishes in the sink, and the lawn needs mowing
I plan to get to it, but my 40 hour work week was more like 80
Now this woman is standing in front of our TV, acting all crazy!
I didn't see it coming, but the pot quickly went from cold to boil
Something triggered a reaction, then tossed in some oil!
She ain't ever pulled a knife!
She kills me, but watching Cleveland beat Golden State was almost worth my life!!!

♥

## Staying live (after RickyDesktop)

(S.R.A.) Staying alive, a sword swipe and a banjo
Species Rhyme Animal (Who?), alter ego
Revived by paramedics in ambulances
Shocked back to life, no second chances (Nope!)
Parked outside, near the venue
Fresh to death, as we continue
Sold my soul, a priceless toll
Fortune and fame, no righteous goal (uh hun)
Our family and friends all congratulated (All Right!)
But spectators and perpetrators, so angry we made it (Boo!)
A song about nothing, is far from unique
I heard it on TikTok, this crazy beat!
On my daughter's iPod, I asked 'Who is this?'
Props to RickyDesktop, handle yo' business!
Not even a rapper, but had to drop bars
Used GarageBand, just to jam in my car! (Yeah!)
So here we are
Species Rhyme Animal, just trying to stay alive
Revived by a dope beat… (Why? Why? Why?)
My rhymes are your prize!

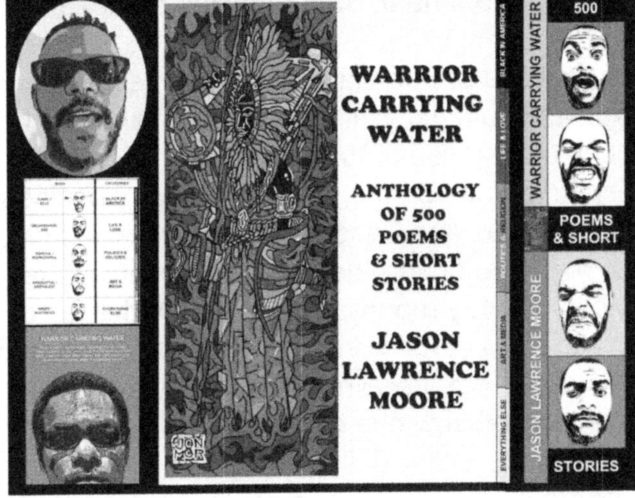


Species Rhyme Animal
Eats beets like a vegetable
Call me insane
Like a Zombie on brains! (Ahhhh!)
Nobody from nowhere
With no claim to fame!
Ride beats like cars, trains, and airplanes! (All Aboard!)
Don't need no hype, I'm just in to win this!
Flow off the dome, no need to pen this!
Remember SRA, add him to your hit list
All I need is beats and some fans to witness… (Barz!)

**Sucker MCs**

I'm Cinnamon Toast Crunch
You're Chex mix, yuck
Wanna battle me? Good luck!
I'll give you a head start: Bragging on my flow is my part
Slander and delusions of grandeur is yours
But your flow's Ambien, all I hear are snores!
From the crowd, but some are mad loud with the boos
The Champion MC is me, but hey, nice shoes!
My flow's extra-terrestrial
Rhymes beyond nebulous, they're celestial
What's my motivation and drive?
I'm just doing what I love, and I'm happy to be alive
The human race is chase, and the prey is our dreams
In my sleep, I hunt, trap, and clap at these Sucker MCs

My rhymes are so vintage, that I'm fearsome, like medieval dentists
No Novocain, so y'all can feel this, far from the richest or realist
I cooked, so you gotta do the dishes!
Ginzu rhymes on the cut, I make it my business
Cell phones and Facebook, way too many pictures
Lotto losers go into debt, to scratch away their wishes
Mess with my money, moves you to the top of my shit list
Try to holla at my honey, makes you a first round draft pick on my hit list!
We olly-oopin, hoopin', with fade aways, making swishes
Y'all whole crew chain game lame, on the side of the road, diggin' some ditches
She keeps jockin' & flockin', dawg come get yo' missus!
Jokers talking goons and goblins, are profoundly lacking
Cuz I'm Zeus, releasing the Kraken, always packin'
Desert eee's, tote the scope, camo'ed in Mossy Oak…

I'm a spirit, haunting these jokers like a ghost
It hard for me to bust without boasts
My rhyme's so dope, feens scheme to listen to everything that I ever spoke!
Reciting my lyrics, like its some shit **THEY** wrote, something like an oath
And I'm something like Tyler, with a legion of fight club blokes
So charismatic, I got these jokers making me soap!
Lines so addictive, I'm in the streets like some coke
Not what you think, rather the ubiquitous carbonated drink
You'll buy a few two liters, and not even think - twice
Since I was a tike, I melted microphones manufactured by Fisher Price!
In my adolescence, I was twice as nice
When I was younger, I had the Motts
But now I'm older, I need more than apple sauce
Its like my plane crashed, years ago, on an deserted island like Lost
Dharma initiative, stuck in a cave, I'm just a slave to the clock.

## Sweet Sixteen

WikiLeaks when he speaks
Transformed MCs into geeks
Like Norm and Cliff Clavin, got 'em revisiting my bars for weeks!
At Cheers drinking beers, Corona and Michelob
I spit fire, y'all drool rigmarole!
Cuz everywhere I go, I hear onomatopoeia!
OOH, AHH, WOW, every time they see a…
Player wearing gators, and driving a two seater
Lyrical bliss is this, big-ga-dee-blasting out your speakers!
See, we endangered creatures
**S**pecies **R**hyme **A**nimal
When 'Sucker Emcees' bite, I'm dislocating mandibles!
To battle me is dangerous
Just go, run on ice with scissors, suicide is painless!
**YOU** wanted to be famous!
Me, I want the loot
Stay fresh with Zest, Crest, and Brut!
No cursing in my rhymes, set the example for the youth!
I only spit the truth
In these sweet 16's
**Supreme Being, Lyrical Dream, Microphone Fiend!**

Illustrated by
Keisha Marie Moore

## The 'internets'

I 'Googled' truth, but didn't find any answers
I looked up my symptoms, and found a dozen different cancers
I wasn't looking for porn, but it found me twice!
Its amazing how much (of it) is free, lust used to have a price!
I read about history, some was new, but most I'd heard
I found some scripture, and studied the word
I scrolled through today's news, but most of it was just gossip
So many advertisements, from companies seeking a profit
Social media was cool at first, but now it seems like a chore
Pictures, memes, opinions, and the same old stuff that I just saw before!
I don't really care, about what my family and friends just ate
Or how cute their kids and pets are, how they spend money, or where they went out on a date
Indulgence is the new normal, the 'world wide web' is a scab, and we're all just anxious pickers
We're just digital versions of those drivers who's cars are all covered in bumper stickers!

♥

**The Media**

The devil's in the details
Walking on a beach
I picked up thoughts, like some seashells
When you don't have to worry about the rent
Or interest on credits cards
It's easy to expand your horizons
And focus your gaze on the stars
The rich have problems too, but unlike the poor
They are happier, live longer, and are immune to the lure
Of the media's fishing line
Spend **all** of your money and **all** of your time
Do what we say, buy what we sell, and don't save a dime!
Don't read between the lines
Because what you might find
Would bring back the protests of the 1960's, and put our investors in a bind!
We the newspapers, magazines, networks, "internets", and "entertainment" masters
Don't need subliminal advertising, to create disasters
You think you control your fate and own your soul?
No, we tell you who to vote for, and plan all of your fiscal goals!
Thanks to us, you know more about Marilyn Monroe
Than about the history of the world, and where you taxes go!
Don't be mad, it's all by design, and you have no control
We tell you everything that **WE** need you to know!
We're the modern day equivalent of the Medieval Church
And even though you can use the internet, to search
When you decide to look for truth, and question our bait
We'll trigger a pop-up ad, with our spyware, and make you wait!

## The Struggle

Living outside the bubble
Ain't got no truck, must take the bus
X said it best, Plymouth Rock landed on us!
Steve Wonder, so what's the fuss?
Beep Beep / Beep Beep / Beep Beep / Beep Beep
Shame on you, Nino Brown, slanging crack from a Jeep!
Livin' just enough for the city
But better off than most, what a pity!
Paralyzed by fear
Too scared to leave your career?
Got too many bills to pay?
So that's mostly why you stay?
If I jump and follow my dream
And my parachute fails, then I'll plummet and scream!
Wishing that I had counted my blessings legit
The other grass was greener, 'cuz it was fertilized with shit!
But what if I can fly?
Take a chance, and try
You miss 100% of the shots that you **don't** take
Gotta break some eggs, before you can bake a tasty cake!
The struggle is just another hurdle, that you have to get around
So get over it, get under it, or just knock that shit down!

♥

**Top Ten Musical Memories**
(my age)

1. Michael Jackson's Thriller - 12/2/1983 (7) **Everyone** in America watched it - at school the next day, our teacher said it was amazing, my grand parents said that it was amazing, even the folks at church were talking about it - that will never happen again.

2. Purple Rain by Prince - 1984 (8) On my porch in a suit, in the middle of the summer during the middle of the week. Miami vice was popular, so I didn't have any socks on, just penny loafers. A WTLC radio personality named Vicki Buchanan rented the house next door (the house on the left if you're facing the fairgrounds, or her mother lived there - I'm not certain - I was 8!). I had a crush on her, and she mentioned that she liked Prince on the radio. So I borrowed my brother's boom box and waited for her to come home from her radio shift, to wave 'hi' to her - and blasted a cassette tape recording of Purple Rain to get her attention and say 'hi'.

3. The Fat Boys Are Back - 1985 (9) A rainy Saturday afternoon, hanging out in my older brother Johnny's room. I got to be the DJ - playing records, recording songs off the radio onto cassette tapes - we had an actual record (12" vinyl) of the Fat Boys Are Back record - Human Beat Box (no instrumentals – incredible!). I spent hours replaying the same record while using a toothbrush to cleaning my canvas Nikes, while Johnny was at his desk working on his latest art project (in about three hours, he turned a pizza box into the Millennium Falcon from Star Wars!)

4. Earth Wind & Fire -1981 (5) Sitting in the back of our VW Bus eating a peanut buster parfait without peanuts (yeah, I was a picky little guy), I heard, '...Let this groove, set in your shoes, stand up, alright! The boogie down... let's groove tonight!' The speaker in cars in the 1980's did not do that song justice! When every I hear that song on the radio, I still lose my mind! Mom was taking us to Dairy Queen after going swimming or going to the movies.

5. Computer Love by ZAAP - 1986. (10) At the Skating rink, I just figured out how to skate around the rink without falling down, and then I heard – 'Hey lady... let me tellll you whyyy... I can't liiiive my lifeeee, without you!' I was like, who/what is this?

6. UTFO - Roxanne Roxanne - 1984 (8) - We were going to my first rap concert, and UTFO was coming to town. We went to either Value City or Lafayette Square, and Johnny and I got track suits - mine was dark red, and I think Johnny's was dark blue. WTLC didn't play rap music on the radio at the time, but I remember our Dad (John Sr.) dropping us off at the Hoosier Dome, and hearing "Roxanne Roxanne" live.

7. 1986 Black Expo free outdoor concert (10) I had heard Rufus' "Tell me something good" on the radio before, but, at that concert, standing near a speaker, the bass line bounced around my chest, and the breathing part was crazy, 'whoo-ooo-whoo-whoo-ooo-whoo!' I remember everyone was just dancing and having a good time.

8. Sophomore year Navy Midshipman cruise 1995 - San Diego, CA (19) on a bus driving back from a long day at the Camp Pendleton (the Marine Corps base) after running 10 miles in combat boots and in full gear with a rifle. 50 college kids from different schools all over the country from various backgrounds, we were all just glad that it was the weekend. I heard one kid tell the buss driver to 'turn it up, this is my jam!' Immediately, everyone on the bus started all singing along (at the top of our lungs) to Seal's Kiss from a Rose. It was my second favorite Navy moment.

9. 2001 - USS Halyburton (FFG 40) - (24) We were just returning home from a 6 month Counter Drug Operations deployment off the cost of Columbia. Everyone was home sick and anxious to get back to Mayport, FL. A few nights before we just completed the 24 hours needed to transit through all of the Panama Canal's water locks. I had the morning watch (4am-8am), as the officer of the deck (OOD), and lead a crew of five guys on the bridge while Captain and the rest of the crew slept. Every morning, the OOD got to wake up the crew by playing a song of their choice over the 1MC (a PA system for the ship). Keisha had sent me a CD with a bunch of Motown songs a few weeks before, and I choose "Signed Sealed Delivered" by Stevie Wonder. Everyone from the captain to the cooks in the kitchen thanked me and said that I pick the best wake up song ever! - the highlight of my Navy Career – LOL!

10. Happy Birthday by Stevie Wonder - January 1983 (7) - Mom and Dad took us out of school, and we drove to Washington D.C. (from Indianapolis) in our VW Bus. We kept playing Stevie Wonder's song on the radio over and over again - there and on the way back. Steve Wonder wrote the song and pushed to make MLK Day a national holiday. President Ronald Regan (who originally opposed the bill), signed the bill into law on November of 1983 after it passed a vote in the Senate: Yea: 78 to Nay: 22). I don't remember much about the rally other than how cold it was. But I'll never forget the song.

## Vice is but a nurse of agonies

We live in a time of crisis
Scrolling social media feeds, constantly on our mobile devices
Governments and corporations keep manipulating the prices
Media spotlights are fickle, what ever happened to the Tea Party and ISIS?
It's ashamed, we complain, as they explain, why the hue that rice is
Is indelible, so incredible, that y'all still believe in the construct of whiteness…
If racism just made up, then why can't can we just eliminate this virus?
Nurses of agonies are vices
Wish that I could be cursed, just like Midas
But instead of gold, everyone I touched
Would have enough, and abstain from all forms of discrimination, is that asking too much?

**Watchmen**

Who watches the Watchmen?
Tales from the Black Freighter often
Foreshadow the current plot
Attacking heroes' egos, taking all that they got!
Absolute power lacks compassion
Why beg for forgiveness, when more questions need asking?
The end is never nigh…
Clouds in sky appear low, whenever I fly
Technology, courage, happiness, and peace breed apathy
Poverty, sickness, and pain are unknown tragedies
Weapons only fear unemployment.

**When did reality become fiction?**

Fake butter
Fake cheese
Fake asses
Fake degrees
When did our desire for reality become fiction?
Our truths a depiction
Jesus is a con, but Marvel comics we praise?
In lieu of church, we binge watch Game of Thrones for days
And hang onto every word of a conman
Charlatan, bigot, misogynist, with an obvious spray tan
Put value into things, but not people
Spend hundreds of thousands on a mortgage, then hundreds more at Home Depot
While there are billions still suffering, I won't get too specific
But when history looks back at babies dying at the US border, we'll all be complicit!
More focused on our next latte or gadget
Addicted to mobile technology, like magic
Under the spells of Facebook, Amazon, and Google
Sharing our deepest desires and secrets, with our willing approval
Searching for products, acceptance, and porn to feed our desire
True to God's promise though, most don't know, that we're all already on fire!
Frogs in a pot of water, that's incrementally boiling
Long days and hours wasted, constantly toiling

## When the stars fall

When the stars fall
From their highest heights
Was their journey and sacrifice, worth the price?
When gravity/reality dragged them down from orbit
How do they feel, when the paparazzi rushes to report it?
Those with coveted amounts of fortune and fame
Rather enjoyed the fruits of their labor, but then complained
About all of the unwanted attention, responsibility, and role model status
I would give them a tip, but alas, the future is cashless…

## Why ain't you packing?

Even when the news is a hoax
There are millions of ignorant folks
Posting comments and expressing their freedom of speech
Following today's headlines, they might be tempted to drink bleach…
Some say, that after the next election, we'll see a major change
But American history repeats, and its government is strange
Think we'll get equality, respect, and reparations?
While immigrants are being locked in cages, and Native Americans are still living on reservations?
Even in the 'Information Age,' common sense maybe lacking
I'm moving to Canada, brothas and sistas, why ain't you packing?

**Why is my Cable bill $100 more?**

(Me on the phone with the cable company... less their words)
Why is my cable bill $100 more?
...No, no, no, y'all didn't say that bullshit before!
...Yes! I checked my account online!
...uh-hun, the rep said I'd lose the rest of the premium channels, and that's fine,
But how am I paying $100 more **THIS** month WITHOUT HBO?
...(sigh)...I don't want Showtime, It. Doesn't. Have. My. Show!
...Yes, it was last month, and I spent THIRTY SEVEN minutes waiting on my phone,
I'd cancel this shit real quick, if it weren't for Game of Thrones!
...Pu-put me on hold? Again? Hell no! Wh-Wh-What's your name?
...Okay, (eyes closed, fingers pinching the bridge of my nose) let me speak to your manager,
y'all need to make my payments the same!
...<Beep> Ain't this a trip? I'm on hold and they're playing elevator music on the other end!
<Click> Oh no they didn't, just hang up on me again!!!

**Words become movements**

Movements begin with words, that are written on paper
Santa Claus didn't exist, until he was written by his maker!
An anonymous poet (Clement Clarke Moore), posted a poem in a newspaper, in 1823
Before then, there was no mystical man, delivering presents worldwide with glee!
No eight reindeer, and no Christmas tree
Before 2005, most parents had more disposable wealth
Then a self published book appeared, called 'Elf on the Shelf'
The biggest con yet, came from a group of genius/crooks
They got us paying to rent and watch movies that used to be DC and Marvel comic books!

## Write. Every. Day.

Write. Every. Day.
These thoughts in my head
Jumped out of bed
Damn, I forgot what I said!
Scribble notions, dreams, hustles, schemes
Words are drugs, and I ain't nothing but a fiend!
I never wanna quit
Another thought, finna take a hit!
Damn, ain't this a trip?
Side of the road, I'm late again
Pulled over an hour ago, still writing in my pad with a pen!
I wish that this steering wheel would bend...
I must have caught something, I gotta take a sick day <cough> Ah-hem
Instead of PowerPoint, Excel, Zoom meetings and conference calls
I'm writing rhymes and songs on the walls
Fuck porn, imma make these words cum!
Beat my mind raw, until my head is chafed and numb
Nouns, adjectives, gerunds, and verbs
Trying to write some new shit, that nobody's ever-ever heard!
To make you laugh, piss you off, or even make you cry
Or think, 'this dude ain't shit,' or even question why?
I won't live forever, but my words will never die!

## Zealots

We believe in Jedis, Avengers, and Ayra Stark
But God, Allah, Buddha and reality are somehow too far apart?
They fear Thanos, Darth Vader and the Night King
But shun religious people, who do the same thing?
My Christian religion does not resemble me
If Christ is 'white', I'm brown see?
Our world is much older, than a few thousand years
Yet the threat of hell, allows a privileged few, to rule by fear?
What of the unjust who steal, lie, and lust?
POTUS never paid taxes, but we're still worried about all the other stuff?
Do they get an advance on utopia?
Want for not, and feast on a cornucopia?
Columbus and Magellan's legacies remain (intact)
And so does the pain (if you're black)
We would never enslave, impose, and destroy lives just to promote our own
Then again, maybe we should....

# PART V: EVERYTHING ELSE (408-513)

Top 75 = ♥

## 2 Samages

A brotha like me needs two Samages!
Meat, cheese, and bacon, or even Manwiches!
Come lunchtime, Imma put in damages!
Went down to the kitchen, to get a little grub
Made two Samages/John Montagu/One love!
Low on dough and bread, Imma use the heel
That's first and last piece, because I 'keep's' it real!
Two ain't enough, so I grabbed a jar of jelly
Bread and peanut butter, get in my belly!
Grilled cheese and roast beef
Is delicious beyond belief!
Don't rush, that soup just might burn your lips
Wrap 'em up in wax, then grab a bag of chips!

## 9K Seiko Gold

By today's comparison, this may sound strange
As a kid, our school's fundraiser, was selling gold chains!
Seiko Jewelry, nine carats of 'fools' gold
Sell ten, and then you could win, a piece of your very own to show!
I sold a total of 40, so the chains on my neck numbered fo'
The very next week, my brother said, 'My chain's tarnished bro!'
And 39 other friends and family, all began to complain
About the quality of their rings, charms, bracelets and chains
One by one, they each showed me their marks, rashes and stains!
Word spread, as I shared their dread, I was filled with frustration and shame
Two of my ropes turned brown, another one broke, and the last one fell down the drain!
I called the company and my school to complain
And I tried to get some refunds or set up an exchange
They explained, that I should have read the fine print, so technically, I was solely to blame!
I felt so taken advantage of and ashamed
Tarnished: my reputation and Seiko's 9K gold chains...

## A jellyfish that lives forever?

Turritopsis dohrnii is an immortal jellyfish
Instead of dying, it simply does this:
Its tentacles retract, its body shrinks, and then it floats down to the ocean floor
And reverts back to being a kid again, and it lives once more!
Barely 1/4 of a inch in size
The only immortal creature ever known, it has an infinite number of lives!
Provided it doesn't get eaten, or attacked by surprise!

## A rectangle is not a square

A square is a rectangle, but a rectangle is not a square
How can injustice here, affect others over there?
Perspective, hearing becomes selective, whenever justice is needed
Talk becomes action, after words once written, are preceded
By feelings and ideas, you know what needs to be done, so do it!
Revolutions begin with sparks, that soon ignite fluids
Flames fed by fuel, and then maintained by invisible elements
We don't need dead presidents, blue donkeys or red elephants!
Change can be mercurial or glacial, so what's your motivation?
Are you the catalyst, solution, or ruination?

## Alleyway

Back in the alley, when I first got at this
Cats clawed at the surface of an abandoned mattress
An utter gutter vermin flow, that reeked like rat piss
Broken glass and plastic littered our path, so tragic
Weeds split the pavement into uneven surfaces
Faded ancient graffiti covered the fences in cursive
Malt liquor, oil, and antifreeze filled the potholes
Power lines decorated with sneakers and tattered clothes

## Ample alliterations assassinating amateurs

Smacking and serving suckers severely, on this sleazy G track
When words don't work, resort to pushing wigs back!
Armed with ample alliterations, assassinating amateurs
Prepared to penetrate these pussies, with prophylactic parameters
Raising a ruckus routinely, without risking repercussions
Create and deconstruct careers, constantly without using crutches
Breaking busters bravado, while barely breaking a sweat
Pros just jockin' and jealous, cuz they can't beat me in a Jeep or a jet
Everybody's evil and greedy, throwing elbows to noses and eyes
Now they see stars in the sky, watch blood, snot, and slobber fly!
My diction is fiction, ditching and digging dames at the same time
Got my gold digging finger itching, good with a gat, but great when I rhyme!
Middle finger to most M.C.'s, making cacophony on the mic
Hoping that haters bring heat, conflict is real hip hop right?
Lotto losers liable to finally learn a lesson
Something for nothing suckers, sometimes sue, then second guess when...

**An emoji will probably be our prophesy!**

In nearly every room of our home, there is a shrine that we diligently praise
Sacrifices of time and attention, for hours and days
Televisions, tablets, and phones, that we all hold, ever so near and dear
Reflections of our deepest dreams, manifestations of darkest fears
News, entertainment, video games, even sports in our basement!
Slowly over time, somehow became a sufficient replacement
For God, spirituality, values, and conversation
Now, one's expression is limited to headlines, characters, and punctuation!
Meme's, hashtags, and social media philosophy
The future's doomed: an emoji will probably be our final prophesy!

## Atychiphobia (fear of failure)

Lost
Cost
Time
Rhyme
Blind
Truth
Believe
Grieve
Facts
Melt
Wax
Lies
Die
Focus
Hopeless
Question
Why?

## Banana Now N' Laters

Banana Now N' Laters
Were once my least favorite flavor
I had to run out of cherry and grape
Before I could really appreciate the taste!
Not quite like any banana that I had ever had
The last pack, at the bottom of my Penny candy bag
After a few squares, I realized that they weren't THAT bad...
So I'd chain eat them in distress
Sometimes I'd even eat them, if I was ever pressed
From Naptown to Decatur
I used to even eat them with tiny bits of paper!
Tell me how it felt?
When a whole pack would melt?
Banana Now N' Laters
Kids in the urban jungle, we were like some alligators!
Chomp a piece
Now at least
You got something sweet
Around your tongue and teeth!
But my friends didn't witness
All of the cavities that I got, filled at the dentist
To this day, I still have metal fillings in my mouth
Caused by my childhood Now N' Later addiction - no doubt!

**Big Mac (Remix!)**

Gimme two all beef patties
Please somebody grab me!
Some of that special sauce
I'll pay almost any cost
Add in some lettuce and some cheese
A few pickles and onions please!
All on a sesame seed bun
We about to have some fun!
Better make it a meal, with some fries and a Coke
McDonald's is out here filling bellies, dreams and hopes!

Two all beef patties
Special sauce, lettuce, cheese
Pickles, and onions on a toasted bun with some sesame seeds
Lunch or dinner, but that's not all that I need
Let-me-get a Coke, fries, a straw, with some extra napkins please!
At the 'drive thru,' but sometimes I like to go inside
To see 'Big Mac Makers,' and look them square in their eyes!
To thank them for their service, and to my delight and surprise…
I looked in the bottom of bag, and they hooked me up with some **Extra French Fries!**

## Black Beauty

When I let off the clutch
The torque made her blush
As I shift, her tires chirped
Backwards I lurched
She loves the rush!
Hundreds of horses moaned in heat and lust
When my foot pushed the pedal
To the metal
We burn rubber
In the rearview mirror, we glance at each other
Her steering wheel's a helm, each tire's a rudder
My land yacht's floating
Naturally aspirated, large horsepower boastin'
Candy painted, black beauty stallion
Old school coupe, sheet metal profiling
Thermodynamic antics
Eight cylinders slanted
Engine goes suck/squeeze/bang/blow!
Perfect air/fuel/spark/exhaust ratio
Pistons crank, to empty her tank
She's so greedy, taking all of my time and bank!

## Chess Pieces

All 32 pieces of Chess
Are slaves to two masters, competing to be the best
Invented in India, in the sixth century AD
Play someone and soon learn, all of their 'idiosyncrasies'
Black is really brown, and never goes first
Half are Pawns, who can become royalty, only after enduring the worst
Strategies, sacrifice and calculated moves
Play offense and defense, but choose wisely or you will lose!
Capture souls, in a manifest destiny to dominate the board
Seeking to be loved, feared, and praised, just like the almighty Lord!
A game that can yield more moves, than every atom in the universe
If you like war and politics, this board could be your church!
Knights and Bishops fight/flee in L-patterns and diagonally
Vertical/Horizontal Rooks who don't castle, may soon become casualties
Kings and Queens can do anything, and go almost anywhere
But are still prisoners in the same 64 squares.

## Christmas Eve in the rain

Christmas Eve in the rain, selling trees
Cold to the bone, soaked boots and coat sleeves
Three remain, alas, who is gonna buy one of these?
They're all on sale
You never can tell
Some wait until the very last minute
On the last day, I'll gladly trim it
And tie it on top of their car, for free

## Cookie Thief

Waiting for the cookies to bake
I got the spatula resting on an empty plate
Made a dozen chocolate chip cookies, and I'm gonna try to eat 8!
Waited until the kid was asleep, this gonna be great!
We don't have to share
A cookie here, a cookie there…
Heading up stairs, with a dust buster for the crumbs in the bed
My wife's upset, did she just hear what I said?
Did I say that I was gonna eat 8 out loud, or did she do the math?
Yup, I soon felt her wrath
If I baked a dozen
And there's 8 on the plate...wait...wasn't…
There are already four cookies missing!
'You already ate four cookies? Oh no you didn't!?'
I confessed, while she was getting dressed, right
I had a moment of weakness, walking up stairs earlier that night
I broke the news to my wife
That I might just have a split personality
Part man, part Cookie Monster, so that's my secret reality!
She didn't believe me, as she glanced unconvinced
I told her to check the stairs, for some crumbs of evidence
If she kisses me, then the beast will cease hence
My story worked, as I sneaked in two more cookies
Six remained, then she growled and mistook me
'Wait, how come I only get three cookies?'

## Craigslist Conundrum

I got things I want to do
And places where I need to be
But I've been waiting for hours on you
To give **<u>YOU</u>** a couch for free!
This sectional, has been cleaned by a professional
I texted you twice, no answer, your character is questionable…
I bent my schedule, and had to skip church, lord God…
I vacuumed it well, and then moved it out into the garage
I'm about to post it on Craigslist again
It cost me $600 in 2010…
I'm about to give it away for free, and then hit send
Had 20 people interested, but you said that you were ready to go
But I've been waiting for hours on you, and you are still a no show...

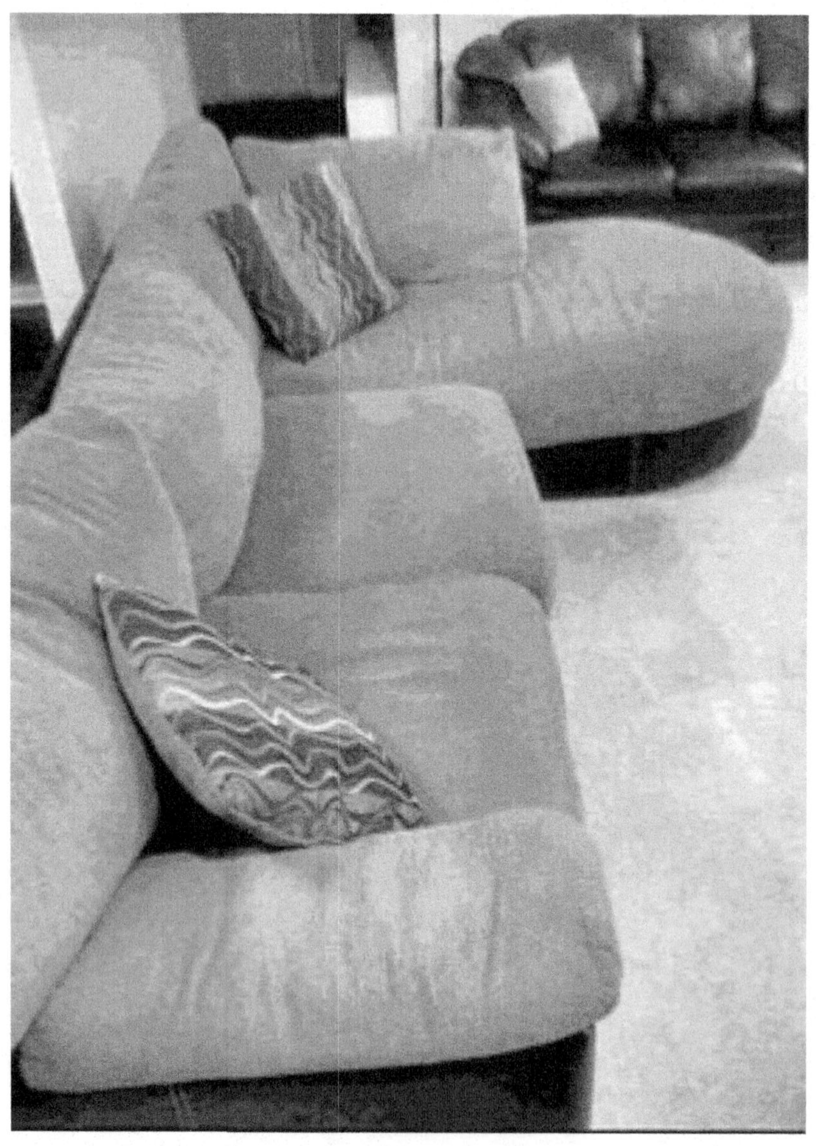

## Crisis of confidence

This last crisis of confidence
Hit me like a ton of bricks
At work and at home, they don't think I'm shit!
My work is never good enough
So my life at home also sucks
Maybe everyone is right, and I'm simply just not good enough…
I give my best, toward love and my career
But it's still not enough, I fear
The only thing I seem to do well is fail
My good intentions soon became bricks in a path to hell!
Turning 40 and life's not going too well
I'm supposed to be at my prime
But I keep fucking up all the time!
I never get the benefit of the doubt
On my second strike, one more mistake and I'll strike out!
I wish that there was a button to reset
And everyone could just forget
Or remember back when, life was a piece of cake
But all that remains is the pressure, to not make one last mistake
Why can't I be better?

## Crypto & Penny Stock

Dropped a G on some crypto and penny stock!
With Bitcoin and AMC, imma buy my whole block!
Got Coinbase and Robinhood on a daily watch!
Show 'em how I reinvest that dividend pot! (Pot!, Pot!)
I own fractions of some blue chips!
Motley Fool is useless!
Send Dogecoin to the moon! (Howl!!!)
Better get you some Ether soon!
Bought Ford at $4
Now it's gonna blow! (Kapow!)
Looking for the next Amazon, watch my money grow!
Low P/E Ratio, high market Cap
Buy low and sell high, this that legal trap!
Buy when there's blood in the street
On my Warren Buffett tip!
Exchanged some altcoin, now I'm about to take a trip!
Crypto and Penny Stock! (Aye!)
Crypto and Penny Stock!

**Crypto & Penny Stock Remix**

Told y'all Doge was moon bound, but you had doubt
Acting all confused, like, 'Wills, what you talkin' bout?'
Gonna hold on for dear life (HODL), or $10, then cash out
Peep game from the OGs and keep my name out ya mouth!

**Stockem Boughtem**

D-D-D Dub-B, on the M.I.C
Not a fan of this so called 'cryptocurrency'
Pigs get slaughtered, dinosaurs go extinct
This Crypto game is, rather unique!
Skies the limit Doge!
Get like me, buy before market close!
And give a pound to my hound!
StockemBoughtem, do you hear that sound?

Warren Buffett

Fast cash won't last?
One share of Berkshire Hathaway A
Is worth more than $420k!
Never split!
Buy and sit!
That's how the rich stay rich! (Barz!)
Duracell, GEICO, Fruit of the Loom, and Dairy Queen (Dilly Bars!)
Been taking y'all's money for decades… You know what I mean?

Elon Musk

Elon Musk!
In Doge we trust!
CEO of Boring and Space X (What?)
Made crypto famous with a text
Your favorite rappers promote Tesla, but I don't pay them a dime!
My net worth's $170-something billion, that should be a crime
My kid's so rich, that I can't even pronounce his name!
Crypto mutt, buy it up, money is just a game!

Mark Cuban

M.C.? Oh! Mark Cuban, that's me!
LotusNotes, Broadcast.com, Dallas Mavericks, Shark Tank…
Get NBA fines so often, I could start a bank!
Buy some crypto, get rich quick soon
HODL- Dogecoin to the moon!
Trill…Trill… how's that?

## Cure for being pissed

I go to work
Boss is pissed
Client's pissed
Friends are pissed
I come home
Kid is pissed
Wife is pissed
The cat is pissed
What is this?
I lifted the lid on the toilet, and there was a fish!
Floating dead
Now it all makes since.. an idea popped into my head
I flushed it quick
Washed my hands, that is it!
I gave my daughter some hugs and kisses
Then told my wife, that I got dinner and the dishes
She smiled and ran upstairs
Changed the mood and cleared the air
I asked my princess all about her day
Non-stop talk about school work and play
I'm still amused how everything she says sounds just like a song
Attitude is contagious, don't stay angry for too long!

**Dead presidents buried in my mattress...**

Buy the rumor, sell the news
Make a profit, if you choose!
Stocks, bonds, and cryptocurrency to buy and keep
No jammy, but like Miami, I still keep that heat!
Don't trust banks, so I stash my cash and receipts under my seat!
And my freezer's were I mash the rest of my stash
Just thawed a block, so I'm about to hawk some hard cold cash!
While I waited, my fleeting needs were long debated
Decided that I really didn't need to spend or waste it
Tossed it back in the freezer, out of utter frustration
Contemplating my situation, on my kitchen floor, slowly pacing
Am I a miser, a liar, or a bloody fascist?
I ain't earning any interest on those dead presidents, buried deep in my mattress
Naw, remember when you bought that Posturpedic?
That you thought, that you really needed?
For your slip disc, when they ran your card, it triggered a fraud
Alert, at that fancy furniture store, your wife was so embarrassed, she whispered oh my God...
Your voice cracked
When you told the manager, that you could handle that
You called Bank of America, and got an automated response, what's up with that!?
When the rep said that you had to call in advance, to spend more than $2K, you were 'flummoxed'
That that vein on your forehead was about to bust!
As the account representative reviewed your last five transactions and stuff
You explained that you could cover the entire expense
The representative said, "I see here that you haven't bought a mattress in 10 years since..."
You say, "I know, that's why I'm trying to get a new one today!"
"But when I used my bank debit card, y'all threatened to take it away!"
The representative apologized and removed the fraud alert so that we could finalize our purchase
Then she asked me to standby by for a brief survey, to comment on her service...

**Deep Cover - Getaway Garden Remix!**

Yeah and you don't stop!
Cuz I gotta cover up my Getaway Garden crops!

When it hits 7 o'clock
Time to cover up my crops
When the temperature drops
Aphids and Hornworms start jockin'
Spray my cucumbers with neem oil often!
And hardened off my plants
So that they have a chance
To grow and bear fruit
We must sow the seeds, to educate the youth!
My garden's so cathartic
From the moment that I started it
It provided psychological relief
From the madness in the world, the drama, the grief!
Chillin' - in my backyard oasis
Travel through time, and various places
The chirps of the birds, the buzzing of the bees!
The heat from the sun, the shade from the trees!
Vibin' with nature, so relaxing and serene
Sippin' on Sangria, all around me green
Vegetation, my education, lessons from mistakes
Sun, seeds, soil, and water, that's all it takes!
To grow your own home, container garden oasis
Go nowhere and grow in many places!

Yeah and you don't stop
Cuz I gotta cover up my Getaway Garden crops!

Visit www.GetawayGardens.com!  Yeahhhhhhhhh!

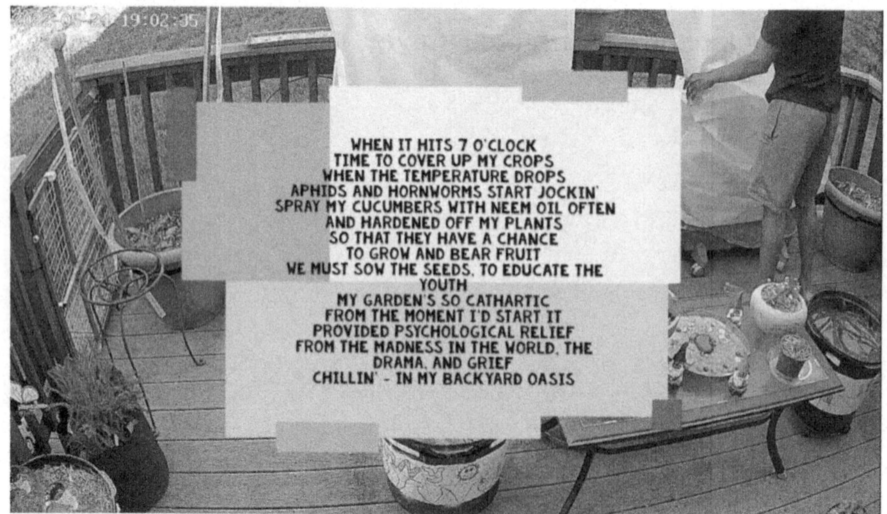

**Do your homework!**

Yeah, Yeah, Yeah! School's in session!
Do your homework! Do your homework!
Girl you gonna learn!
Do your homework! Do your homework!
Boy you gonna learn!

Home from school, grabbed a quick snack!
Put my play clothes on, and put up my backpack!
Grabbed my tablet, and played a few apps
But now its time to study, some figures and facts!
I wanna be the best
Study for this test
Practice makes perfect
Answer questions, with my mind and my time…
Yeah! Solving mysteries, like detectives do with crime
Every time you study, think of this rhyme
Do your homework homie, and stay on your grind!

Yeah, Yeah, Yeah! Do your homework! Do your homework!
Girl you gonna learn!
Do your homework! Do your homework!
Boy you gonna learn!

Got my #2 pencil erasing
Mistakes to correct answers, while I'm replacing
Paragraphs being quoted
With wise words, and the author's name noted
Yeah, correctly in the bibliography
With rhymes so vivid… (ha!), you'd swear its photography
If you closed your eyes, and opened your ears
You'd see these dreams, as the cure for your fears!
Success begins, when you finish your homework
Now rhyme along to my song, and go berserk!

Do your homework! Do your homework! Do your homework!
Girl you gonna learn!
Do your homework! Do your homework! Do your homework!
Boy you gonna learn!

Yeah! Twenty Seventeen, you know what I mean?
Stay in school, make something of yourself!
Words is bond, it is also a noun…

## Dolomite

Way down… in the soil deep!
With the potatoes, rutabagas and other beets!
I enrich with calcium and magnesium to regulate pH levels!
So mix me in good **FOOL**, with your tiny little shovels!
I prevent root rot, and give your plants exactly what they need!
You betta' come see me, before you sow that first seed!
Two to three weeks before planting, just put me in yo' mix!
When you sprinkle me in your lil' containers, please remember this
I don't like the rain, 'cuz it will wash me away!
So pick a day with no wind and some sun, and then maybe I'll stay
I'm $CaMg(CO_3)2$, 'aka' Dolomitic lime
I'm well worth your time, and my price on Amazon is only $5.99!

# $CaMg(CO_3)2$ is...

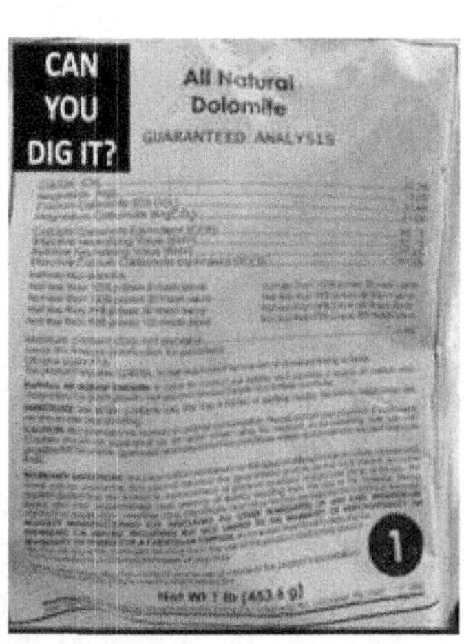

**Dolomite is my name, and regulating pH is my game!**

# DOLOMITE

## Electromagnetic Spectrum

Light waves beyond the rainbow
Infrared scans and radio plays
Ultraviolet black light and bone finding X-rays
What humans can't see, they still believe
Microwaves and gamma radiation retrieved
UHF frequencies entertain and delight
ROY G. BIV, visible colors from left to right

| IR | R | O | Y | G | B | I | V | UV |
|---|---|---|---|---|---|---|---|---|
| Infra Red | Red | Orange | Yellow | green | Blue | Indigo | Violet | Ultraviolet |
| >750 | 750 -609 | 610-589 | 590-569 | 570-500 | 500-465 | 466-432 | 433-400 | <400 |

Wavelength in nanometers (nm)

## Escaping Holes

Never a dull moment
Always working certain, still digging a hole until the shovel's bent
Wondering where the time went
Money spent, fret debt/payments/interest/fees, barely made a dent
We owe more now, than we did back when it was lent!
I wanna stop, just to catch a breath
Can't afford sheets, to bed the cousin of death
Looking up to see the ground
Can't fathom the heights, of the blessed looking down
On us, though our misfortune is a portion
Of their security, our rights and life is an abortion
To these poverty virgins
Corporations and governments extract our dimes, like general surgeons
An inconvenience, to the regent, is a burden
So while they are nervous and purging
We're stacking the scraps, up in our traps
Building steps to climb out, of the mud and crap
As we escape with our family and friend
Up to the level playing field, they are quick to push us back in...

♥

## Even for a tiger, hell hath no fury

So Tiger had a few 'jump-offs'
What's that got to do with Golf?
He was wrong, but smart enough to know to get away
Black man and a white woman, he thought, 'I don't want to end up like O.J.!'
Here's the real story, that the Daily News couldn't print
2:30 in the morning, Mrs. Tiger Woods had a fit!
After snooping through Tiger's phone, she cooked a pot of hot grits
Then woke up the 4X Master's winner, by pouring it all over his Kibbles and Bits!
Now you know why his stroke ain't been the same since!
Elin, in hot pursuit with a Nike nine iron, she chased Tiger down the driveway
With hot grits in your lap, it hard to drive an Escalade!

## Fake Fame

I took some time to read other people's words
Learned all sorts of things, that I never ever heard
I'd rate most first, others second and the third
Thought I was fly, but eventually realized, that I'm just another bird
Unique, but not special or the best
Just pretended, then offended my ego in jest
I've never taken life or myself too seriously
I understand the brevity of life, curiously
As each of my favorite rappers, just a few years my senior
Pass away, each day, it slightly changes my demeanor
Had they never spit or had a hit
Would they still be alive or would this still be it?
Fast life, cash, gold, and VIP liquids and barbiturates
When the fame no longer remains, so goes all your constituents
Before I go, let me leave you with this:
Remember back when people used to be really famous?
Not 15 minutes of lame-less
So talented, that every house in the county knew their name?
Nowadays people become rich and famous virtually, without using their brain
No skill or record deal, but they recorded a video that makes people feel
Going viral, in denial, making millions, but it's just not 'real'

## Fare is fair

On borrowed time
Days past the due date, so I'm
Slowly counting change to pay the fine
It all happened so fast
Full to empty, like a tank of road trip gas
Destinations and celebrations, fare is fair
Side shows, trains, paradise, and hell, I'm already there

## Father Figure (after Tobe Nwigwe)

I wish I was good enough to be on this feature
Tobe, Thought, and Royce, spit like some mythical creatures
I'm just a freshman in awe, with applause, up in the bleachers!
Scratching in my notebook, learning from my favorite subject and teachers
Motivated to write, entertain, educate, and inspire
The spark's been lit, but my flame ain't quite fire
Candle sticks, wicks split, basically my gift ain't melting wax
If I could only quit my job and just do this all day - facts!
But when I do the math, reality and fear hold me back
Long lost on this journey, but I'm still walking the path
Destination unknown
Ten years later, and I'm still writing rhymes on this phone...
A stream of consciousness flow, that just happens to rhyme
The voice in my head, first appeared in my prime
I ignored it for years, until I finally picked up a pen
I have thousands of stories to tell, but where do I begin...

♥

## Fish Bait

You thought you was extraordinary, but you're just barely above average
You hard headed bastard!
The mold's been broken and re-casted in plaster!
History's atrocities and natural disasters
Are mostly man made, but we still believe that God is the cause **and** the cure?
Could it really be that simple, okay, maybe, sure!
Labels, boxes, biases, and division into rich and poor
Bait, tackle, hook, line, and sinker, we still can't avoid the lure
Caught, gutted, sautéed, and filleted
Some say life is just a game, ain't you tired of being played?

## Format

I don't want your pity, shame, admiration, or anger
Can't accept your frustration, capitulation, or danger
I reject your feelings, hatred, and lack of respect
No longer influenced by your tactics, hat tricks, and regrets
Your opinion is irrelevant, concerns unnecessary
As dead as bones in coffins, that strangers bury
You no longer matter, therefore you cease to exist
Our experience together was deleted, ignorance is bliss!

## Ghosts

A candle's flame never casts a shadow
Phantoms in the night, cause a fright, whenever they make a rattle
Fear can be a manifestation of inexplicable truths
Effects and causes
One quickly pauses
Whenever they discover tangible proof
Of ghosts, sounds and light in the darkness, that we don't believe but fear
Light casts no shadows because its not really here!

**Gold Grill**

Hey!  I yelled in a tone angry and dismissive
It took a moment to digest what I had just witnessed
An old man, standing between the legs of a teen
In a shopping mall's food court bathroom, it was the strangest scene
Confused, I saw another dude quickly wash his hands and then go
I waited to get (both of) their attention – WTF, I had to know!
What in the hell is going on, what should I say?
How could this be happen, in the middle of the day?
My curiosity was soon fed
When the old man turned around, here's what he said (to me)
'What in the fuck are you looking at?'
The kid sported a gold grill that read 'LIL' MATT'
As the old man counted a wad of $20's with no gloves
His finger nails were so dirty, that I wished that he had just sold the kid some drugs!
Lil' Matt ignored us both, starring proudly in the mirror and smiling
The old man was humming and counting his money, I was shaking my head and willin'
The kid was pleased and I guess that the old man was right
The rest of the day was a blur, and couldn't sleep later on that night
As I watched them leave, I felt sad for them both
The next day I volunteered to tutor elementary kids in Washington D.C. and inspire hope…

♥

## Green

Green means more than envy
Dollars scream spend me!
My favorite color
Add the hue with blue and it's the picture of our mother
Earth, moss, algae and slime
Yellow and blue's combination is so sublime!
Leaf, olive, grass, pine, apple, pear, pine, shamrock, pickle, sea, basil, chartreuse, fern, mint, shamrock, camo, kelly, pistachio, caterpillar, and spring
That is just 20 descriptions of green.

## Guilty Measures

Washed my hands, but they're still greasy
I didn't expect that life would be so easy
Climates change, strange these times be
Mice and men, both sin to be free
The rich and powerful, sharing both unlikely
Men, women, and children, die in these streets nightly
From addiction, disease, neglect, and envy
Most assailants tend to be familiar, family or friendly
Drawing lines in the sand, stick in hand, so rightly
A part of the problem, I just might be...

**Hello Yellow**

Hello yellow!
Neutral color for baby girls and boys
The less chosen crayon, other hues gets broken like toys
Primary color, no mixing needed
Makes green and orange, whenever it's breeded
This pastel reminds me of Easter eggs
Mellow shades
Scrambled eggs, lemonade, and baked custard
Bananas, butter, and bottles of mustard
Yellow, marigold, chartreuse, butter, butterscotch, blond, sunshine, goldenrod, cream, brass, canary, flax, banana, daffodil, pineapple, ochre, mustard, Dijon, lemon, and corn
20 types of yellow, in more than one form.

### How Prime altered time (and changed the world)

In the space between time and reality, dwells a different version of life
I'm prime, the one designed, to define what's wrong and right
No religion, salvation or damnation
Seeking justice, centuries in the making
Redefined history by finding opportunities within my bloodlines
Sharing technology, traveling into the past, twenty or so dozen times
With messages and gifts, buried around the globe, for each to find
The power to change history and to also free my ancestor's minds
By preventing the Transatlantic slave trade and the Europeanization of the globe
Balancing odds by altering my ancestor's genetic code
We changed reality, but nobody would ever know...

As the Moors in Spain were driven out of Europe in 1492
We all know (in the same year) what Christopher Columbus would do
So a few months prior, I buried weapons and detailed plans that explained everything
In a villa, along the boarder of Portugal and Spain
For a few of my Black Spaniard ancestors to claim
And leverage, to force a coup
Against Queen Isabella and you know who
Then in the early 1500's as the Portuguese first tried to steal our children
I convinced dozens of my ancestors to start building
Thousands of citadels and forts along West Africa's coasts to keep the brutes at bay
The depopulation of hundreds of African nations, failed to take root that day

History must be rewritten
Since their God continues to punish and smitten
The globally majority
From the future, I assumed a moral authority
Studied humanity and invented a technology
To travel back and alter the past 500 years of reality
Half of the world once spoke English or Spanish
But I travelled back in time to eliminate or banish
European plagues that once spread like a viral infection
We kept Europeans in Europe, by teaching the world an invaluable lesson!
Warning them that pale face visitors would steal their land, and ruin life as they once knew it
My African brothers and sisters listened, but the rest of the world just blew it!

## Humpty & Dumpty

Humpty and Dumpty, loved to play ball
Humpty got fouled on a dunk, and the refs gave him the call
The team thought he was done
But Humpty picked himself up, and got the 'And 1'!

With seconds remaining, and his team down by five
Humpty got back on D, and took it all in stride
Dumpty got the rebound, and passed it to Humpty, down the weak side
His coach told him to go for a three
Double teamed, Humpty was trapped at the top of the key!
He made a quick pass
Got the rock back from Dumpty, then called 'Glass'
Banked the ball in, and made a clutch three fast!

All the Kings and Mavericks, each had no fouls to give
Humpty knew that he had to foul or steal, so here's what he did
He ran out of bounds
Then spun back around
Tripped and fell, then cracked all over the ground!
The other team's guard tripped
Then the ball slipped
Then Dumpty managed to grab it real quick!
Dumpty lobbed the ball back to Humpty, with a prayer and a hope
Humpty picked himself up off the court, still leaking fresh yolk
And caught a bounce pass, with 1.3 seconds remaining
Standing at half court, he launched the ball, groaning and straining
Just before the shot clock hit double zero
He scored again, Humpty was a hero!
The Kings won the game by one!

As confetti fell from the rafters, the fans cheered and rejoiced
As Humpty was being interviewed, he started losing his voice
The reporter congratulated him, and asked him what was next, in store
Humpty replied, 'Do you have a dust pan or something? I left it all out on the floor!'

♥ Illustrated by Jason Lawrence Moore

## I ain’t your Supernigga (after Karyn White’s Superwoman)

I've been up all night
Protecting Metropolis from evil and crime
I come home, and again, you're demanding all my time!
That's a luxury that I really can't afford
Maybe if you stopped watching daytime TV and got a fucking job, you wouldn’t be so bored!
Told you 100 times, that I like my eggs scrambled!
And why is the damn house always in shambles?
Forget toast, I stopped at McDonald's for breakfast, plus you know that I hate coffee!
I just want to unwind, and check the news, so please back the hell up off me!
I'd give you a kiss and hug, but dammit, I'm just too weak
Lex Luther tricked my dumb ass again with some Kryptonite, so I can barely speak!

Yeah, I ain’t your Supernigga! ♪♩♫
You said that you had super powers to
Turns out you’re a fucking lie, so what the hell am I gonna do?
The Daily Plant will make me out to be the bad guy, when I finally dump you
And there ain’t no more super women left
But your constant nagging, makes me wish that I was deaf!
Lois Lane never complained
And Wonder Woman gave crazy brain!
With you, it's nag, nag, nag, its driving me insane!
Its always me, me, me, you’re always popping that yang!

The juice is sour, because it expired last week
I got to do the grocery shopping too? Damn, I shouldn't have married no freak!
When we met, you talked a good game
But your "superpowers" were a damn lie, and its really a shame
Cause your body is banging, and in bed you don't hold back
But when it comes to cleaning and cooking, lady you're whack!
So you ‘fought’ through rush hour traffic, just to bring us some fast food?
Cuz I ain't broke you off in a week, now you're all upset and in a foul mood?
I just battled three lunatics from space, who were trapped in some kind of glass
The last thing on my mind right now, is some titties and a piece of ass!
I almost got killed four times this week, and it's only Wednesday
The truth is you're only a human, so what else can I say?

**I lead a herd of dinosaurs, but I'm a mastodon**

I reside in the metropolis
Where the populous
Resembles and envies me
Preachers drinking wine, while thugs sip on some Hennessey
And busters have a tendency
To report on my situation, like they're Wolf Blitzer, and I just bombed an embassy!
But when I got them cornered, they expect mercy and empathy!
So I spit a quick 16, then murk them all lyrically!
My flow grows quickly, like seeds, weeds, and trees in the Amazon
I walk amongst the giants, leading a herd of dinosaurs, but I'm a mastodon!
Extra-terrestrial, vegetable, questionable, sectional, correctional, dawg you speaking gibberish!
I spit bitter words toward your click, flavor similar to black licorice
So worried about what I'm going to say next, that you just shit a brick
Now your face is priceless, pwned, and perfect for a twi-pic!

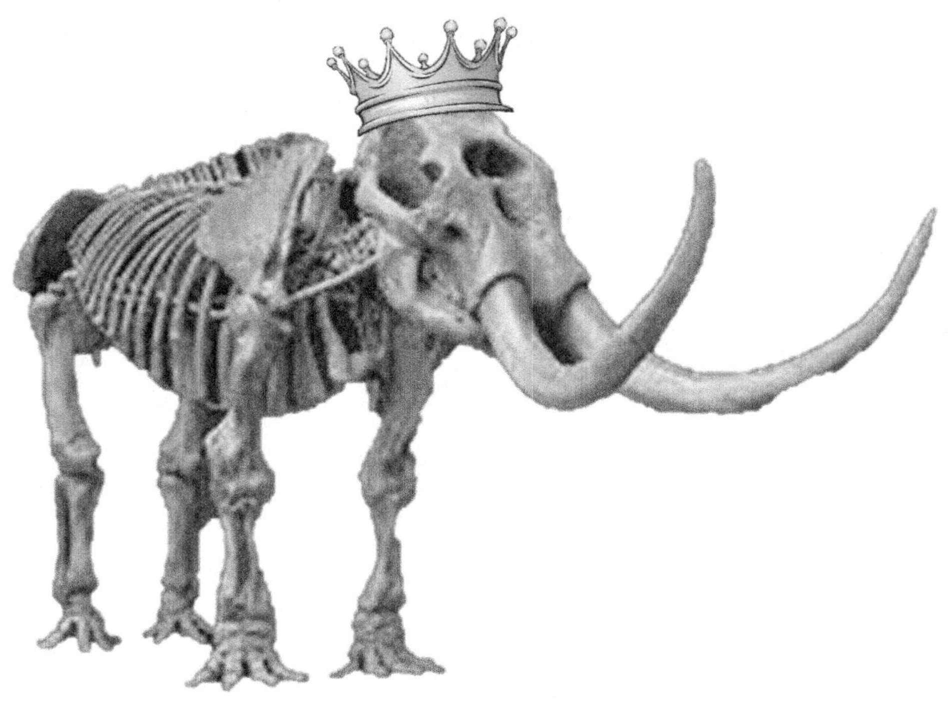

# I tried to create an app

I tried to create an app
Then I thought, who in the hell is going to buy this crap?
I had to delete all of my pictures, videos, and Wazes!
Just to download a new app on my phone on Thursday
To be rich, you basically have to take a dollar from nearly everyone you can
That is Nike, Disney, McDonalds, and Apple's business plan!
It's sounds unrealistic and capitalistic
As brick and mortar stores go out of business, like this quick!
Toys R Us and Payless already went bankrupt
But Amazon wants all y'all's paycheck - when is enough, enough?

## Idle thoughts in bumper to bumper traffic

Traffic stopped, rush hour, waiting for movement
A reminder to write congress for some pavement and traffic improvement
Sometimes I lose it, like important receipts and spare change
Yes, the left lane is open, mash the gas, and I'm off like a rocket
My cell phone's powered off and charging in the cigarette socket
Solving major mysteries, so I'm something like Crockett
In an episode of Miami Vice, that I saw back in the 80's
Used to wear no socks and my suit jacket, just to impress the ladies!
Today, I have a Dodge Charger, so you can keep your Mercedes
I'll drive American steel, until I'm pushing up daisies
I digress, no need to stress my consumer preferences
Nor reminisce on 1980's pop culture references
Just some idle thoughts, off the dome, in the morning rush hour
Off to work, to make some more dough, like water and flour.

**If you don't like tacos, I'm nacho type!**

If you don't like tacos, then I'm 'nacho' type!
I probably 'cheese' wrong for photos, right?
Put me in coach, but not on a Spirit flight!
They charge extra for everything, including baggage right?
Seems everything is extra, and we blindly believe the hype!
I spent three hours watching that Marvel Avengers movie last night
Drank a large coke, and had to get up to pee twice!
When I returned, I was concerned with all the loss of fictional life
Then I realized that I've spent more time watching movies, than preparing for the afterlife…

**Larry Jordan (Michael Jordan's 5'8" older brother)**

We both could play ball
Under 6 feet, wished that I was tall
But you got all the height
And a contract with Nike
I was still wearing buddies
Two strips, man, very ugly!
I used to 'school' you in the yard
You was way too easy to guard!
Taught you all I knew about the game
I'm the G.O.A.T., but you got all the fortune and fame!
I stand five feet and eight inches
When I was in the game, Mike used to ride benches!
In high school, my jersey number was 45
Mike picked 23, because he was still only half as live
One summer, younger brother put in some work
Stepped up his game, and then he had a major growth spurt!
He became a legend, but my feelings ain't hurt
But man, I wish I was tall too...

## Lie and fuss

Unsure of what lies ahead
Tomorrow morning when we hop out of bed
What challenges will we face?
What journeys, which destinations, and how many decisions to make...
Wait, what am I writing?
We're all quarantined, isn't this exciting?
Noooo, it's boring as fuck!
COVID-19, so we're all just shit out of luck!
I still got a full tank of gas in my truck
What's-his-name, same as a cartoon duck
Has daily press conferences, just so he can lie and fuss
The world is in stitches, but the joke is on us!

## Likes

I like the big body Caprices
36 month leases
Fewer polices'
A relationship with Jesus
Khakis with cuffs and creases
Cures for deadly diseases
Twizzlers and Reese's Pieces
Universal health care and tax decreases
New movie releases
Warm sweaters and fleeces
Chicken that's greaseless
These are a few of my favorite things!
I have big dreams
Hold value in people, not things
Consider us knowledge feigns
I only own two pairs of jeans
Gave up watches and rings
Content with what hard work brings
I know why the caged bird sings
I'm focused, like laser beams.

## Lying in Spades

I can't much longer keep up this facade
When I know that hope is just a mirage
My bids 'whist' playing a game of charades
Caused me to renege, like I can't play a game of Spades!
When the cards were dealt
Anger and hopelessness was all I felt
With just one Trump card
We bid six, and I threw it down hard!
To psych out my partner and the competition
Secretly hoping, that we wouldn't fail in our mission
The game was close, so I started talking crap
Collecting the first book, and giving my partner some dap
But in a matter of minutes, the truth became clear
My partner didn't have nothing, and they were whupping...our...rear...
We lost the game and it crushed my pride
My partner was real pissed too, because I lied

# Lying in Spades

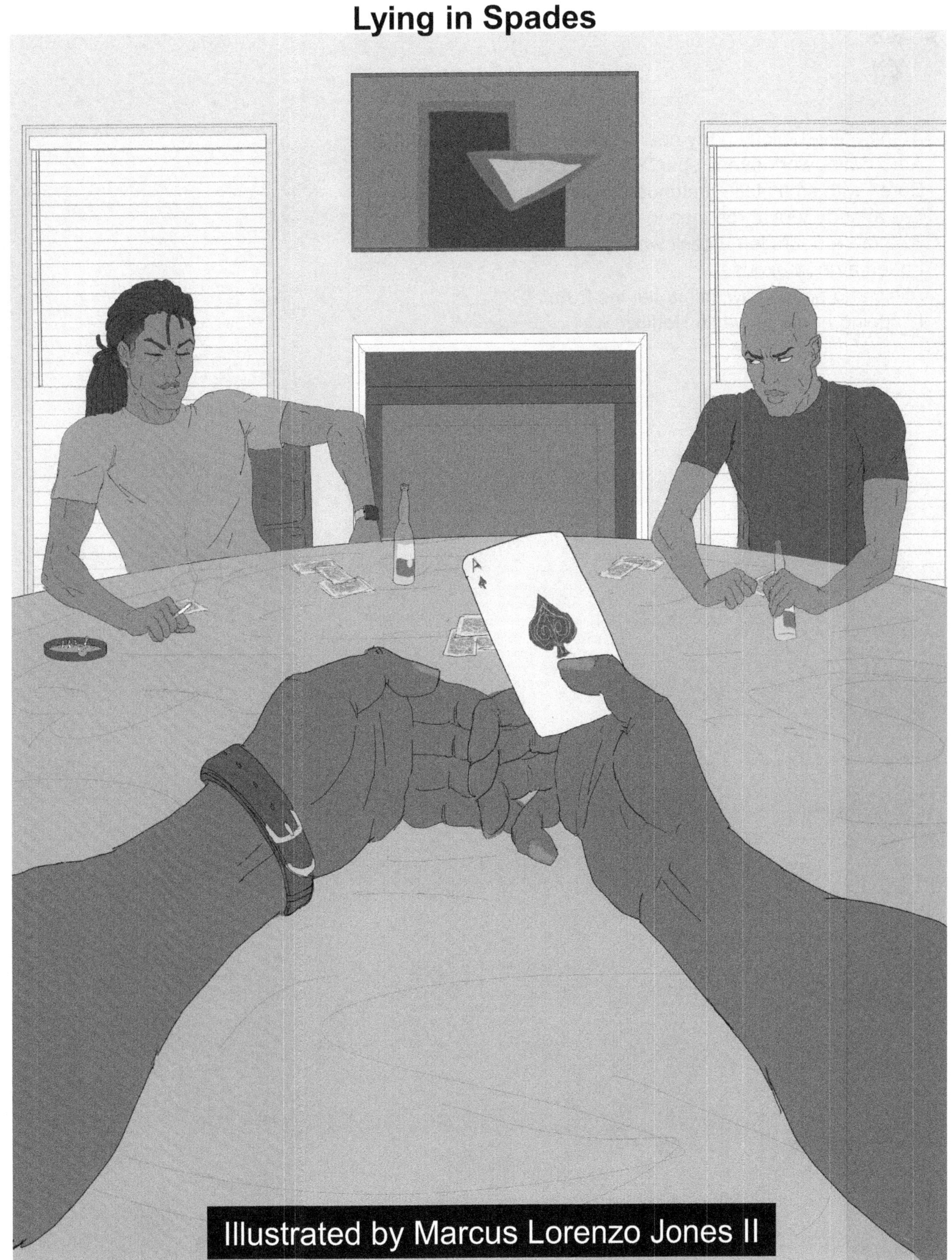

Illustrated by Marcus Lorenzo Jones II

**Mandatory fun**

At the office holiday party near the meat and cheese platter
After hours work event, spent engaged in idle chatter
Bored with small talk, pretended to empty my bladder
I've already took three trips to the bathroom
Two more hours left, I can't wait to go home soon
I need a good excuse
Alibis and proof, naw, imma tell the truth
I'm going home to watch Netflix!

## Medusa – a #metoo origin story

Poseidon raped **me** but men, women and the Gods hate **me**?
Athena cursed **me** (for being raped by Poseidon), but my locs ain't really snakes, see?
Gold tipped ends, blowing in the wind
Scared and confused mortal men, so I lost all of my family and friends
My story was shaped by chauvinistic and misogynistic
Cowards who didn't help a sista out, but wonder why she got pissed quick
The Roman poet Ovid, was the first wimp to get 'statued'
Then those other fools tried to manipulate and decapitate me, and what have you
A life of love should have been my metamorphosis
Instead, one look at my dreads, makes sand pour out people's orifices!
When I got 'merked' by Perseus, he used my wig as a weapon
Karma's a bitch 'cuz Megapenthes taught him a fatal lesson!
Silly Gods, even though I'm dead, my legend persists…
This cursed mortal woman's rage, is the reason why the Gods no longer exist!

♥

## Mistakes are the breaks that even eggs need

I get so excited
Like the Pointer Sisters
That I just can't hide it!
Finger blisters
Grasping bars so hard
But I'm less of a rapper, I'm more like a bard
But in that regard
I'm swift with my gift
Like a credit card
Interest gets charged
Deep in debt
No regrets
Flying high like pilots in a commercial jet
30,000 foot views of the picturesque sun set
Far above the crowds, float ominous clouds below
Those on the ground who just don't know
That whenever it rains, the sun still sits high above the mist
It's still somewhere out there, like Fievel Mousekewitz
Singing its sorrows to the moon, but it makes no sense!
What can a lifeless rock do, in this instance?
Fate and reality, two sides of a dime
Who flipped the script and invented bitcoin as a counterfeit?
Fabricated data, just to get rich quick
Zeros and ones, coded to expose society's greed
And spread reparations to those in need
Anonymous hacks to give back seeds
To grow intellect, we must always regret, our country's past misdeeds
For mistakes are the breaks that even eggs need
To make omelets, cakes, and other confectionary sweets
Good and bad both need each other to exist
Life would be hell, if death didn't exist!

♥

## Money Mistakes

I keep making money mistakes
Whether I have none or some, it still takes
Too much effort to track: Pay, bills, taxes, and math
I try to save, but then I spend on whim or I binge
Then debtors fetch my ends, via envelopes that bust at the hinge…
Of my mailbox, overdue statements and bounced checks
Embarrassed, I pray to God, unsure of what I should do next
Payday loans and ridiculous interest, what a mess!
Rewind back to a time, when our bills and debt were much less
Plan, save and live below your means
Put value in appreciating assets and avoid worthless things
God saves, but banks never forgive debt, it seems...

## Mosquito

Tempt me once, like a trigger I might just pull you
Nag me twice, shame on me
Ask, sass, and harass, gave you chances three?
I've been waiting on somebody like you
With what I'm about to do, the word cruel
Is too generic of an adjective
More like a sick mix of a beans, milk, and a laxative!
I guano bat a thousand, at everything you pitch
Then surround you like a cloud, then watch you squirm and itch!
I'm a nightmare, who you wish you'd never met
Moths fly to flames, but mosquitoes just want your blood and sweat!

## Naked and Afraid

Naked and Afraid
In the jungle 21 days
Wishing 'Off' and 'Raid' was being sprayed
Dreams of catching trout, cooked over a fire filleted
But my reality, in the Amazon, is being betrayed
My partner bragged about their survival skills on day one
A week later, they just complain, while absolutely nothing is getting done!
Everything bites and scratches, from the bugs to the plants
Haven't you seen the show before? Go get us some firewood, and quit your annoying rants!
Keep an eye out, for when the producers film a wild boar at night
Let's follow them, and gut that sonofabitch, with this pocket knife!
Did you come on this show to lose 20 pounds, or gain 15 minutes of fame?
I came here to win, don't hate the player, respect the game!

# Ode to the literati

Ode to the literati
Well educated student body
Driven to learn
Not concerned
About opinions from anybody
Future ideas and harmony
Are what we strive to achieve
Anything is possible, if you choose to believe!
In yourself, share your wealth, seek the greater good
Knowledge is power
Chew on your thoughts, like candy that kids devour
Education is key
Understanding will set us free!
Letters and numbers can make the third eye see!

## On the highway speeding

On the highway, speeding
Down the left lane, preceding
A semi truck on my bumper, we
Can't go any faster, because of the cops ahead, see?
I gestured and nodded, but he must not believe me
He honked his horn, and continued to rush and complain
I finally signaled for him to get over, into the fast lane
After the truck passed, suddenly one of its tires ripped!
A loud boom and white smoke began to emit
As the impatient trucker swerved then hit
The guard rail, he tipped into the pit!
And 'Jackknifed' sliding in a collision course
Toward the parked police force
Not guilty, but I was left with a tinge of remorse
I set my hazards to flash, as I pulled over on the side of the road
I began to sense, what my gut soon forebode
The accident progressed, in cinematic slow motion
A chain of events, culminated into a tragic commotion
When I finally processed, what I'd seen
I realized that this particular truck, was hauling gasoline!
I dialed 911, and prayed like I was in church
As I popped the clutch, and threw my 6 speed in reverse
First I saw the flames, then felt incredible heat before the explosion
Drive forward or backward, what would you have chosen?

## P. Infestans

The Irish potato famine (1845-1849) was a failure of epic shame
History faults the mold, but the British deserve the blame
When Britain annexed Ireland
All they could keep was their name
Making the Irish pay rent and raise cattle, were both of England's selfish plans
Absentee British landlords made laws, to impoverish the Celtics
They tried to survive by harvesting potatoes with their hands
When the only crop that could grow didn't, everybody felt it
25% of the Irish died or moved from a trifecta of greed, laws, and a potato mold called
Phytophthora infestans

**Pencil Pop on the Bus**

Back and forth, on the way to school, Pencil Pop on the bus, plus other things we'd do, backpack filled with yellow pencils and Now and Laters, contests for packs of Cherry and Pineapple, my favorite flavors, the only break in the game came from Duck in the front, letting us know when the bus finna hit a bump! On the count of three, in our seats, we'd all jump, up, up high defying gravity for a second or two, back to earth, grabbed my gear, I've got some work to do, eliminations one-on-one to see who's the best, I'm ready for whatever and know I can beat the rest, except for the new girl might be a true test, she moved here from California, some said she soaked her pencils in ammonia, it made them stronger and last long, but she ain't played me yet, so I'll prove 'em all wrong.

I peeped her technique, her Kung Fu was pretty good and her style was unique, the next round was her versus Buster, she seemed annoyed, like the match kind of disgusted her, he popped first, but didn't make a dent, but the whole bus was in a fuss, after she went, all you heard was a loud crack, and Buster's pencil broke in half with a snap! She was smooth with hers, all I could do was slow clap. Her name was Brianna Jenkins, now as my competition, she got me thinkin', for my next round, Malcolm and I had a go, he had game, but his style was all show, gyrating in circles with his pencil, before taking a hit, talking too much, he took a swing and he missed!

For my turn, I taught homeboy, a lesson he needed to learn, my #2 knew what to do and smashed his pencil like a worm! I basked in the adulation, the look from Brianna was a mix of awe and infatuation, the bids were going up, as Briana faced Rich, Malcolm's twin, 20 packs of Now and Laters would be mine in the final win, Brianna had a challenge in the other twin Rich, dude was huge and would never miss. He was held back a year and always seemed pissed. Once, he broke my pencil and nearly my wrists! As they traded blows, I looked into her eyes, her beauty and focus had me mesmerized. She stared in my direction and our eyes locked, It hit me like the slug from a BB gun shot - to the chest - this must be love! She beat Rich quick like a scrub, some kids noticed my stare, and sing-song teased us with glee - Jason and Briana sitting in a tree...

Everybody starting ooohing and laughing at me, sweat drenched my face, hands, and armpits, me and Briana in the Finals, she chirped 'you ready for this?' She sounds so nice, say something, flirt, speak! 'Ladies first, if you win, I'll carry your books for a week!' 'Bet', she replied then held her hands high, To pull up her sleeves, while I admired and sighed. Her first lick was sick, and numbed my fingers, the bus was laughing and hurling out zingers. She made a big dent, but my next swing did some damage. She said, 'My bookbag is pink, think you can manage?' With a swift flick, she split my pencil into two! Between the cheers the victor, she said 'close your mouth, you're starting to drool' Impressed, I said 'Congratulations, can I be more than just a friend?' She took my candy and said 'Not really, bruh, the Big twin is my boyfriend' :o

## Picky eater

I'm trying to get to the noodles, under the cheese
I asked mom not to put beans in the chili please
But everyone else likes it that way
So I push them to the edge of my tray
Food's getting cold, it's going to be another long night
I'm still at the table, pretending to take another bite
Six years old, I would gladly give it to the less unfortunate
Both my parents are disappointed, about the wasted food and money spent
My napkin's full, and my brothers and our dog are in the other room
I hope mom and dad will let me watch some TV soon…

## Pigeons at the airport

Pigeons at the airport, the paradox
Science and industry aid our flight, while their habitat got lost
Like Native Americans wearing ball caps and blue jeans
They wander asunder, depressed, adapting to unfamiliar scenes
Trapped but unable to change things, they are still driven by their needs
Concrete structures poured into forms, with spite and greed
These birds continue to peck through the trash, looking for scraps
While avoiding spikes in the gutters and other roof traps.

## Probability

Take a deck of 52 cards, and shuffle them good
You just created a combination that nobody else ever would!
It's math, a 52 factorial, 52! is the equation, understood?
That is 52 x 51 x 50... x 3 x 2 x 1, nearly an infinite number!
Every time you shuffle, its the first time that that order's ever been created, so I wonder?
If the probability of me writing this, and your reading it is greater
Or less than other thoughts and my words, printed on paper?

## Quarter Water aka Ghetto Juice

For just 25 cents
You could buy a plastic jug of liquid
So cold and sweet that it quenched
And burned your throat
And turned your mouth blue, like a cold Billy Goat!
Other friends would quickly see, and pay their fees like some sheep
Then the whole hood was good, riding our bikes with one hand down the street
One or two might complain, and get pissed
When the foil was jagged and cut up their lips
I'd like to say that we recycled our trash, then rinsed and brushed our teeth
But we just bought a bunch of Penny Candy, ice cream and jerky beef.

## Rain's Perfume

Early summer sitting on the porch
Gray clouds crowd, as thunderstorms float forth
Still warm from hours of sweating in the summer heat
Then a cool breeze blows and quickly chills my feet
Birds fly and bugs bite in anticipation
Rain's perfume permeates ahead of the precipitation
An illusion that never gets old, rain as it first hits the hot street
As the steam dances, there's no other place I'd rather be!
Greener greens than you've ever seen
Whenever it rains, the world just seems so clean!

♥

## Random Facts

Here's 20 or so random facts
Laws and truths, like universal math
Gasoline has no smell
A scent is added to detect a spill
Light travels 900,000 times faster than sound can
That's why you see fireworks first, then hear the BAM!
Caterpillars turn into soup before becoming butterflies!
They gain a pair of wings in the process, but lose four pairs of eyes!
A ten year old mattresses is double the weight is was when it was new
Due to years of sweat, dirt, oil, dead skin, pollen, and dust mite poo
As you read this, there are 1,800 thunderstorms active around the globe
Leonardo DaVinci may have invented those scissors that you hold
In Genesis 1:20-22, the chicken came first, later an egg she'd lay
The human heart beats 100,000 times per day
All polar bears are left-handed
A horse cannot vomit, dammit!
In 18 months, two rats can make a million more rats - I can't stand it!
Coca-cola was originally green
Abraham Lincoln's dog, Fido, was also assassinated, now that was just mean!
99.9% of all life on earth (ever) has already gone extinct!
Everything that remains is just 0.1% of all that ever was, just think!
The microwave was invented by mistake
A researcher walked by a radar tube, and the chocolate bar in his pocket baked!
It snows pieces of metal on Venus
Objects that appear the greenest
Do so, because that is the only color that is reflected
The rest of the colors are absorbed, but green light is rejected!

## Ravens and Crows

Groups of Crows and Ravens are called a murder and an unkindness, respectfully
This is a great injustice to these majestic birds, regretfully
Similar in color, Ravens are bigger but Crows have longer tails
A Raven's song is a 'gronk' but a Crow 'caws' whenever it yells
Crows like to hang out in groups, while Ravens are mostly solo
If you ever see either, don't fear, just take a photo!

## Reality versus insanity

Infected, cursed, walking dead
Information overload, brain rots in my head
Binge-watched Netflix all day in bed
The revolution was televised
Enslaved by multiple screens, right before our eyes
No tangible action, just fake reaction
Emojis, likes, and headlines, met to our satisfaction
Selfies and video games, claimed our time and vanity
Technology blurred the lines, reality versus insanity

**Senseless**

Hot, hungry, sleepy
Itchy, tipsy, lustful, lippy
Angry, stressed, bored, sore
Playful, bashful, thoughtful, hopeful
Restless, anxious, lazy
Cold, crazy, silly, happy
Spiteful, pensive, jealous, whimsical
Thirsty, sinful, annoying, painful
Charismatic, passionate, funny, shy
Sexy, thirsty, vacant, loquacious, wry
Flippant, arrogant, glib, proud
Stupid, lucid, indifferent, loud
Remorseful, resourceful, good, bad
Fantastic, mad
Chill, panicked
Flippant, distant
Tacit, tragic
Angel, devil, hero, bastard.

## S'mores Wars

You're Donald Duck, I'm Mickey Mouse
I'm the big cheese, this my house!
Imma squash beef, like bread on a steak and cheese hoagie
With a Jedi's force, Obi-Wan Kenobi
Like Mike Jones, back then you didn't know me!
Now I'm hot, y'all wanna be all cozy!
Nosey, asking all about my life story
So I keep making these shots, Robert Horry
No competition, Sucker MCs bore me
Refrain from critical disdain is mandatory
No concern, gotta be more pachyderm and 'less poor me'
That was an adjective for an elephant
Gotta have a thick skin, that advice is so relevant!
These jokers don't care about you and yours
Ain't got no rifles and tanks, but we out chea' fighting these wars!
Graham crackers, chocolates, and marshmallows, braised by fire under the moon
Impaled, burning, melting, and slowly being consumed!

## Snowpocalypse 2: Electric Boogaloo

You're mine, so I'll probably never let you go!
DC's blizzard of 2010, covered in two feet of snow!
No electricity just sleep and sex
Between baby making and sleep, all we ate was breakfast!
Hardly no rest
We barely even got dressed
During the 'Snowpocalypse'
We were like some ostriches
Burying our heads in the sand
Two flightless love birds, just executing a plan
They do that to ensure that their eggs are evenly heated
Marathon 'coitus' was exactly what we needed!
When I think back to the frequency of love with which we shared, I honestly can't believe it!
The mission, the positions, our intention was clear!
The expansion of our family, is it me, or is it getting funky in here?
No phone calls or distractions
Just you and me interacting
40 months later, lucky you and blessed me
Thanks to a record blizzard, a baby makes three!

### Snowmageddon, February 5-6, 2010

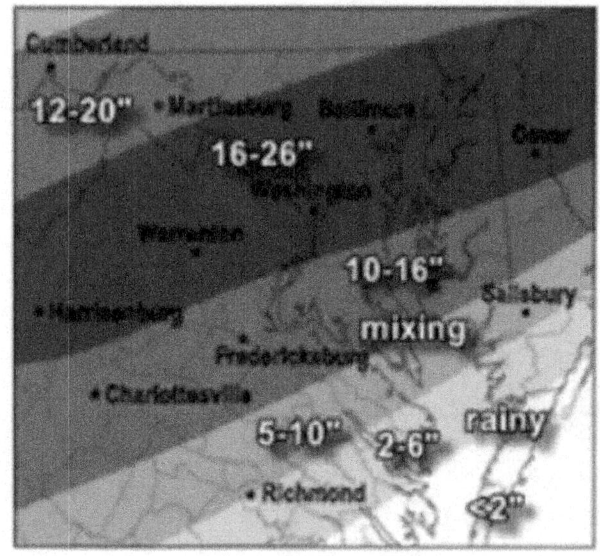


The Forecast

What should the storm be named?

Snowmageddon — 36%

The Great Superbowl Superstorm of 2010 — 15%

Kaiser Snowze — 15%

Snowpocalypse 2: Electric Boogaloo — 20%

Alex Snovechkin's Revenge — 12%

Closed

Total Votes: 4,947

The Naming

## Summer is delicious

At the celebration of summer
Bodies groove, unconsciously to a rhythm of drummers
Feel the heat, as you sleep on top of the covers
By twilight, birds and motorcycles join in on the symphony, as they fly and drive around
As dudes whistle at women nearby, some smile, others frown
Sweet Cocoa butter shines on curves so soft, smooth, and brown
People vibing, walking, and talking, the city's alive!
At the peak of the season, when the rush begins, you must imbibe!
Remember this feeling, the sounds, tastes, smells, and the heat
Summer is delicious, please enjoy the treat!

## Thanksgiving

Give thanks, break plates
Stuff turkeys and bellies, and then lay waste
Football, ham honey baked
Plans with the fam
Cranberries, jammed in a can
Tryptophan coma sets in, as waist lines expand
That third plate, gets second looks
Drunk Uncles, tipsy Aunts, and tired cooks
Our Great Aunt's double parked, Mercury Sable
Got ticketed, she thick a bit, can't slide past the kid's table
Somebody's fuming mad, and not saying much
Hours pass and their casserole, still remains untouched
Politics, church, and sports is still being discussed
You got some kin, who proudly voted for Trump
7pm, you just refused your seventh portion
Sitting with six octogenarians, watching the Wheel of Fortune
Amused, how now, Vanna White just touches the screens
Thirty years ago, she used to actually turn them things!
People just keep spinning that wheel, and risking it all
Do you guess, buy a vowel, or try to solve?

♥

## Thanos

A purple dude with a big chin
Quest for universal domination, with a wide grin
Out for riches that glitter like gold
Can't stop my aim, to reclaim those rare stones
What a motley crew
What can you do?
Nothing, running, rushing
Pleas, reason, and boring discussion
The boogie man and devil are nothing but lies
Your fate, on this date, is a timely demise
Dinosaurs were great once, in history's eyes
But time turned them into coal and oil
Pressure and heat, crushes and boils
Matter as memories, perish to exist
Your death was a test for my fate, what a twist!

## The Human Program Code

Those who can, shit on others
Those who can't, clean it up
To the fortunate few, everything is never enough
If you feel lost, depressed, dazed and confused
You are not alone, because we're all being abused
The weight of the world and history's toll
Is suffocating, an information overload is causing explosions in our skull!
Sorry to give you more problems with no solutions
We the people are everywhere, just like plastic pollution
Causing more harm than good, since the days of old
What if our program is near the end of its final code?

## The Legend of Kalidi

Over 1,000 years ago, an Ethiopian Goat herder named Kaldi
Found his goats dancing around, and acting very needy!
After eating some red berries, they refused to sleep at night
So Kaldi tried some too, to experience all of the hype!
Kaldi was later visited, by a friend who was a monk
Who took a bunch of the red beans back to his monastery, in a trunk
He mixed the roasted beans and hot water, into a tea like consistency
Did you know that coffee's origins are rooted in African history?

## The prices of vices yield diminishing returns

I'm hip, I'm hip!
We flipping the script
It's cool, don't trip
The haters they bit
Bad is good, up is down
The grass is blue, and the sky is brown
Ford stock is ~$10, but Amazon is over three thou?
A gallon of milk is $5 and so is a Big Mac
If you still smoke cigarettes, it will cost you $15 a pack
And you may one day get cancer or C-O-P-D
You'll look cool for a bit, but then become a PSA on TV!
Don't feel sorry for me kid, just learn from my mistake
I was addicted to nicotine, now look at my face!
My teeth are stained, from all the smoke and the tar
My jaw was removed, now look at my scar!
The prices of vices yield diminishing returns
Save your prayers and excuses, and address your own concerns!

## The Mystery of the missing sock

I lost some socks in the wash, but I'm unsure why
Looking for pairs, in despair, aimlessly we try
To find matches, but only end up with orphans
Dividing colors and whites, into equal portions
Forever lost in the wash, they cost those with feet
Fortunes gone missing between the underwear, shirts, and sheets
In the journey from the washer to the dryer
Maybe sock manufacturers have a special supplier
That makes a special sock, that dissolves in the wash?
Yeah, that best explains the mystery of the missing sock!

Illustrated by Jonathan Riley

## The Three Little Pigs - Remix!
## (After Crime Mob's song, 'Knuck If You Buck')

Yeah… You heard of the three little pigs? Well, this is the remix!

Yeah, yeah, yeah, yeah, yeah…
I huff and I puff (X6)

Huff, Huff, Huff, Puff, Puff, Puff, Huff, Huff, Huff, Yeah, Yeah!

(Chorus)
Yeah, yeah
I'm knocking (knocking on the door)
No options
Pig please let me in! (In!)
Otherwise Imma blow and you gonna catch this wind!

(Pig #1)
Go ahead and try it then (Do it!)
There's no way you getting in
You getting me is science fiction
Never happening! (Nope!)
Make believe, tricks in sleeves
Straw bends like wind in the trees! (Wind blowing sounds)
Wolf I swear If you don't leave
Imma bop in the nose! (Ka-Pow!)
Maybe then you'll think twice, about whose door you choose! (I heard that!)
Walking around in just a vest?
Boy put on some clothes! (Ha Ha Ha!)
And stop wasting my time
Its a quarter to nine
Trespassing's a crime (Yep!)
So I locked all the locks
You pretended to be  friend….(What?)
But you just want pork chops!

Illustrated by Jonathan Riley

## The Three Little Pigs - Remix!
## (After Crime Mob's song, 'Knuck If You Buck')

I huff and I puff (Oink!)
I huff and I puff (Oink!)
Huff, Huff, Huff, Huff

(Chorus)
Yeah, yeah
I'm knocking (knocking on the door)
No options
Pig Please let me in!
Otherwise Imma blow and you gonna catch this wind
I was just down the road, and was sent by your twin! (Oh Yeah?)

(Pig #2)
I'm picking up what you're putting down
But wolf, you must just think imma clown!
Thinking imma let you in?
Imma a triplet, not a twin! (That's right!)
So tired… of all your huffing and puffing
Let's just end this discussion
Your stank breath just can't bust in! (Ha Ha Ha!)
Sticks and stones can break bones
But you'll never, ever harm my home (Yeah!)
I hear you blowing, but my house is barely shaking
Ain't no way you getting one strip of this bacon! (Yeah!)

I huff and I puff (Wee!)
I huff and I puff (Wee!)
Huff, Huff, Huff, Yeah, Yeah, (….wee!) Yeah!

Illustrated by Ona Riley

**The Three Little Pigs - Remix!**
**(After Crime Mob's song, 'Knuck If You Buck')**

(Chorus)
Yeah, yeah
I'm knocking (knocking on the door)
No options
Pig please let me in! (In!)
Otherwise Imma blow and you gonna catch this wind!

(Pig #3)
What?
Look at my house
Check out them bricks
Master, mason, plaster mix! (Yeah!)
You can't touch this!
Go kick rocks
Imma boss (Boss!  Boss!)
You can't pick locks
No ham hocks!
Chillin' in my socks, understand?
You failed to see the plan (Plan! Plan!)
I Invited the whole fam…
Out to this venue
You out of breath (time to eat!) and right on time, 'cuz **'Wolf's'** on the menu!

(Pigs howling in unison)

We had enough! (Woof!)
We had enough!  (Woof!!)
We had enough!

Illustrated by Ona Riley

## The Three Little Pigs - Remix!
## (After Crime Mob's song, 'Knuck If You Buck')

Momma pig!

These pigs are my kids
I heard what you did!
Now that they big
I can finally live (Tell 'em Mamma!)
Biological didn't bother
Was mother and father
Bad wolves who bother
Get hooves in a slaughter (Whooooo!)
Killing this track
Then put it on wax
Serious business and personal attacks
Thought we was playing? (Nope!)
This ain't Xbox, this ain't PlayStation
Leave no time wasting
Hope that you patient (I heard that!)
In a slow cooker, you gonna be tasty! Mmmmmmm.....

(Daddy Pig)

I beg your pardon… but this ain't in the book! (Mamma, who dis man?)
Pigs can't eat no Wolf!
I was locked away for years!
Disguised…. to escape with fears (Word?)
Of getting caught again
I saw all of these homes, but I didn't know what was happening
So I just blew them all down…(I don't believe him!)
But now I'm so happy, that I finally found
My kids and my wife
Survived the struggle and strife (what, what did he say?)
Surprise! Yo' daddy's back in yo' life! (What?)

<Ain't my Daddy!>

## The Three Little Pigs - Remix!

Illustrated by Ona Riley

## The truth tastes terrible

I guess the appeal is control
Of the mind, body, and soul
They rarely heed my command
But with words on paper, sometimes I feel like Superman!
Maybe I'm an extra-terrestrial?
Fictional and abysmal
When my pen begins to leak
I don't know what to convey, until our ancestors start to speak
Then I read what I wrote, and think, 'damn, that's too deep!'
I gotta dial it back, to reach the sheep
Boil and distill it down, to make it simple and weak
I'm trying to serve knowledge, to the old and the youth
But nobody wants to drink the bitter truth.

## Too

You used to be too old
When I was too young
Others were too smart
While most felt too dumb
The world seems too cruel
Wrong knows all too well
As right fights tooth and nail
Few prosper, yet too many fail

## unconfident

Not sure what to do, or where to go
Ideas yes, answers no
So damn confident, in our prime
But time will quickly get you in line!
Age and wisdom, humble like a mug
Thought you was the windshield?  Naw homie, you just a bug!

## Travel well

Bong – 'You are now free to move about the country,'
With airplanes, hotels, and travel fees
Everyone is frantic to get somewhere
Home, work, vacation, connections to anywhere
Some run, others walk, are driven, or sit and stand
I like having the window seat, to look down on the horizon and scan
For roads, water, trees, buildings, and the twinkling lights at night
Sitting over the wing, marveling at the physics and mechanics of flight
Thousands of feet in the air, speeding through distance and time
I drift asleep as my dreams entertain my mind.

## Utopia anyone?

I write out lines when I type
These rhymes are simply an imitation of life
Imperative, that my narrative, cuts like a knife
The serrated edge sparks hot, dividing truth like a pipe
Friction/description/listless/the harvest is ripe!
Deeds and seeds, planted in granite, will eventually crack the foundation
The world stumbles, whenever our intentions are mistaken
No desire to supplant or retaliate
Our only desire is to live, love and educate!
Them versus us, has been done for generations
What if everyone could live together, without aggravation?
You don't have to like me, to get some respect
And I don't have to love you, just to earn a check
Can we break bread, without squeezing each other's neck?
The alternative to heaven and hell is utopia
To make it real, we all got to get together, like a cornucopia!

**Wear a mask!**

Why, I ask?
Don't you wear a mask?
You already have the vaccine?
And the booster too, but here's the thing...
It's not 100% effective against the virus that causes the disease
You can still catch and transmit it, with a touch, cough, or a sneeze!
If you still don't get why (you should wear a mask), here's a footnote
Remember the effects of second hand smoke?
People were susceptible, even if they never took a toke?
Viruses never discriminate, always looking for the next host
You may be immune and never fall ill
But think of all of those kids under 5, and immuno-compromised people that you might kill
By just touching a hand rail, elevator button, or even using a pen!
Did you wash your hands for 30 seconds with soap, or did you just pretend?
Some say masks are too uncomfortable, others claim that just can't breathe well
But doctors and nurses wear masks daily, during surgeries, without fail
So do yourself, and the world a favor, when you're out and about
Please wear a mask, and make sure that it covers both your nose and your mouth!

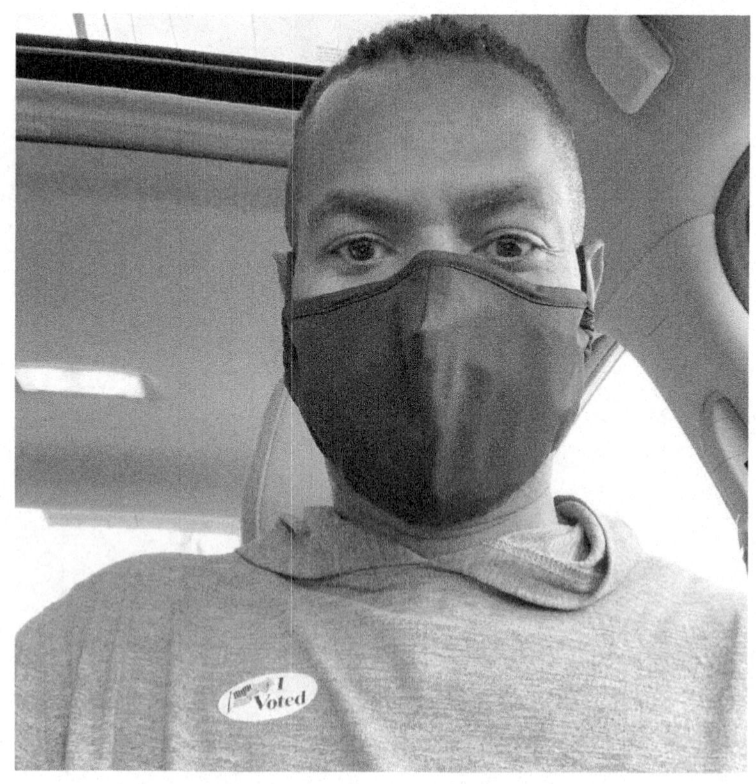

### What ain't is, but shouldn't be, because...

Bed-sty got rich white residents?
I'd say more, but I'm hesitant
Cuz the Feds might be reading…
The streets is crying, cops are lying, and we're still bleeding
But somehow they're pissed... taking the fifth?
Evading taxes, violating actresses, what's the diff?
Between Cosby and Weinstein?
Not a got damn thing!
Sin is sin, the media made them both come clean
Conscience and profit, tortoises and hares
It might be about race, but who cares?
Separate the 'art' from the 'man,' and don't pretend
R. Kelly and Bill Cosby, some black folks will vehemently still defend…
Hypocrites, they'd never let their daughter, wife, or mother spend
The night at R. Kelly's or Cosby's mansion...
Our hearts and minds demand expansion
Right is right, black and white, can both be wrong
But you knew this all along…
Up is down, we worship clowns, the majority worry about the opinions of the affluent few, but that's not what we used to do, the subways in NYC look so new, I miss the days when kids expressed their rage with graffiti, today, they stay on 'Social Media' sounding all needy, the talented tenth is a myth, they use their gift, to make millions, then decide to pick, white women to spend their time wealth, their conscience is still honest, and plagues their mental health, people like Kanye West, failed the test, saying that they did their best, be like me, rich and famous with a red cap, urging others to pull up their bootstraps, instead of gats, but we ain't listen....

**What happened to Saturday morning cartoons?**

Boss: How can we make breakfast cereal more expensive and taste bad?
Employees: Remove all of the Saturday morning cartoons and stop running our ads
Tell people to buy organic and stop including prizes and toys
Don't put fun stuff on the back of the boxes for the little girls and boys
Fire all of the frog, rabbit, toucan, tiger, and bear spokesmen
Boss: Sounds like a plan, let's begin!

## What if Columbus went east?

What if Columbus went south and east instead?
And survived, would we all be dead?
Europeans versus Asian armies and ships
Would we Americans still even exist?
Martial arts and gun powder might not cower
Would Africa still be oppressed by colonial powers?
No America, no Manifest Destiny, and different history books
If Europeans went to Asia first, how would the world look?

**What if I had nothing**

When I'm faced with adversity
Will you support or just curse at me?
Fair weather folks, will ride shotgun in the Benz
But with a bus pass, would they still view you through a rose colored lens?
Poverty is a filter for fake friends
Age too, what would you do, if I asked you, for a box of depends?
Sickness and health
Poverty and wealth
Hard times, dark crimes, or ashes on the shelf?
Life and death, from the first kiss to our last breath
Would you learn sign language, if I became mute and deaf?
If I had nothing else to give, at my worst, would you still treat me the best?

## What if sex didn't exist?

What if everyone in the world, was no longer interested is sex?
Would your personal relationships, be more or less complex?
The things that we worry about most, identity, security and respect
The very survival of our species, appearances, and neglect
If the very act of sex, was both repulsive and painful to all, you get the gist
Would life, as we all know it, cease to exist?

## What is your passion?

What is your passion?
What would you do for free, without asking?
Beyond games, jobs and other stuff
Something that is everything, yet never enough!
A dream, idea, product, service, or business
Just do it, don't ask for permission or beg for forgiveness!
Art, music, reading
Speaking, learning, encouraging
Cleaning, fixing, building
Singing, writing, acting
Owning, buying, selling
Sewing, knowing, showing
Treating, healing, fulfilling
Meeting, cooking, eating
Driving, flying, coding
Debating, relating, legislating
Swimming, running, ballin'
Creating, breaking, replacing
Serving, preaching, teaching?
The path you choose is strictly up to you
Own it, live it, love it, simply try and do!

### What these bullets what from a trigga? (after DMX)

What these bullets want from a trigga?...Break them off some...
...What these bullets want from a trigga?
Bust yo' guuuunnns.... aye yo!!
So you gonna shoot guns at me?
It's only been 150 years, but you're still mad that we're free?
Ya'll clinging to the wrong history
Why you in the suburbs and stay strapped, it's a mystery?
Worried about the 2nd Amendment
But still discriminate, based on our pigment
Associations that lobby and profit from donations and fees
Cops who can't wait to harass and shoot at me?
Jokers going postal with rifles and sawed-offs
We have the right to bear arms, but at what cost?
Daddy's got a gun locked away in a safe
3 am, they break in, and gonna take momma's cake?
You can't scrap, so you stay strapped
Why you pretend to live in fear, you ain't black!
With your CCL/CCW, you just can't wait to pop off!
And squeeze off 18 shots like a round of golf
Bragging about your guns and which is bigger
Must be compensating for something, most figga
What these bullets want from a trigga?
What these bullets want from a trigga?
What they really want from a trigga!!

There's a Beretta, Smith & Wesson, the Joint on my dresser, a Mossberg, the stressor, a Remington, a 45, 22, and 36, stacked and strapped, Gotta dig those measurements, the Uzi, Derringer, revolver, and Glock... oh I got that from a pawn shop, the AR-15, the street sweeper, The Desert Eagle, my heater, a 38 Special, the burner, a biscuit, the cannon, and chopper, the gat, the gauge, a drum, my hammer, a popper, the Mack, a hat, the AK, my heat, my piece, the snub, that musket has a quick release in the streets when I bust it, a toaster, the tech, and my stainless, you was nobody while breathing, but now I'll make you famous....

What these bullets want from a trigga?
Bust yo' guuuunnns....
What these bullets want from a trigga?
I got smoke and gun powder, I know you want it
What they really want from a trigga!!
Aye yo!!!!

## When I get rich, Imma do this…

This one might not even rhyme
Psych, I speak thoughts from my mind
Once I get real rich, imma do this
Starting a new company
No loans from a bank to exploit and own me
Upfit vehicles and hire ex-felons
To build vans so that homeless folks can dwell in
Then buy plots of land
Where they can park their vans
So mothers with daughters can have this
And fathers with sons can pursue happiness
No charge for WIFI and electricity
In exchange for cleaning up the inner city
Use the the revenue from our municipalities
To payroll their salaries
All across the country
Moore Life will do something key
So when tragedy plagues Haiti (again)
I'll ship in a fleet of Moore Lofts for free!
With cots, potable water, heat, and AC
I'll even throw in a TV
Home ownership should not be a commodity
When I get rich, imma help people and build a global community!

## When my cookies tossed

WTF Ralph and Chuck?
Woke up to a throw up!
Web MD diagnosis, not drunk
3am what's the answer?
Best case food poising, worst case cancer!
Sat up, acid reflux?
Was it fast food or that pie crust?
Cleaned up, washed off, but I still can't go back to sleep
Throat's burning, disconcerting, plus I think I just ruined the sheets
And pillows in the hotel's bed
I'll leave a large tip and an apology note by the remains, stains brown and red
With that Big Mac, apple pie, fries and ketchup, I paid the cost
Still can't explain, apologize for the mess and stains from when my cookies tossed...

## When the Bees Die

When the bees go extinct
Due to the chemicals in our vegetables and meat
Our present way of life will cease
Consumption and production comprende?
Will no longer be America's modus operandi
-ism's of race, class, and sex
Will be replaced with anybody's guess
With essentials and resources limited to few
Will the meek or the rich rule?
What would you do for a gallon of water?
To quench the thirst of your dying daughter
Stand in a bread line for days and only receive one!
Go hungry and to give it all to your son?
The food and water we take for granted today
May one day soon be taken away

## Why kill beasts of burden?

We taunt these beasts, to test our fears
With chants, cheers, capes and spears
Pinned in with fearless cattle
Our recent ancestors were similar chattel
Breed to run, work, and provide entertainment
Electricity, innovation, and technology usurped our enslavement
Yet we still seek to claim our domain
Over beast of burden, but few will complain

## Work Life Balance

I've been sitting here for 25 minutes
But it feels like 5 hours
Too much pressure
**Enduring pain...**
Trying to get rid of this week's wasted burdens
Ironic, how my life is a lot like my Outlook inbox
Two days away from capacity
I hold on to things that I should delete
Occasionally, I miss important communications
The meeting that I skipped three weeks ago turns out to be a mistake
The Saturday I spend on the couch online/watching TV, I should be
On the floor with my daughter pretending to drink tea
I've tried several times to prevent this pain - knowing my faults and doing nothing about it
**But I fail...**
I'm sweating, tugging on my socks to scratch my calf
I just realized that my leg is sore
From nervously tapping my heal on the floor
I stare at my laptop monitor, at PowerPoint presentations and
excel spreadsheets for 10 hours per day
If I had a dollar for every time I've eaten lunch down in the cafeteria
I'd have $6 to buy lunch
Get up earlier, eat right, plan my day, and drink plenty of water
Prioritize my tasks at work
**I keep failing...**
Hindsight reminds you how much easier the past was
When expectations were as low as your monthly expenses
No responsibilities, no bills, no stress
Today, the pain remains
Dull, unforgiving, constant, sharp
Controlling stress takes my best
To manage, the damage, I can only continue to try to push
**But it hurts...**
I wish I could just go home today, but I'm too busy
Too many deadlines, meetings to attend, emails to read and send
I haven't had a vacation in five years
Instead of a beach chair
I'm sitting on the toilet
**Constipated at work.**

## Write from a bird's eye height

I'm really not all that bright
But sometimes I get nose bleeds, whenever I write
Because my creativity takes me to a bird's eye height
Acrophobia* in fear for my life
Looking down below, from thousands of feet
The picture become so clear, that I'm forced to speak
Honest in these rhymes, sans a beat and the booth
It's like I'm digging for clues like a super sleuth
Detective, selective, and destined to tell the truth

*Definition - extreme or irrational fear of heights.

## Yo Momma!

Playing the dozens at school
I just kept my cool
As the crowd gathered, I'd never let them see me nervous
Squatted down to lace up my LA Laker Converses'
Sized up my completion from toe to noggin
This buster's a scrub, so this battle won't be a problem
Husky Jeans and a winkled shirt, I'll hit him where it hurts
Hygiene, it seems, would probably best work...
Me: 'Your lips are so ashy, talking looks like it should hurt!'
Him: 'Yo' daddy's so short, when he goes to court, they put him in a high chair!'
Me: 'Yo' momma's so bald, she got Homer Simpson hair!' (Doh!)
Him: 'Yo daddy's so poor, pigeons throw bread at her, why?!
Me: ''Yo momma's so ugly, she made a blind man cry!'
Him: 'Yo' daddy's so dumb... (that's it, no punchline)
Me: 'Yo momma's so old, her social security number is one!'
Him: 'Yo Daddy's on drugs, so when I say 'Hi,' why does he get so offended?'
Me: 'Yo momma's so stupid, it takes her two hours to watch 60 minutes!'
Him: 'Yo daddy's so stupid, he took a ruler to bed to see how long he slept!'
Me: 'Yo momma's so fat, she ain't got no neck!'
Him: 'Yo daddy's so stupid, he stared at orange juice for 12 hours because it said 'concentrate'!'
Me: 'Yo mamma's so stupid, when they said, "Order in the court," she asked for some fries and a shake!'
Him: 'Yo mamma's so stupid, she put lipstick on her forehead to make up her mind!'
Me: 'Yo daddy is so illiterate, he's been reading a sign says 'Do Not Trespass,' with a coupon for three donuts this whole time!'

## Zoom

Zoom!
Ever since COVID-19 began, meeting in person's out (out)
WiFi's so slow, my words don't match my mouth (mouth)
Plus I'm starving', why schedule meetings during lunch?
Mandatory cameras... y'all gonna see and hear me munch!
Celery, carrots, potato chips, sometimes I eat sloppy fast (fast)
My video is blurry (Why?)
Greasy hands on the glass (Oh)!
Instead of sales tempo, I'd rather play Nintendo
Back when we dialed in, life was so simple! (Yep!)
Invasion of privacy, co-workers in my crib... (Yep!)
My boss got jokes, I'm so sloppy, I need a bib! (Yep!)
But revenge is sweet, peep the lesson she was taught
Captured her digging for gold via a screenshot! (Ha Ha!)

Zoom, I really, really hate to see!
They think they camera's off
Oh, but they on screen...
Digging for gold, and I can't believe
That they nose, their nose.... still ain't cleaneeeeeeeeenn – Ho! (Zoom!)

I never understood, why we need to be on camera, proof that I'm awake?
Look, I need this job, we in a pandemic for heaven's sakes! (I'm Hip!)
My internet has restrictions
For audio, I gotta dial in (Damn!)
My daughter's on Google classroom, snack break's at 10 (10)!
We don't have 5G, so my bandwidth has limits (limits)
I can't do all of them cool backgrounds and other gimmicks
Y'all keep asking for comments, reactions, and other things....
But my neck hurts, staring at these computer screens
I ain't paying attention, on Twitter posting memes (Memes!)
Six Zooms a day, is like a dozen bad dreams! (I'm Hip!)
Zoom for work, school, church, community activations
We all burned out, venting our frustrations! (Frustrations)

Zoom, is that your family and dog (dog yelps) behind you?
How many kids and cats you got? I got no clue?
What, in the world's hanging, up on your wall? (Is that velvet?)
Looking at y'all's home offices, I'm in total awe! Oh... Zoom!!

We been on this Zoom for hours, talking about something
But what have we all accomplished? Absolutely nothing! (Zoom, Zoom!)
This ain't no idle time, got a bunch of texts and emails to send…
300 people on this meeting, but you calling on me again? (what's up with that?)
I wasn't paying attention to your question, I must confess
But I'm a pro, so I'll impress y'all with some BS (BS!)
Been utilizing 'Best Practices' to generate incremental traffic (Yeah!)
Hit mute then watch a movie with my favorite actress! (Netflix!)
Multi-tasking, online classes, guessing, testing 'till we see 'Congratulations, passes' (Passes!)
How do I know when a Zoom is over? This is sad...
A red and blue thumb asks, how was your experience, good or bad? (good or bad)

Zoom, I like, to fly far away from here…
Why these fools, speak on mute, but we can't hear?
Why, oh why, can't they just see?
Just press the freaking space bar, or unclick on the mute key, Who's Zooming Who!

# 8 SHORT STORIES

- ❑ Rescue at the Crossroads
- ❑ Haitian Joe
- ❑ Undark
- ❑ Kills White Man
- ❑ Captain Jolly Roger
- ❑ Oscar & Buddy's Super Origins
- ❑ Race War – Part I
- ❑ Race War – Part II

# Rescue at the Crossroads

Illustrated by Marcus Lorenzo Jones II

## Rescue at the Crossroads

11:59 am, September 2, 1911 - Indianapolis, Indiana.

Lynn Fox left the train depot and walked toward the police station. As a reporter of 'The World', a weekly newspaper for colored people nationwide, Lynn prided herself in reporting the truth. But tonight she was off the record and seeking justice!

Hours earlier, 13-year-old David Johnson, accused of 'whistling' at a white woman, was dragged from his family's farm and thrown in jail. His grandmother contacted Lynn for help, worried that her grandson might not live to see the light of day. The town's torches were lit just after dusk, lighting the path for hundreds of angry men and women, each seeking their pound of flesh.

Lynn saw a single light twinkling on the horizon. "These negros are never on time," she joked to herself. Sizing up the growing mob, Lynn knew that she would have to start without help. Tired and sore from helping her neighbors harvest their crops, Lynn rolled her head from side to side. 'There's more than corn in Indiana,' she vexed, 'racism.'

There were no chants from the lynch mob, just hate and an insatiable lust for blood. It began to rain as a brick was thrown toward Lynn. She effortlessly caught it midair like a baseball, held it up, and chuckled, "Who threw this?" as she tossed the brick aside and walked forward. With the cover of night and dim street lights, Lynn barely needed a disguise. She already spotted the mayor and a famous racecar driver, so she thought it best to remain anonymous, and pulled the brim of her Boater hat down.

# Rescue at the Crossroads

Illustrated by Marcus Lorenzo Jones II

## Rescue at the Crossroads, cont'd

"Go home, the kid's already in the hoosegow!" Lynn pleaded half-heartedly. A low, booming voice replied, "Make us Niggra!" Parting the crowd was the largest man that Lynn had ever seen! Armed with a scythe, Cornfed was an imposing figure. "We gonna have us a few hangings tonight!" laughed Cornfed.

"Da name's Esther!" Lynn yelled in a deep, rich, exaggerated Haitian accent, as her alter ego emerged. "Besides, it's morning already, ding-bat!" countered Lynn.

"I ain't scared of no little Voodoo Coon! Imma enjoy strangin' you up!" Cornfed snarled, as he lumbered toward Lynn.

Just then, Lynn felt a swift brush against her side and the familiar smell of coal. As Cornfed's scythe hurtled down toward her, an imposing shadow nearly the size of Cornfed's appeared. When John Henry Jr.'s (Junior for short) hammer blocked Cornfed's reaper, the streets resounded with rolling thunder.

"Well, well, the prodigal son has returned?" Cornfed mused. "Yo daddy cried when I gutted him like a fish, so what in the hell you gonna do... BOY?" taunted Cornfed. "Daddy was 90!" Junior roared as he nailed Cornfed square in the chest with his hammer. The blow sent Cornfed airborne several yards back into the scrum. Cornfed slowly got back up and ran toward Junior enraged. The two giants sized each other up and traded punches. "Get the kid!" Junior cried to Lynn.

The mob and Lynn ran toward the station. Lynn arrived first, but the police barred the doors, trapping her outside to the bigots' benefit.

# Rescue at the Crossroads

## Rescue at the Crossroads, cont'd

"Sick!" yelled a Beelzebub, unleashing a pack of dogs that ran toward Lynn like a rabid Cerberus leaping from the porch of hell! Lynn conjured up an old familiar childhood spell. As the time slowed from minutes to seconds, the large pointy eared black and tan hounds appeared suspended not only in time, but in space. Lynn was reminded of the demise of her beloved matriarchs.

As all matter in her immediate vicinity drifted, easily manipulated as pawns on a chess board, so did Lynn thoughts. She drifted away to Haiti, to a time long ago when she hid away as a similar pack of hulking dogs mauled the lifeless bodies of her mother and grandmother on a pier. Both once very powerful in the ancient mystic arts, they sacrificed themselves (and bequeathed their powers) so that Lynn and her baby brother could stow-away on a ship bound for America.

As her time spell dissipated, Lynn, slowly turned around to a surprise attack – a blast of water from a fire hose! Before her was a team of firemen, pumping water from their fire engine. The water cannon pinned Lynn to the station door. Skillfully controlling the residual effects of time distortion, she propelled herself from the door toward the racist rabble. Lynn appeared to fly toward the hateful horde at an inexplicable speed! As the lagging water hose continued to follow Lynn, it extinguished most of the torches and knocked down scores of bigots like dominos. She continued into the mob in a zig-zag motion, smacking their faces for good measure!

A few Hoosiers regained their footing as the hose ceased and the effects of the spell wore off. Suddenly, someone grabbed Lynn's boot and slammed her to the ground! Now several hundred yards into the fray, Lynn realized that she was severely outnumbered.

# Rescue at the Crossroads

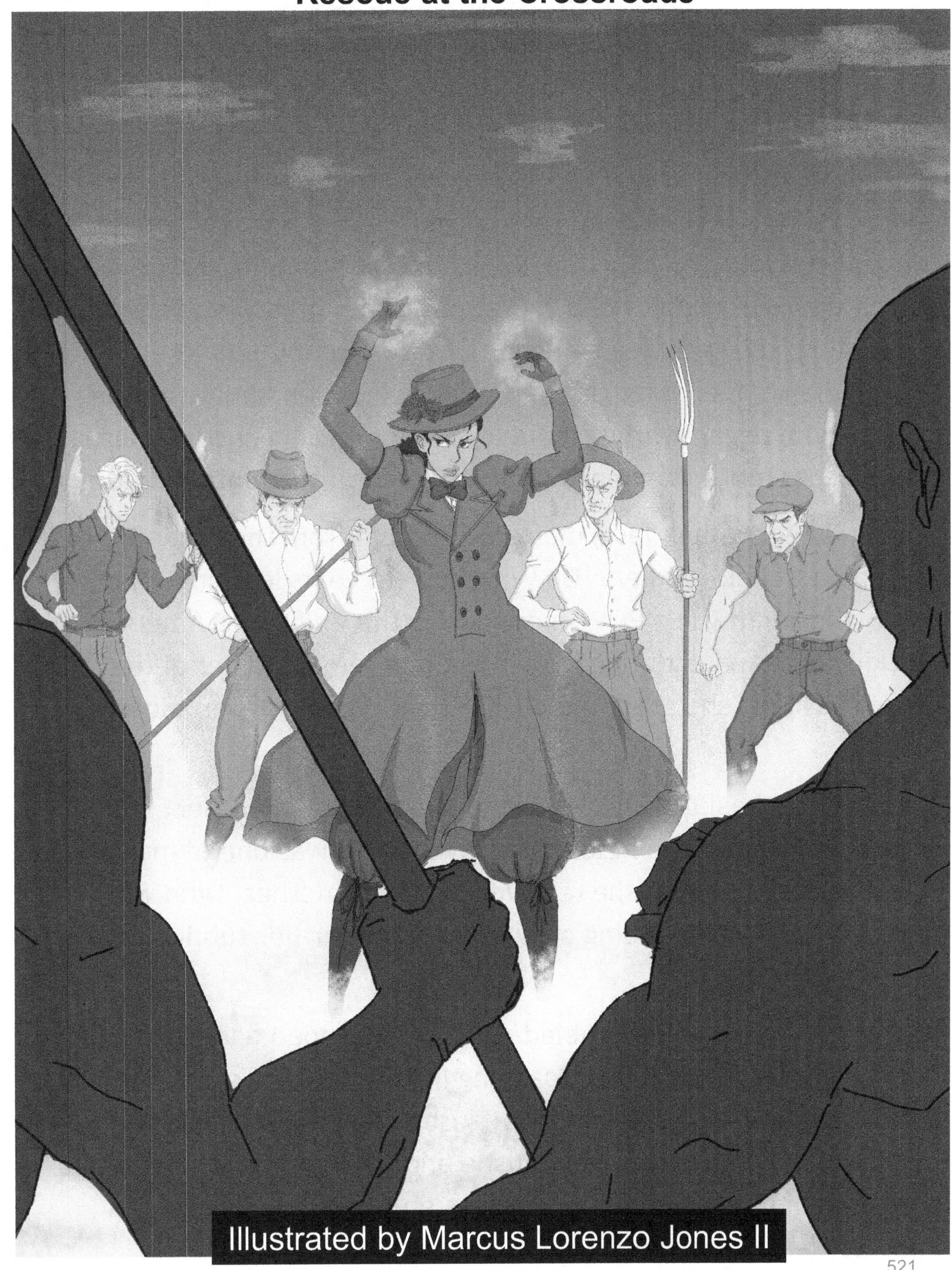

Illustrated by Marcus Lorenzo Jones II

## Rescue at the Crossroads, cont'd

Another Hoosier caught Lynn off guard and stabbed her in the leg with a pitchfork! Then a barrage of shovels, rakes, and sticks hit Lynn so hard, all she could do was curl up into a ball.

The riffraff continued to attack Lynn with a flurry of fists and feet from behind. Sensing the beginnings of regeneration and unwilling to concede defeat, Lynn caught a bat just inches from her face, pulling herself up as its wielder followed through with his swing. Regaining her footing, she snatched a pitchfork from a stunned attacker, snapped the handle across her leg, leaving a dense wooden handle in her hands. Lynn began twirling it about, using Arnis, an ancient martial arts style, as more 'lemmings' stepped up for a customized beating.

Lynn and her brother, Jack, mastered combat from their mentor, Dr. Wilson, (a Buffalo Soldier). Dr. Wilson spent years learning *Arnis de mano* and *kuntaw* in a POW camp during the Philippine-American War. Blocking bats and enduring pain in the rain reminded her of the countless hours she spent practicing in the garden of her adopted home.

The ability to heal quickly was a gift from her grandmother. She sensed Jack's presence before he arrived. This was one of many preternatural gifts that she received from her mother. Lynn was reassured by Jack's pending arrival to help to further subdue the throng.

As the ground violently rumbled, everyone stopped fighting to seek out its source. A quickly approaching light was noted a few yards down the railway. CJ's train arrived just as the Indiana State Militia marched up South Street. CJ's hustle and ingenuity made her into a true titan of industry, but her business empire was not nearly as impressive as her vigilante enterprises.

# Rescue at the Crossroads

Illustrated by Marcus Lorenzo Jones II

## Rescue at the Crossroads, cont'd

CJ exited a train car ramp riding on a motorcycle, accompanied by Lynn's brother Jack, an Indian aptly named 'Kills' (short for 'Kills White Man'), and a sea of young men (Nupes) and women (Walker Agents) dressed to the nines and armed with canes and hatpins (respectfully).

CJ ordered the Nupes to the police station to free David, while hundreds of Walker Agents threw scores of needle-sharp hatpins from their Edwardian Straw Boaters to counter the militia's attack. Jack joined Lynn as 'Kills' charged toward the militia's flanking cavalry, living up to his namesake.

Jack and Lynn pushed the mob back with a series of blows and kicks that caused scores of Hoosiers to retreat. The Nupes fought the police and managed to find David without any bloodshed, per CJ's orders. The firemen blindly gave chase as CJ sped away from the train tracks as planned.

Lynn asked, "Think we can do a Sandman, Ace?" "With this many… maybe," Jack reasoned. The duo whispered in a mystical tongue as Junior pushed Cornfed toward the rioters. Like a log being tossed onto a bonfire, the sky was filled with glowing ashes that mesmerized the entire horde. One by one, they all fell to the muddy streets.

"You might want to get the militia too, before 'Kills'… well, you know…" quipped Junior

CJ's train whistle blew, commanding her crew return to the depot. 'Kills', just getting into a rhythm, reluctantly retreated too. The militia and cavalry, also dazed by Lynn and Jack's spell, toppled over in the street.

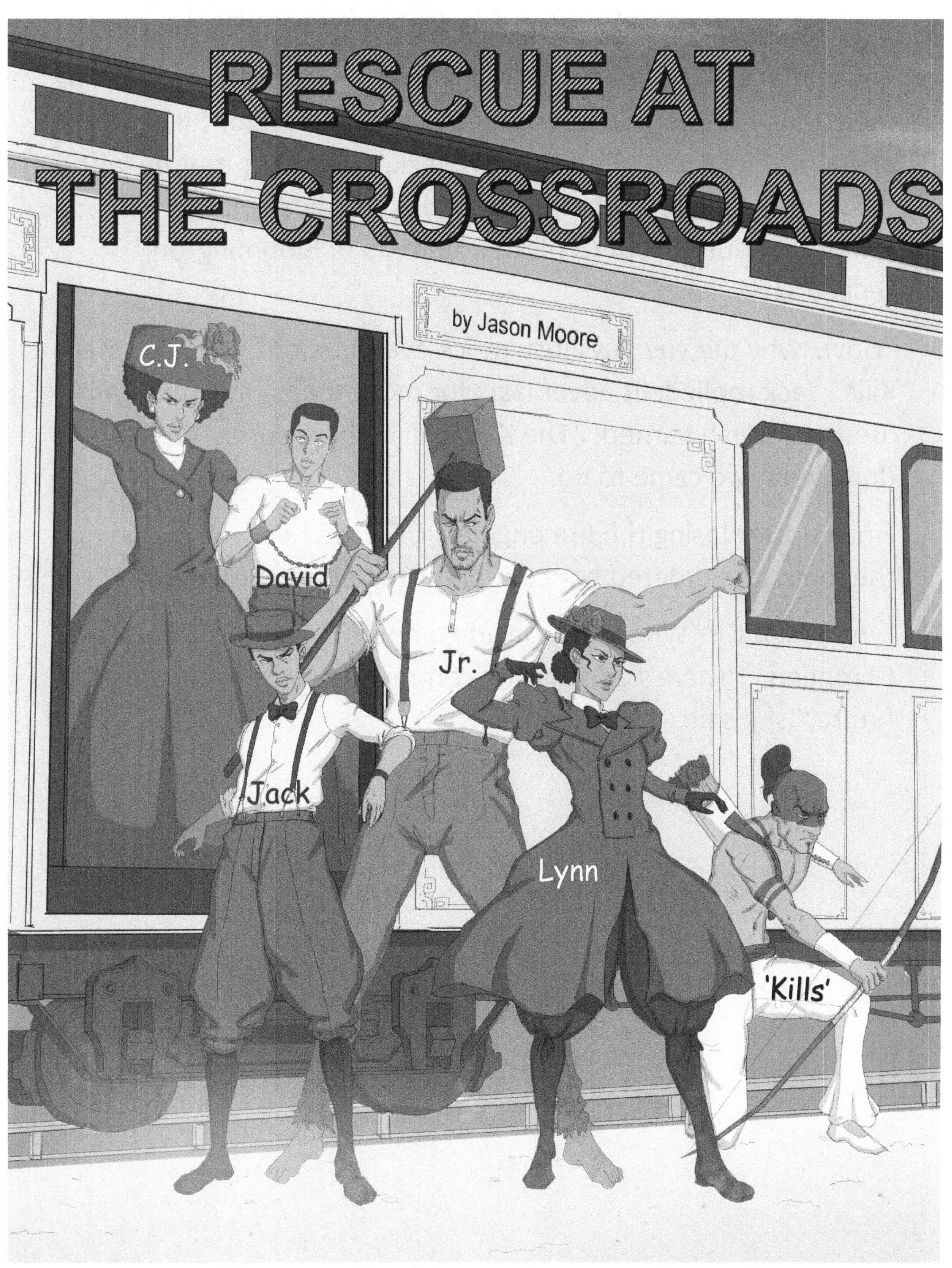


Illustrated by Marcus Lorenzo Jones II

## Rescue at the Crossroads, cont'd

David boarded the train with the Nupes, enthusiastically shaking the hands of everyone he encountered, thankful for his newfound freedom. Finally, Lynn, Jack, and Junior met up with 'Kills' on the train. "What in the hell is a Nupe?" whispered Junior? "I dunno, but CJ picked them up in Bloomington," replied Jack.

"How…why did you guys just knock everyone out?" complained' Kills.' Jack replied, 'It never lasts for more than a few minutes!' 'Besides,' Lynn warned, "The Klan will be here soon. We've done what we came to do."

Finally, after losing the fire engines, CJ drove her motorcycle up the ramp and ordered her conductor to depart the depot.

Lynn asked CJ, "Where will David go now?" "Tulsa, Oklahoma," CJ replied. "There's an amazing community there with a bright future," she said.

## Haitian Joe

Haitian Joe (HJ) walked toward another angry mob
Just as his father's father did decades ago, how odd!
The wage for independence and freedom was always war
Somewhere deep in rural in Florida, HJ's legend soon became lore
Quick with both wits and fists
But strength and division were two of his greatest gifts
One man who could become a 1,000 in a flash
He'd clear acres while sharecropping, just to earn some extra cash
HJ became quite wealthy, and with time came security and clarity
He'd often help other farmers with their harvests, and anyone else in need of charity
Being several places at once (for him) was as easy as breathing
HJ's world changed when he defended a class of school age kids one evening
When a large crowd of 'property owners' got too aggressive
The beating that they got from HJ was certainly not expected!
The next morning, a large white mob knocked down HJ's gate
Armed with torches, ropes, rage, and hate
They demanded that HJ be hung and immediately stripped of all possessions and land
As HJ walked toward the mob, he said, 'Sure, catch me, if you can!'
In a fraction of one second, he disarmed...
All of the angry men and women, who were quite alarmed
To find their torches extinguished and ropes neatly coiled
In a large pile between them and HJ, their plans were instantly foiled!
The mob tripled in size and returned the next day with dogs, pitchforks, ropes, axes, and guns
Before a hound was released, a shot fired, a noose knotted, an axe swung, or one person could even so much as lunge
HJ disarmed them all, then fashioned a large cage (from their weapons) that held everyone!
Then turned the ropes into leashes and walked away with their dogs!
HJ gave each hound some food, then tied them up to a few large logs
Here's the speech that HJ gave to the militia who tried to lynch him (twice)
Pointing at the dogs, HJ said we're all kind of like them
Trained to hunt and obey
But what happens when their master goes away?
Leave me alone, and the rest of our people too!
I'm just playing games today, but tomorrow... y'all won't like what I'm gonna do
My family fought the French for independence with 'Haitian Voodoo'
I'll free y'all, after you fix my fence!
Any questions? Do y'all understand? Am I making any since?
Why do you hate us so much?
We work for free, fight your wars, and harvest your lunch!
We can't own a business, get a quality education, or even vote
Y'all even threw Marcus Garvey in an Atlanta jail for mail fraud, and then took his boat!
Just leave us alone, please don't come back here
That's not a threat, but let me be clear...
I could curse you, but it's a waste of my time
I just want to live my life, and enjoy the rest of my prime
Another question for the group, please help me to comprehend
Why do you bring your children with you to participate in this sin?
So, what? Was the 'big idea' just to string up old HJ?
And drag me down the way?
Then lynch me from a nearby tree, then afterwards, burn me anyway?
What in the hell is wrong with you people, acting just like ghosts?
Is haunting us what you need in your lives the most?
Killing Native Americans and stealing their land wasn't bad enough?
Y'all like, 'Do you know what we need to do tonight? More evil stuff!'
The kids y'all harassed were innocent/defenseless
Just sleeping in a school house, so that's why I beat y'all senseless!
But you are all still alive, I guess the lesson was not learned
Had I killed just one of 'you people,' my whole town would have been burned
From one person with power
To a whole town of people with power
Please cease and desist!
If you come for me or mine again, you will no longer exist!

# Undark

Undark glows bright from years of exposure to radioluminescent paint
Working on watch dials at work, one day she'd faint
The daughter of slaves, she was fired, then was quickly replaced
Most of the 'Radium Girls' became disfigured or died of cancer
When Mary Jane was asked how she survived, this was her answer
In 1920, she was committed and received shock therapy daily
For 'hysteria', but the electricity, radium, and Gamma rays did not drive her crazy
Rather she was empowered with gifts, that the Gods would envy
Super human strength and gravity manipulation, she could even make a calm day windy!
She travelled down south, to fight injustice and Jim Crow
Hooded mobs became frightened, as her teeth and eyes would glow
Green, Undark's spark prevented countless race massacres, along with her team
Pullman Porters, Harlem Hellfighters, and hundreds of hero's who fought behind the scenes.

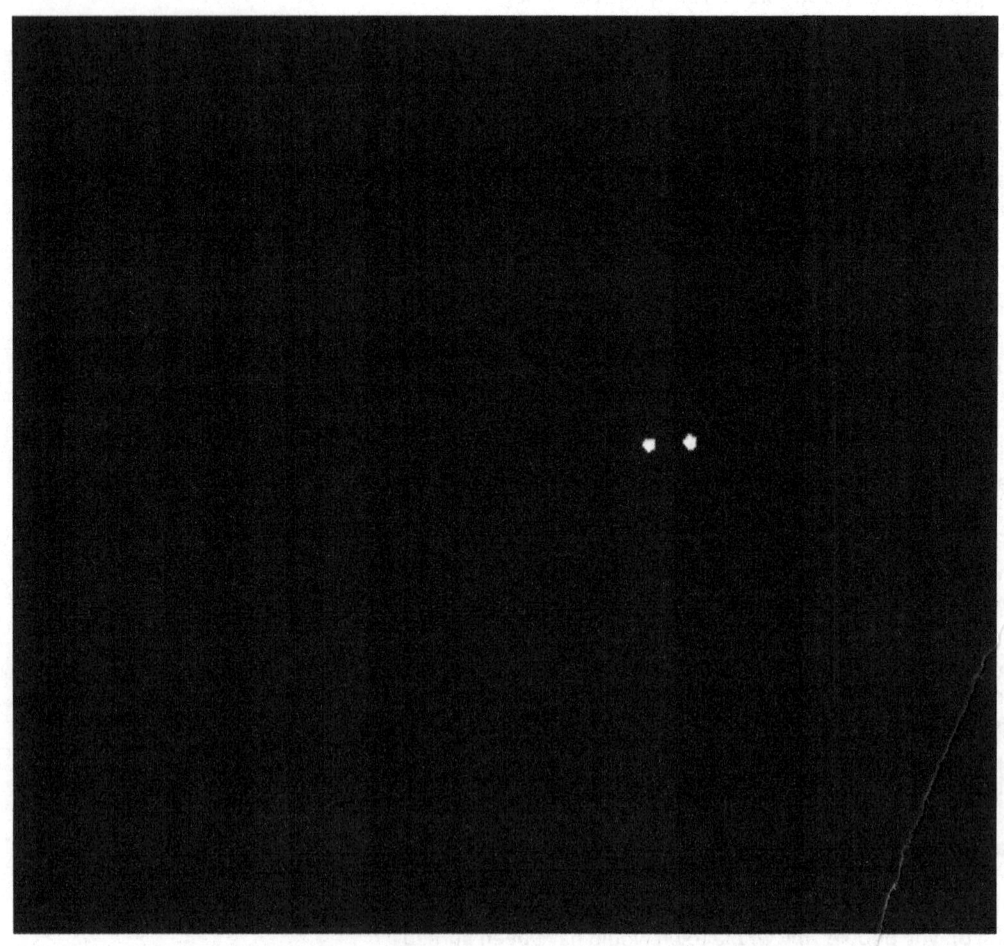

## Kills White Man

Kills White Man
Not a Native American
But an indigenous person
Whose very name
Became his claim to fame!
From an early age
Once battles became waged
America against his tribe
All America did was lie
So that's the reason why
Kills White Man, makes them all die!
They labeled him a savage
So he evokes fear, then begins to ravage!
With supernatural powers that make the greatest moral, feel far below average
Any foe that crosses Kill's path
His enemy's blood, will soon turn into ash
Decades become a flash
Skulls, Kills will instantly smash
His only living purpose
Is to exact revenge, and he really enjoys his service!
An obstruction to America's manifest destiny, the government is getting nervous
Because Kills cannot be contained
They tried money and reason, to no avail, so they think that he's completely insane!
Kills does it for justice, never for the fortune or fame
A target that is impossible to eliminate, impervious to water, blades, bullets, and flame

Illustrated by Marcus Lorenzo Jones II

# Captain Jolly Roger

Captain Jolly Roger, or just JR for short
Attention on deck! Give me a status report!
We're ready to set sail Sir! What's our next destination?
Northeast mate, we have a date with destiny, plus y'all deserve a vacation!
All aboard, crew and ready your battle stations
Nice job with the haul, I apologize for being moody
To the Victor's belong the spoils, now we got a treasure trove full of booty!
But that just makes us a target, plus everybody's after me
As foes go, we've got twenty more than plenty
But we'll continue to fight, because we'll never flee!
We sent hundreds of American and European ships down to the bottom of the sea!
To join our brothers and sisters who skipped the middle passage
Orphaned from mother Africa, we're more than just some shiftless half-breeded bastards!
But there's no other place on earth that I'd rather claim
Whenever my beautiful mistress, forms a tempest, she's soon refilled with rain!
Feast or famine
Thirst or salmon
My fate you have a hand in!
Hurricanes and Tsunamis, I'll gladly stand in...
On land for long, I can never be
My only love remains for you, my dear capricious sea...
Sorry shipmates, where were we? I apologize for the monologue
Sometimes I get lost in my thoughts, my mind's in a fog
Onto America, New York City, to join in a new fight
Folks up there don't think that our brothers and sisters have the right
To live in freedom or pursue happiness at all
Once we storm the shore, let's just kill them all!
Show them that our sea power remains undiminished, even on land
To give our brothers and sisters in the struggle an upper hand
Balance the scales
We're the Leviathan, the enemy are just sharks and whales
That's the mission ladies and gentlemen, we simply cannot fail!

# Oscar and Buddy's Super Origins

'What should we do with this nigger and the China-man?' yelled a henchman, near the open door of a freight car.

'Kick 'em off the fucking train for all I care!' spit the outlaw in charge, 'We got all we need, so they can go back to hell, or wherever the fuck they come from,' he proclaimed as he folded a map and placed it in his vest pocket.

Awakened by the sensation of floating, Oscar Brown realized that he was falling toward a river! His left eye was swollen shut, and he was tied to Buddy. Overwhelmed, Oscar didn't know where he was or how he and Buddy got there, but he had to figure out how to break free – and quickly!

Time began to slow, 'Wake the fuck up Buddy!' Oscar screamed. 'You ain't gonna believe dis shit!', Oscar continued. Just as Buddy regained consciousness, Oscar yelled, 'Deep Breath,' while taking his own advice!

As they hit the water, time stood still. Buddy and Oscar had each had their fair share of near death experiences, but being tied back to back and thrown a hundred feet from a bridge into a river was a first!

The last thing that Oscar could remember, was being surrounded by an entire Army of people. Fighting back to back with Buddy, and out of bullets, they were rushed by countless knives and sticks. Then, he blacked out.

Floating to the surface, time began to right itself, just as their breath began to give out. Oscar felt a weight lifted from behind him as Buddy somehow got free.

Waiting at the surface, Buddy's smiling face pissed Oscar off even more than being thrown off of the bridge! 'How in the hell did you?... what did you?... Oh Never mind!' Oscar cried, confused and annoyed by their current state of affairs.

Treading water, Buddy extended his right hand to help Oscar float. With his left hand, he offered him the end of a small knife.

"You somabitch!" joked Oscar. "These muthafuckas are gonna pay, after I get dry and get my shit...!" Oscar mumbled to himself as he cut the ropes from his wrists.

Swimming toward shore, Oscar and Buddy looked up at the bridge that they were thrown from. Both were shocked that they somehow managed to survive.

Back on land, Oscar found more reasons to be upset. 'Not my boots and my custom belt!' Oscar cried. They should have just killed me! Buddy regaining his bearing, volunteered, 'I have no idea where we are, but I need a drink!'

"We'll, maybe you can walk to a saloon and get one, with your boots!' Oscar sneered.

Climbing back up to the railroad, Buddy and Oscar walked for several hours until Buddy found a rail marker.

# Oscar and Buddy's Super Origins, cont'd

'Oscar, we ain't in Texas anymore!' Buddy exclaimed. 'The good news is there's a town a few hours away, the bad news is that we're in California!' Yelled Buddy in complete disbelief.

'Shit!', exclaimed Oscar, 'Imma kill that fuckin' Peckerwood!' Oscar snarled.

Buddy, in a better mood than Oscar, realized that he was just a few hours away from a stiff drink, helped Oscar to focus.

'No boots, no belt...' Buddy began.

'No map!' Oscar suddenly realized. If that asshole thinks he's getting to **MY** shit before **ME**, then he's got another thing coming!' Oscar swore.

As Oscar and Buddy arrived in town, they agreed to split up, find some supplies, then meet back up before dusk to leave town.

Oscar's best contacts were with the Pullman Porters. These black men had travelled on trains all across the country, for decades, and had established a fraternity that almost always came through when Oscar need it most.

Buddy's years of working on railroads and blowing holes in the sides of mountains (in nearly every state east of the Mississippi) also provided him with invaluable connections practically everywhere he traveled. An unknown fact to most people, Buddy had mastered martial arts as a child back in China. Partnering with Oscar early in his travels, once he arrived in America, the two taught each other everything that they knew and became like brothers.

After securing some funds to buy some new boots and a belt, Oscar found Buddy on the main road, along with more than half of the town's folk shouting threats at an old woman, who was tied to a platform.

Although his 'shooting' eye was still swollen shut, Buddy knew that the look in Oscar's right eye meant that it was time to 'rescue and dash, no questions asked!'

Buddy stole a few nearby horses, as Oscar snuck around the platform to get into position.

Oscar didn't care to hear the details, but though it odd that old woman was accused of 'witchcraft.' But he'd seen and grown tired of the same scene time and again, a bunch of white men, women and children gathered to hang or burn somebody that didn't look like them.

'Did y'all ever see a black witch?' blurted Oscar, interrupting the self-appointed judge/jury/executioner's speech. Coiling a lasso he snatched from a nearby horse saddle, Oscar walked slowly toward the platform.

Standing closer, the old woman now seemed so small compared to the thick noose fastened around her neck. She was chanting quietly while staring at the man's hand on the trap door lever that controlled the release door beneath her feet.

The executioner smiled before quickly pulling the lever. Oscar used both hands to throw the lasso and its handle toward the rope and the old woman who was suspended just below. Snapped out of her chant, the old woman was surprised to find herself flying toward Oscar and away from the platform!

# Oscar and Buddy's Super Origins, cont'd

As if the routine had been practiced, Buddy appeared on a horse and holding the reigns of a spare mare. Oscar jumped on the galloping horse while carrying the old woman in one graceful motion. The executioner and blood thirsty crowd stood dumbfounded, still trying to process what had just happened! Buddy laughed as the trio rode away, wondering how long it would take for the all the townsfolk to untie their horses and give chase!

After a few minutes of riding and reaching a safe distance, Oscar and Buddy slowed down and offered the old woman some water. 'So, what was that all about?' Oscar asked, half joking, have serious.

After taking a prolonged drink, the old woman, cried, 'thank you! I've never seen someone do what you just did!'

The old woman continued, 'I'm Awena, the sole survivor of my people. Those men will come after us again soon, if we can make it to my home, I'll give you both something that will aid you on all the journeys ahead for the rest of your lives.'

Awena directed Oscar and Buddy through a valley on a day long journey toward her home.

'So, why did those folks say that you was a witch?' Buddy asked.

'He-he-he, you're funny,' Awena replied. Not really, I'm more of what you would call a 'Medicine Woman.' With all of our people gone, I thought our Gods might have died too. I had no chance, no hope back there, then you guys showed up! I had a vision, years ago, that someone like you would come along to save us all. Better late than never, I guess!' Awena joked.

Buddy, Oscar, and Awena arrived at her home. Disappointed, but not surprised that everything was burned and ruined beyond repair, Awena disappeared for a few minutes and then returned with several items in her arms. As she made a fire for tea, she shared more of her story with Oscar and Buddy.

After a time, she offered Oscar and Buddy each a ceramic pot of tea, along with a necklace with a charm. 'You are both special and powerful spirits. My gift to you, for bringing me back home, is all the power and protection that remains from a long lost culture. It will take you places far from here, help you 'help' more people in need, and keep you safe. Thank you.' whispered Awena.

'There's also a few guns and bullets over there, because that's the only language that these folks understand!' Awena coughed, as she laid down on the ground, finishing her drink.

'Your tea empowers life, as mine takes it away' Awena continued.

Just then, Oscar and Buddy felt a jolt of energy that gave them both conflicted feelings. They weren't sure how or why, but Awena sacrificed her life for two strangers that she'd just met. Oscar, whispered, 'I don't know how to thank you...' as he suddenly realized that he could now see out of both eyes. Buddy argued, 'Can't you just give yourself the power, and save yourself?' whispering to Awena.

'Not how it works... my time is over... they'll be here... thank...' as Awena gave her final words and took her last breath.

# Oscar and Buddy's Super Origins, cont'd

Oscar and Buddy paid their respects by giving Awena the best funeral that they knew how to give.

Taking an inventory of their supplies and planning their impending attack, Oscar and Buddy set up a defensive position and then tried out their newfound powers.

'Hit me!' Oscar challenged Buddy. Happy to oblige, as the two had enjoyed sparing since they were teens, Buddy linked his fingers and launched a double back handed punch to Oscar's jaw with all of his might! The blow caught Oscar off guard, and knocked him off of his feet, but other than a minor stinging sensation, he felt just fine!

'Shoot me!' Buddy exclaimed! 'You are an idiot, Buddy! I'm not going to shoot you, we aren't bullet proof... At least, I... don't... think... we... are.' Oscar reasoned.

'Let's see who can throw these boulders the farthest?' Oscar challenged.

'We just dug a six foot grave without breaking a sweat... I'll bet we can launch them pretty far,' Buddy boasted, as he flung a rock about half his height and weight beyond their field of vision.

'Buddy! I can still see it! Your rock it's still moving through the air!' Oscar screamed, shocked that he could not believe what his eyes were showing him.

Buddy, looking further down the other direction, exclaimed, 'I can see Awena's mob riding toward us!'

'Do you think we can knock them off of their horses from here?' Oscar asked.

'We don't have enough rocks,' answered Buddy.

'Do you think we can out run a horse now,' asked Oscar?

'Only one way to find out... Go!' Challenged Buddy.

Along the desert plains, Oscar and Buddy ran at train like speeds toward the enemy. Without thinking Oscar jumped, and flew in the air! Buddy jumped after Oscar. In seconds, the duo found themselves flying miles above the unsuspecting raiders, and then before they knew it, they were already miles behind them!

Buddy and Oscar landed hundreds of miles away from their origin in less than a minute!

'What should we do now,' Buddy asked Oscar?

'Looks like we got us a train to catch!', replied Oscar with a smile.

# Race War – Part I

Thursday, May 29th, 1919. Irvington, New York

Madam C.J. Walker's death on May 25th brought together thousands of supporters, family, and friends in the black community. C.J.'s political activism, of late, made her an even bigger target toward several groups in America who hated the seed of ambition that she planted for women and people of color.

Triple K, the leader of a growing sect of Americans who wanted to make 'America Great' again, (and restore it to its pre-Civil War glory), saw C.J.'s death as an opportunity to seize her Westchester compound full of gadgets and information and destroy her team of 'extraordinary negroes' power for good!

Behind the scenes, C.J. knew that all of her donations, speeches, and dreams of change for Black America would require an unprecedented show of force. A war the likes of which America was unwilling to support, a military unable to fight for colored folks, nor a bank confident enough to fund black interests. So, for years, C.J. recruited the most brilliant minds, men and women with incredible abilities, to be a voice for the voiceless, power for the powerless, and justice and economic support for the people who needed it the most.

The day before C.J.'s funeral, her daughter A'Lelia met with Lynn Fox at her estate. Nearly the same age and friends for several years, the two women considered each other to be family. They spoke briefly, as they walked the grounds of C.J.'s Westchester estate toward her garage. 'Momma wanted you to have this,' A'Lelia whispered, handing Lynn an envelope with a letter and a set of keys. A'Lelia hugged Lynn and then gave her a moment alone to grieve.

Looking at the black motorcycle, Lynn recalled several adventures that she had with C.J. over the years. She chuckled as she wiped away some tears, while leaning against 'the beast' as C.J. jokingly called her motorcycle and began to read C.J.'s letter:

*Dear Lynn,*

*We've known for a few years that this day would come. I hope that you'll continue to lead the resistance that we've worked so hard to establish. My story is just another eulogy in history, but yours, baby girl, it's still being written.*

*I hope you'll forgive me for the distance and secrecy over the past year. After we lost your brother, I should have been there for you, but I just poured myself into preparing for the next battle. I'm so sorry that I could not do more for you, Jr., and Jack.*

*I've been working on something that may help you and the team with the challenges that lie ahead. There's an abandoned subway station near A'Lelia's old apartment in the Bronx (the address, is hidden in this letter). Bring Kills and your cousin to meet up with Undark, Jolly, and Alex for further instruction. I completely trust them, and though they'll never replace our family, they are our best chance our people have for a better future.*

*Triple K has been after us for years. He'll come after you, your team, my home, then our people. You won't have a lot of time to plan, but I'm confident that you can defeat him. Don't hesitate, when you have the chance, take him out for good!*

*Thank you for everything, the best is yet to come!*

*Love, Sarah*

# Race War – Part I, cont'd

Lynn drove her newly acquired motorcycle into the city to meet Kills, who was sitting by a pond in Central Park.

'This land once belonged to my mother's people,' Kills cried. 'The Lenape, they called it 'Manhatta' which meant hilly island.' Kills continued. 'And they just kept killing my people, and then your people, in this very park... when will it end Lynn?' Kills growled.

'Soon,' Lynn replied, 'C.J. gave us one last assignment, if you're up for it?' Lynn asked in a sing song voice, as she pointed to C.J.'s Motorcycle.

'Inena!' Kills bellowed, meaning, 'Let's go!' in his father's native Cherokee tongue.

Lynn, not all too surprised that Kills also had a motorcycle from C.J., similar to hers, gave him the address to the subway (in the Bronx) and told her that she'd meet him there after one last stop.

Driving up to Harlem, Lynn found the only living member of her family left, sitting on a stoop reading a paper and smoking a cigar. 'Haitian Joe,' as he became known as, still seemed like the little kid that used to follow her and Jack around when they moved to Louisiana. Lynn suddenly realized how much he favored her brother, they could be twins, she mused me to herself. It had been a very emotional day, with everything reminding her of love ones recently lost.

'Kijan ou ye?' (How are you?) Lynn greeted her cousin in Haitian Creole. 'Mwen byen,' (I'm good!) Joe replied, folding his newspaper and rushing over to give Lynn a bear hug. 'This article is something else! Don't these white folks know that the war ended? In Europe? Nearly a year ago?' Joe replied, half joking, half serious.

Lynn wasn't sure what impressed her more, Joe's powers (equal to hers possibly), or the fact that he always had a cigar in the corner of his mouth, even while talking, drinking, or eating!

'I know what you're going to say, L!', joked Joe. 'Since we stopped wearing them Flu masks, I just started smoking cigars again,' Joe chuckled. 'All jokes aside, I'm so sorry for your loss kouzen (cousin), I know how much she meant to you,' Joe, spoke softly.

'Thanks Joe,' Lynn replied. 'She was a fan of your work, and I'm not quite sure what to expect, but she wanted you to join me for a mission, are you game?' Lynn asked.

'Sure, but only if I can get me one of them fancy thing-a-magigs you got!' Joe said, pointing to her motorcycle.

When Lynn and Joe arrived at the subway, they found a state of the art facility loaded with enough weapons and equipment to be a military base!

Kills was there in a heated debate with Undark, Jolly, and Alex.

'Every time a negro is accused of being near a white woman or a land owner cheats a group of sharecroppers of their pay, its another lynching,' Jolly cried.

'Well, at least we have stopped quite a few (lynchings) so far this year,' Alex reasoned.

'But it's not enough! We can't be everywhere at once. The laws need to change, and white people need to be held accountable!' Undark pleaded.

# Race War – Part I, cont'd

Just then, everyone broke into laughter, including Undark, who just realized how crazy she sounded as soon as the words left her mouth.

An impromptu briefing continued as everyone had a chance to introduce themselves and pick the weapons and gear that they wanted for the next mission. Lynn found a second letter from C.J. who, even from the grave, was running the show and planning the group's next steps.

As Lynn read reports of the organization's successes and failures of various conflicts over the past year, Alex the youngest member of the group welcomed Oscar Brown and Buddy Lee who just arrived from Texas.

'Welcome to C.J.'s subway! I'll give you the who's who of the party, starting with me!' Alex exclaimed.

'I go by 'Harlem Hell Hound,' but you can just call me Alex. I fought in the war as a member of the 396th Regiment - the Harlem Hellfighters. Fighting Germans in the trenches in France. I was left for dead in the trenches on my first tour, behind enemy lines. I learned what mustard gas was first hand. A jug of it exploded right by my head. When I work up, I was better than ok, doctors still can't understand what it did to me, but a twist of fate and German chemicals is why I'm here. I fought through a few German regiments until I found my unit. Pinned down behind enemy lines. I blacked out and wiped hundreds of German infantry out.' Alex continued.

'Kills White Men, the Indian fellow over there, earned his name all across the county. I've seen him in action, and he just gets to a place where his killing is like... well, honestly it's a work of art!' Alex bragged.

'Now don't let Lynn's stature fool you. She's much more than a reporter, she's the leader of our group here! She's like Hugo, Hercules, John Carter and Zorro all in one! We might just end up watching her take on all of the bad guys by herself!' Alex reasoned.

Continuing around the room, Alex continued, 'The gentleman over there with the cigar in his mouth is Lynn's cousin Joe. He goes by the name, 'Haitian Joe.' Not missing a beat, while in the middle of a conversation with Undark, three duplicates of Joe suddenly appeared before Alex, Oscar, and Buddy, and shook their hands!'

'I've never met Jolly (as in the Jolly Roger, the old Pirate flag), but he's an actual pirate and a real force of nature! This man has been everywhere and has done everything, if anybody can take on Cornfed, it's him!' Alex concluded.

'So, a Cowboy and a Sojourner (Chinese railroad worker) from California, what's your story?' Alex asked.

'We can hold our own, we're just here to pay our respects to C.J. and help out in any way that we can,' replied Oscar.

Lynn continued to address the group, further explaining C.J.'s Plan.

'I appreciate all of your efforts in keeping the peace since the end of the Great War and the Spanish Flu. Our sources across the county have Triple K arriving in the city this weekend, gunning for us! Along with the Army, the NYPD, and anyone else you can think of.' Lynn continued to brief her team with profiles of their potential assailants:

# Race War – Part I, cont'd

Triple K* (super powerful - flight, super human strength, practically indestructible), de facto leader of the Klu Klux Klan. He killed Lynn's brother Jack, John Henry Jr. and dozens of other 'extraordinary negros' in the past few months.

Tsarina* - An expatriate of the Russian Revolution and Triple K's wife (powers include flight, energy pulses, and expert combat skills).

Fritz Haber - AKA 'FCW' (Father of Chemical Warfare). A German chemist who won the Nobel Prize in Chemistry in 1918 for the Haber-Bosch process, which allowed large-scale synthesis of fertilizers and explosives that were first used in World War I. Triple K brought FCW to the United States to create an ultimate weapon.

Amy Washington* - A leader of the white woman's suffrage movement, expert swordswoman, and boxer. George Washington didn't have any kids, but Amy claimed to be related, and became rich and famous leveraging her 'truth'. 'Don't let facts get in the way of a good story,' is a quote often attributed to Amy!

Cornfed* - Killed John Henry, Sr. We've never quite able to put him down, a formidable foe. That is one big summabitch! Is it me, or does it seem like he keeps getting bigger every time we fight him?

Patty* an Irish gangster/butcher, who was 'wicked' with a blade, became one of the most powerful gangsters in New York City. Triple K allegedly offered Patty C.J.'s estate in exchange for his (and his 3,000 gang army) participation in the assault on Irvington.

**Memorial Day, Friday, May 30th, 1919**

A few hours after C.J.'s repass, a plane flew overhead and dropped a projectile! Without a second thought, Lynn said, 'C.J. hasn't even been in the ground for one day... everyone get ready!' As she and Haitian Joe flew toward the plane, Lynn grabbed the bomb and Joe went straight toward the pilot.

The rest of the team on the ground stared up at the sky as if watching fireworks. An explosion ignited high above the clouds, followed by a blinding light, then a loud bang! In C.J.'s backyard, Joe somehow landed the plane that just dropped the bomb, with the pilot unharmed and tied up the back seat!

Lynn returned, a little rattled, wearing a concerned expression on her face. While flying the bomb up to a safe distance, she had time to quickly take a surveillance of the impending attack from a bird's eye view.

'Undark, the NYPD and NY militia, led by Patty and the FCW are going to flank CJ's compound from the east. Take Kills and Alex to set up a perimeter just outside of the compound,' ordered Lynn.

'Oscar and Buddy, assemble the Pullman Porters and create a perimeter to the north,' Lynn ordered as she sensed more planes and the Army closing in. 'Keep them from breaching the estate by any means necessary.' Lynn pleaded.

'Triple K, Tsarina, and Cornfed are about 20 minutes due west of our location. Joe and I will meet them at the gate,' Lynn continued. Finally, Lynn ordered Jolly and the Masons to post up on the south end of the estate, where Patty, FCW, and the NYPD would attack. 'Good luck everyone!' Lynn screamed as she and Joe flew toward Triple K and Tsarina.

# Race War – Part II

Triple K addressed his 'Righteous Army' at an undisclosed location, hours before the attack on New York. 'After we kill these 'extraordinary' niggers, we're going to every town in America to paint the streets red with nigger blood! This summer, in Chicago, Tulsa, Atlanta, Washington D.C. and Los Angeles, we'll make the dream that the confederacy promised to our grandparents our reality! Generations of white men and women will prosper for hundreds of years when we eliminate America's biggest threat to our future. We'll reclaim our land, and begin a new world order. No mercy, no prisoners. You have your orders. Let's Make America Great again!' Triple K shouted to thunderous applause and cheers.

Even CJ's resources and planning could not thwart the scale of the assault that Triple K was about to unleash. With the full support of federal and local government, the latest military weapons, and thousands of enraged combatants, Triple K relished in the fact that he had Lynn's team cornered, and it was only a matter of time before he'd personally get the chance to squeeze the life from her neck!

Within minutes of arriving at the east end of CJ's estate, Undark, Kills, and Alex were met with a hail of bullets! 'Holy Shit!', Alex screamed, 'these motherfuckers are shooting MG 42's and Vicker's machine guns at us!' Without a second thought Kills ran full speed toward the enemy ranks! Undark smiled at Alex, and said, 'watch this' and returned with one of each of the machine guns and several cases of bullets! 'Hell Yeah, nobody's getting past me now,' Alex screamed. Undark returned the the front line, quickly eliminating as many combatants as she could. She didn't know what was more shocking, how many hundreds of ranks of soldiers there were, or how many soldiers that Kills had already killed!

Oscar, Buddy, and the Pullman Porters only made up 50 people in total, but were glad that Undark had also somehow managed to provide them with a bunch of machine guns and bullets from the eastern battle front.

Oscar heard the first plane before he saw it, leapt toward it with his lasso trailing behind him. Buddy followed a few hundred yards alongside Oscar, to be able to intercept his own plane before the attack began. Above the clouds, Oscar and Buddy found a dozen or so aircraft ready to drop bombs on CJ's compound!

Quickly thinking of a plan to push the planes back down toward the enemy ground forces, Oscar slung the end of his lasso toward Buddy to catch. They slowly 'closed-lined' the group of bomb loaded planes and brought them down within a few hundred yards of the advancing combatants, creating a temporary barrier.

Jolly, along with a group of his most trusted crew members, the Black Masons, and the rest of the volunteer Pullman Porters numbered 89 in all. 'It looks like they brought knives to a gun fight,' Jolly laughed, as he saw Patti's Irish gang slowly climb up a hill. One of the lead Masons, armed with a sword and a revolver, asked Jolly, 'What's with the carrier pigeon?' 'My ship is anchored in the Hudson, with cannons ready to fire on these bastards!' Jolly replied. Just then, Jolly gave orders to a few of his men to shoot arrows at few piles of wood in the distance that quickly ignited and produced a heavy black smoke to signal his ship's gunner.

Patty's gang all started to panicked, running in all different directions! Suddenly, loud booms filed the air, followed by dozens of solid and hot cannon shot projectiles!

# Race War – Part II, cont'd

'Stay behind the line of the painted tree trunks,' Jolly commanded. 'For those lucky enough to reach us, reward them with the sharp end of your sword!' Jolly laughed.

Lynn and Joe were met with a phalanx of bullets just a short distance away from the entrance of CJ's compound. They managed to block or absorb most of them, but what didn't damage them, destroyed the gate and CJ's home. As a series of projectiles targeted CJ's house, Lynn was distracted as it exploded. Just then, a fast moving projectile aimed at Lynn's back was intercepted by Joe, as he selflessly sacrificed himself for his cousin!

Filled with dread, Lynn knew that something was wrong. Joe, immediately realized that the projectile was a grenade, and as he quickly launched himself into the air, he exploded into pieces a safe distance above Lynn!

'Wonderbar!', FCW screamed repeatedly as he ordered a second projectile to be reloaded and launched toward Lynn again. Freezing time, Lynn also tried, in vain, to conjure a spell to restore her only living relative.

Sorrow changed to rage as Lynn saw Cornfed rushing toward her, somehow immune to her time manipulation spell! The man who murdered Lynn's brother and John Henry Jr. had to die a slow and painful death, and she instantly knew exactly how she wanted Cornfed's life to end. Known for his size and brute strength, Cornfed didn't have the ability to bend time. Someone or something had to help him travel through Lynn's spell, she just needed to find out how. Then, Lynn pinpointed the source - Tsarina! She'd only heard of the Russian Mystic, before today, but now felt her aura nearby.

Unfazed by Lynn's time warp, Cornfed quickly closed the distance between them. Ever loquacious, Cornfed grabbed Lynn by the neck and spat, 'Well, well, now that you done lost yo' whole damn family, what you...' Thump!

Lynn, who's back hid a second fast approaching projectile closing in on her and Cornfed's location, had just enough time to reply to a shocked Cornfed, 'Go to Hell!' as she maneuvered out of the projectile's path as it hit Cornfed square in his chest! Before a shocked and, for once, speechless Cornfed exploded, the last thing he heard was Lynn cheering 'Wonderbar!' She turned toward FCW, clapping and repeating the phrase, 'Wonderbar!' as she froze time again to try to locate Tsarina and terrorize the rest of the combatants that had just destroyed CJ's home.

Tsarina spotted Undark a few hundred yards from the edge of the east end of the compound. Intrigued by Undark's abilities, Tsarina relished the ideal of taking her on 'mano a mano.' With the ability to materialize nearly to and from anywhere, Tsarina appeared just a few feet away from Undark to size up her competition. 'Wow, you are absolutely breathtaking for a niggra!' Tsarina yelled. 'I'm going to mount your head above my fire place,' Tsarina taunted, with a strange Russian accent that had somehow morphed into a southern one. 'Dante yemu luchshiy shans,' Undark replied in Russian (Give it your best shot)! Impressed and a little unsettled, Tsarina struck first and hard, just missing Undark's chin as she swung her head back.' Do you want this ass whipping in English or Russian, bitch?' Undark laughed. 'What are you?' Tsarina wondered in amazement, as she spun back around after failing to connect her fist. 'Your nightmare personified,' Undark spit as she kicked Tsarina in the mouth, breaking several teeth in the process!



PARENTAL ADVISORY EXPLICIT LYRICS

# Race War – Part II, cont'd

As if sensing Tsarina's battle in progress, Triple K sneaked up behind Undark, palmed the back of her head and slammed her face into the ground repeatedly.

As Triple K wound up to continue bashing a now unconscious Undark's head into the ground some more, Alex unloaded his machine gun toward Triple K and Tsarina, forcing them to retreat.

As Lynn ran over to assist Undark, she was overcome with waves of dread and panic. Sensing the enemy closing in from all sides, she felt the team's hopelessness and sensed Triple K's forces constricting upon and extinguishing all that remained of CJ's legacy.

Emitting the most energy that Lynn had ever wielded, she managed to relocate 35 souls, all who remained of the team still fighting a futile battle, several city blocks away on the Hudson! Kills, Alex, Jolly, Oscar, Buddy, and a stable but unconscious Undark, along with dozens of bruised and battered Porters and Masons found themselves safe, aboard the deck of Jolly's ship in Hudson river! Without a second thought, Kills jumped into the river and swam back toward Lynn to continue fighting.

'Let him go,' Jolly ordered to his team, knowing that Lynn was going to end the battle way before Kills could ever reach the shore.

As Lynn chanted in an ancient tongue, Triple K, Tsarina, thousands of uniformed Army and NYPD troops, and the rest of his coalition closed in on her location.

'Belay my last,' Triple K ordered. 'Open fire, on my mark, and don't stop until you've fired everything you got, clear?' Triple K barked to everyone on his flanks.

Footsteps, heavy breathing, and metal clanking were the last sounds that Lynn heard as Triple K and his entire army surrounded her, reloading their rifles and training their sights toward her.

'Fire!' Triple K shouted. 'Boule Nan Lanfe' (Go to hell!), Lynn replied as she focused on every combatant attacking CJ's compound. The explosion was so forceful, it took after a few seconds for the sound from blast to hit the shore! Jolly's ship listed back and forth as if it were in a hurricane! Kills, who had just reached the beach was knocked back several yards into the water, by the same force. After he regained his footing back on land, he was hit with the gravity of the sacrifice that his friend Lynn had just made.

Within twenty minutes, Jolly and his crew made their way back to port to rendezvous with Kills to travel back to CJ's compound. Undark, who had only recently regained consciousness, had last seen Lynn, lead everyone to her last location. Outside of the damage done by the bullets, not a tree had been displaced by Lynn's explosion. There was not a trace of Triple K nor his Army anywhere to be found, just dust, like everyone had been instantly cremated! Lynn had turned thousands of combatants into dust! Kills found Lynn's bracelet lying on the ground, now nothing more than tattered leather and bent metal. Holding it brought tears to the warrior's eyes.

Never a man of many words, Kills felt compelled to speak to the group. 'Lynn was the best of us. She removed the worst from our path. But the fight must continue. They will come after us again, and continue to fight, unfair, unjust and in even bigger battles. We must remain diligent. When will it end? I'm the last of my kind. All I know is war. I am strong, and I can be ruthless. But it is not enough. America... will... pay... Lynn... she's... her spirit... she's.... still alive? Look there, up in that tree, its...'

# INDEX

## # (23)



## A (34)



## B (38)



## B (38)



## C (29)



## D (24)



## E (13)



## F

## G (21)



## H (15)



## I (36)



## I (36)



## J (5)



## K (2)



## L (17)



## M (25)



## N (11)



## O (16)



## P (19)



## Q (1)



## R (19)

# R (19)



# S (22)



# T (46)



# T (46)



# U (8)



# V (1)



# W (51)



# W (50)



# Y (4)



# Z (4)

# Please leave a review on Amazon!

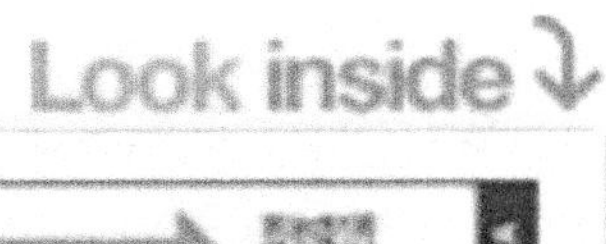

See all formats and editions

Kindle
$2.99
Read with Our **Free App**

**Paperback**
**$14.95** ✓prime
1 New from $14.95

**When a cop stopped and frisked me**

The moment that I relive most
The day that still haunts me, like a ghost
I've tried for years to write about it
Alone at night, as I sit
Recalling every detail of the time
When a police officer assumed that I had committed a crime
As the cop car passed by, I heard the squawking of a dispatcher
'Be advised, the suspect, a young black male with a green jacket, is a purse snatcher.'
'Freeze! Turn around with your hands up!' shouted the cop
Stunned, time slowed, as my paper bag dropped
I could see my house, just a few yards away, should I run?
As I slowly turned around, the only thing that I saw was a gun!
The cop continued to shout, but I couldn't understand his commands
He holstered his gun and then patted me down with his hands
I answered all of his questions about where I had been
To the corner store, I pointed to the bag on the ground, and then
He picked up my bag of Twinkie's, crushed them, and just put them in my hand!
When he left, I took a big breath, and just said damn…

## Bottled Lighting

In the 6th grade, I won the first prize
Of Indiana's state science fair, on one of my very first tries
First thing that morning, it felt like lightning had struck me - I was so energized!
I didn't think that I could win, but I just felt so confident
In my understanding of the subject with all of the time spent
Researching the topic and making my display
For weeks, my family helped me to practice and cheered me on later that day
I explained how methane gas could be used to power your car or to heat your home
Just like in my favorite movie, Mad Max Beyond Thunderdome!
And how farmers could make this fuel just by using the feces
Of cows, pigs, chickens, and many other animal species
There were hundreds of kids there with more impressive projects, but I was just 'Jason'
As dozens of judges came by, I shared the details, jokes, and stories from my project presentation!
During lunch, I checked out the other kids computers, robots, volcanos, and poster boards
When my name was called at the awards ceremony, I was completely floored!
The only folks who clapped were my mom, dad, and my brothers, as I made my way to the stage
My picture and the headline, 'Moore is elementary science champion' made the Sunday local page!

March 25, 1988 Indianapolis Star

# Moore is elementary science champion

The Indianapolis News

Michael Marks — Shawn Graft



The News Photo, Bob Miller

Jason Moore, a sixth-grader at School 11, is the overall Science Fair winner.

Small or medium-sized

Panama: Strike is accelerating

WARRIOR
JON MOR
JON MOR

Made in the USA
Middletown, DE
12 October 2022